BUDDHISM: THE WAY TO WISDOM

BUDDHISM: THE WAY TO WISDOM

Suman Chaterjee

CYBER TECH PUBLICATIONS
4264/3, Ansari Road, Daryaganj, New Delhi-110002 (India)
Ph.: 011-23244078. Fax: 011-23280028
E-Mail: cyberpublicationsdelhi@yahoo.com

BUDDHISM: THE WAY TO WISDOM

Suman Chaterjee

First Edition 2009

Published by :

G.S. Rawat for **Cyber Tech Publications**
4264/3, Ansari Road, Daryaganj, New Delhi-110002 (India)
Ph.: 011-23244078. Fax: 011-23280028
E-Mail: cyberpublicationsdelhi@yahoo.com

Printed at : Asian Offset Printers

Preface

Any research into a school of thought whose texts are in a foreign language encounters certain difficulties in deciding which words to translate and which ones to leave in the original. It is all the more of an issue when the texts in question are from a language ancient and quite unlike our own. Most of the texts on which this thesis are based were written in two languages: the earliest texts of Buddhism were written in a simplified form of Sanskrit called Pali, and most Indian texts of Madhyamika were written in either classical or "hybrid" Sanskrit.

Terms in these two languages are often different but recognizable, e.g. "dhamma" in Pali and "dharma" in Sanskrit. For the sake of coherency, all such terms are given in their Sanskrit form, even when that may entail changing a term when presenting a quote from Pali. Since this thesis is not intended to be a specialized research document for a select audience, terms have been translated whenever possible, even when the subtleties of the Sanskrit term are lost in translation. In a research paper as limited as this, those subtleties are often almost irrelevant. For example, it is sufficient to translate "dharma" as either "Law" or "elements" without delving into its multiplicity of meanings in Sanskrit. Only four terms have been left consistently untranslated. "Karma" and "nirvana" are now to be found in any English dictionary, and so their translation or italicization is unnecessary. Similarly, "Buddha," while literally a Sanskrit term meaning "awakened," is left untranslated and unitalicized due to its titular nature and its familiarity. Another appellation of Siddhartha Gautama, Tathagata, is the only unfamiliar term consistently used in the original. This has been done because translations of the term do not do justice to its mystic import and esotericism.

— *Author*

CONTENTS

1

The Meaning of Buddhism

The teaching founded by the Buddha is known, in English, as Buddhism. It may be asked, who is the Buddha? A Buddha is one who has attained Bodhi; and by Bodhi is meant wisdom, an ideal state of intellectual and ethical perfection which can be achieved by man through purely human means. The term Buddha literally means enlightened one, a knower. Buddhists believe that a Buddha is born in each aeon of time, and our Buddha-the sage Gotama who attained enlightenment under the bo tree at Buddh Gaya in India-was the seventh in the succession.

Gotama was born the son of an Indian king on the border of modern Nepal 623 years before Christ. The wise men of the kingdom foresaw that he would become either an emperor or a Buddha, and his father, wanting him to be an emperor, kept him utterly secluded from all unpleasant things, so that he might not become wise by seeing life. But the gods knew that Gotama must become the Buddha, and so they visited earth in various forms to let him see them. On three successive days, while on his way to the royal park, Gotama saw an old man, a sick man, and a corpse, and thus he learned that men-all men-must suffer and die. On the fourth day he saw a monk; from this he understood that to learn the way of overcoming man's universal sorrow lie must give up worldly pleasures. Accordingly, in his twenty-ninth year, he renounced his kingdom and became an ascetic.

Gotama wandered about the countryside, a seeker after truth and peace. He approached many a distinguished teacher of his day, but none could give him what he sought. He strenuously practiced all the severe austerities of monkish life, hoping to attain Nirvana. Eventually his delicate body was reduced almost to a skeleton. But the more he tormented his body the further away he was from his goal. Realizing the futility of self-mortification, he finally decided to follow a different course, avciding the extremes of pain and indulgence.

The new path which he discovered was the Middle Way, the Eightfold Path, which subsequently became part of his teaching. By following this path his wisdom grew into its fullest power, and he became the Buddha.

As a man Prince Gotama, by his own will, love, and wisdom, attained Buddhahood-the highest possible state of perfection-and he taught his followers to believe that they might do the same. Any man, within himself, possesses the power to make himself good, wise, and happy.

All the teachings of the Buddha can be summed up in one word: Dhamma. It means truth, that which really is. It also means law, the law which exists in a man's own heart and mind. It is the principle of righteousness. Therefore the Buddha appeals to man to be noble, pure, and charitable not in order to please any Supreme Deity, but in order to be true to the highest in himself.

Dhamma, this law of righteousness, exists not only in a man's heart and mind, it exists in the universe also. All the universe is an embodiment and revelation of Dhamma. When the moon rises and sets, the rains come, the crops grow, the seasons change, it, is because of Dhamma, for Dhamma is the law of the universe which makes matter act in the ways revealed by our studies of natural science.

If a man will live by Dhamma, he will escape misery and come to Nirvana, the final release from all suffering. It is not by any kind of prayer, nor by any ceremonies, nor by any appeal to a God, that a man will discover the Dhamma which will lead him to his goal. He will discover it in only one way-by developing his own character. This development comes only through control of the mind and purification of the emotions. Until a man stills the storm in his heart, until he extends his loving-kindness to all beings, he will not be able to take even the first step toward his goal.

Thus Buddhism is not a religion at all, in the sense in which the word is commonly understood. It is not a system of faith or worship. In Buddhism, there is no such thing as belief in a body of dogma which must be taken on faith, such as belief in a Supreme Being, a creator of the universe, the reality of an immortal soul, a personal savior, or archangels who are supposed to carry out the will of the Supreme Deity. Buddhism begins as a search for truth. The Buddha taught that we should believe only that which is true in the light of our own experience, that which conforms to reason and is conducive to the highest good and welfare of all beings. Men must rely on themselves. Even though he may "take refuge in Buddha," the expression used when a man pledges himself to live a righteous life, he must not fall victim to a blind faith that the Buddha can save him. The Buddha can point out the path, but he cannot walk it for us.

The truth which the Buddhist sees when he looks around him is the truth of cause and effect. Every action, no matter how insignificant, produces an effect; every effect in its turn becomes a, cause and produces still further effects. It is meaningless to inquire for a First Cause. A First Cause is inconceivable; rather, cause and effect are cyclical, and this universe when it dies and falls apart will give rise to another universe, just as this one was formed from the dispersed matter of a previous universe. The origin of the universe, like that of every individual person or thing in it, is dependent on the chain of previous causes, which goes on and on in an endless cycle of birth, death, and rebirth. This is the principle of dependent origination.

What of the soul? The Buddha taught that there is no soul or self, and he used the metaphor of the cart. If you take away the wheels and axles, the floorboards and sides, the shafts, and all the other parts of the cart, what remains? Nothing but the conception of a cart, which will be the same when a new cart is built. So the uninterrupted process of psychophysical phenomena moves from life to life. Each life passes instantaneously in death to a new life, and the new life is the effect of the causes in the old life. A candle flame at this instant is different from the flame that burned an instant ago, yet the flame is continuous.

Thus in the chain of interdependent causation all phenomenal existence is constantly changing. The elements combine and recombine with no underlying substance, or soul, to give them permanence. This is the Wheel of Life. The main cause of the restlessness, the suffering, which is the lot of beings turning on the Wheel of Life, is craving or selfish desire for existence, and it is this desire which sets the life force in motion. Desire is manifested in action. This action is in reality volition or will power, which is responsible for the creation of being. It is called karma in Sanskrit, but in the Pali language, which the Buddha spoke and in which all the Buddhist scriptures were written, it is softened to kamma.

In this universe in which nothing is permanent all change is governed by kamma or the kammic force. Kamma means action. In its general sense, kamma means all good and bad actions. Kamma refers to all kinds of intentional actions whether mental, verbal, or physical, that is, all thoughts, words, and deeds. In its ultimate sense kamma means all moral and immoral volition.

Kamma, though it activates the chain of cause and effect, is not determinism, nor is it an excuse for fatalism. The past influences the present, but does not dominate it. The past is the background against which life goes on from moment to moment; the past and the present influence the future. Only the present moment exists, and the responsibility for using the present moment for good or ill lies with each individual.

Every action produces an effect; it is cause first and effect afterward. We therefore speak of kamma as "the law of cause and effect." If you throw a stone into a pond, the ripples spread out to the shore, but that is not all, for the ripples return inward until they touch the stone again. The effects of our actions come back to us, and as long as our actions are done with evil intent, the waves of effect will come back to us as evil.

But if we are kind and keep ourselves peaceful, the returning waves of trouble will grow weaker until they die down and our good kamma will come back to us in blessing.

In the world around us there are many inequalities in the lot of man-some are rich, others are poor, some live full lives, others die young, etc. According to Buddhism, the inequalities which exist are due, to some extent, to environment-which is itself shaped by cause and effect-and to a greater extent to causes, that is kamma, which are in the present, the immediate past, and the remote past. Man himself is responsible for his own happiness and misery. Thus kamma is not fate nor destiny nor blind determinism. Man has a certain amount of free will; he can modify his actions and affect his future. Each act, whether mental or physical, tends to produce its like. If a man does a good deed or thinks a good thought, the effect upon him is to increase the tendencies to goodness in him.

The understanding of kamma gives us power. The more we make the doctrine of kamma a part of our lives, the more power we gain, not only to direct our future, but also to help our fellow beings more effectively. The practice of good kamma, when fully developed, will enable us to overcome evil and even to overcome kamma itself, thus bringing us to our goal, Nirvana.

The principle of dependent origination and the law of kamma provide the background for understanding the nature of rebirth. According to Buddhism, death is "the temporary end of a temporary phenomenon." It is not the complete annihilation of the being, for although the organic life has ceased, the kammic force which hitherto actuated it is not destroyed. Our physical forms are only the outward manifestations of the invisible kammic force. When the present form perishes, another form takes its place according to a good or bad volitional impulse-the kamma that was the most powerful-at the moment before death.

At death the kammic force remains entirely undisturbed by the disintegration of the physical body, and the passing away of the present consciousness creates the conditions for the coming into being of a fresh body in another birth. The stream of consciousness flows on like a river which is built up by its tributaries and dispenses its water to the countryside through which it passes. The continuity of flux at death is unbroken in point of time; there is no breach in the stream of consciousness, and therefore there is no room whatever for an intermediate stage between this life and the next. Rebirth takes place immediately.

The present being, present existence, is conditioned by the way one faced circumstances in the last and in all past existences. One's present character and circumstances are the result of all that one has been up to the present, but what one will be in the future depends on what one does now in the present. The true Buddhist regards death as a momentary incident between one life and its successor and views its approach with calmness. His only concern is that his future should be such that the condition of that life may provide him with better opportunities for perfecting himself.

Buddhism teaches that with the practice of meditation and concentration the memory can be trained. By meditation and mind culture one can acquire the power to see one's rebirth as a link, or a succession of links, in a chain of births; one can also acquire the power of looking back into one's previous lives. Not only this, but Buddhism also teaches that with the attainment of Nirvana in this life itself, through enlightenment and true wisdom, one can reach the end of this chain of rebirths.

Nirvana, the state to which all Buddhists aspire, is the cessation of desire and hence the end of suffering. Nirvana in Sanskrit means "the blowing out." It is understood as the extinguishment of the flame of personal desire, the quenching of the fire of life. Among Westerners Nirvana is often thought of as a negative state, a kind of "nothingness." But in the Buddhist scriptures it is always described in positive terms; the highest refuge, safety, emancipation, peace, and the like. Nirvana is freedom, but not freedom from circumstance; it is freedom from the bonds with which we have bound ourselves to circumstance. That man is free who is strong enough to say, "Whatever comes I accept as best."

Nirvana is the dying of the kammic force. The Buddhist ascends to Nirvana through many stages of the Middle Way, the path of wisdom, morality, and control. There is not space enough here even to mention these phases or the various aspects of the regimen recommended by the Buddha in his vast scriptures; but it may be taken for granted that the life of the conscientious Buddhist is full and rich. Through the cycle of rebirths he ascends, he perfects himself, he conquers his cravings through wisdom and love. Slowly the kammic force ebbs away, the flame dies down.

At the root of man's trouble is his primal state of ignorance. From ignorance comes desire, which sets the kammic force in motion. Hence the way to Nirvana lies through knowledge, and we come again full circle to Dhamma, the Buddha's teachings. For in Dhamma, as truth, lies release from ignorance and desire and perpetual change, and the Buddha has shown us the way to truth.

What, then, is the meaning of Buddhism? Ultimately Buddhism, although not strictly speaking a religion, is a systematic exercise in spirituality, certainly one of the greatest ever conceived. It offers the individual a means by which he may fulfill himself through understanding, reaching eventually the plane of the supraperson on which both the self and self-knowledge are no longer useful. Meister Eckhart, the great Christian mystic, said: "The kingdom of God is for none but the thoroughly dead." The Buddhist would agree, though he would probably prefer a less grim way of saying it. Nirvana in life, the peace which "passeth all understanding," is the conquest of life, the discovery of the permanent in its flux of psychophysical accidents and circumstances. The Buddhist believes that through meditation and good hard thought he can follow the Buddha through the successive stages of enlightenment and achieve at last the perfect wisdom which surmounts all need.

But by no means all Buddhists are monks or adepts. What does Buddhism mean for the ordinary person going about his work in the world? All through the Buddha's teaching, repeated stress is laid on self-reliance and resolution. Buddhism makes man stand on his own feet, it arouses his self-confidence and energy. The Buddha again and again reminded his followers that there is no one, either in heaven or on earth, who can help them or free them from the results of their past evil deeds. The Buddhist knows that the powers of his own mind and spirit are enough to guide him in the present and shape his future and bring him eventually to the truth. He knows that he possesses a strength which is ultimately unsurpassable.

Moreover, Buddhism points unequivocally to the moral aspect of everyday life. Though Nirvana is amoral, in the sense that final peace transcends the conflict of good and evil, the path to wisdom is definitely a moral path. This follows logically from the doctrine of kamma. Every action must produce an effect, and one's own actions produce an effect in one's own life. Thus the kammic force which carries us inevitably onward can only be a force for good, that is, for our ultimate wisdom, if each action is a good action.

This doctrine finds its highest expression in metta, the Buddhist goal of universal and all-embracing love. Metta means much more than brotherly feeling or kindheartedness, though these are part of it. It is active benevolence, a love which is expressed and fulfilled in active ministry for the uplifting of fellow beings. Metta goes hand in hand with helpfulness and a willingness to forego self-interest in order to promote the welfare and happiness of mankind. It is metta which in Buddhism is the basis for social progress. Metta is, finally, the broadest and intensest conceivable degree of sympathy, expressed in the throes of suffering and change. The true Buddhist does his best to exercise metta toward every living being and identifies himself with all, making no distinctions whatsoever with regard to caste, color, class, or sex.

In addition, of course, the teachings of the Buddha are a prime cultural force in Oriental life, just as the Bible is the ultimate source of much Western art and thought. The Buddhist scriptures are larger and more detailed than the Christian Bible, however, and in translation would fill a dozen volumes. In Pali, the language of the scriptures, the Buddha's teachings are called Tripitaka, which means "The Three Baskets."

Vinaya Pitaka, "The Basket of Discipline," consists of five books which expound the rules of monastic life. Sutta Pitaka, "The Basket of Discourses," is a collection of discussions, stories, poems, and proverbs, written in simple language, imparting all the precepts of practical Buddhism. The third basket, Abhidhamma Pitaka, or "Basket of Ultimate Things," deals with epistemological, metaphysical, and psychological matters and is of interest mainly to trained philosophers.

Thus the Tripitaka offers cohesive guidance at every level of intellectual, ethical, and spiritual activity. The Buddha's word is light, a lamp for Burma-and for everyone.

THE WAY OF WISDOM

The Five Spiritual Faculties

Spiritual progress depends on the emergence of five cardinal virtues - faith, vigor, mindfulness, concentration and wisdom. The conduct of the ordinary worldling is governed by his sense-based instincts and impulses. As we progress, new spiritual forces gradually take over, until in the end the five cardinal virtues dominate and shape everything we do feel and think. These virtues are called, in Sanskrit and Pali, indriya, variously translated by faculties, controlling faculties, or spiritual faculties. The same five virtues are called powers (bala) if emphasis is on the fact that they are "unshakable by their opposites."

1. Faith

Faith is called "the seed," and without it the plant of spiritual life cannot start at all. Without faith one can, as a matter of fact, do nothing worthwhile at all. This is true not only of Buddhism, but of all religions, and even the pseudo-religions of modern times, such as Communism. And this faith is much more than the mere acceptance of beliefs. It requires the combination of four factors - intellectual, volitional, emotional and social.

1. Intellectually, faith is an assent to doctrines which are not substantiated by immediately available direct factual evidence. To be a matter of faith, a belief must go beyond the available evidence and the believer must be willing and ready to fill up the gaps in the evidence with an attitude of patient and trusting acceptance. Faith, taken in this sense, has two

opposites, i.e., a dull unawareness of the things which are worth believing in, and doubt or perplexity. In any kind of religion some assumptions are taken on trust and accepted on the authority of scriptures or teachers.

Generally speaking, faith is, however, regarded as only a preliminary step, as a merely provisional state. In due course direct spiritual awareness will know that which faith took on trust, and longed to know: "Now we see through a glass darkly, but then face to face." Much time must usually elapse before the virtue of wisdom has become strong enough to support a vigorous insight into the true nature of reality. Until then quite a number of doctrinal points must be taken on faith.

What then in Buddhism are the objects of faith? They are essentially four: (1) the belief in karma and rebirth; (2) the acceptance of the basic teachings about the nature of reality, such as conditioned co-production, emptiness, etc.; (3) confidence in the "Three Refuges," the Buddha, the Dharma and the Order; and (4) a belief in the efficacy of the prescribed practices, and in Nirvana as the final way out of our difficulties. I shall say more about them when I have dealt with the other aspects of faith.

2. In this skeptical age we, anyway, dwell far too much on the intellectual side of faith. shraddha (Pali: saddha) the word we render as "faith," is etymologically akin to Latin cor, "the heart," and faith is far more a matter of the heart than of the intellect. It is, as Prof. Radhakrishnan incisively puts it, the "striving after self-realization by concentrating the powers of the mind on a given idea." Volitionally, faith implies a resolute and courageous act of will. It combines the steadfast resolution that one will do a thing with the self-confidence that one can do it. Suppose that people living on the one side of a river are doomed to perish from many enemies, diseases and famine. Safety lies on the other shore. The man of faith is then likened to the person who swims across the river, braving its dangers, saving himself and inspiring others by his example. Those without faith will go on dithering along the hither bank. The opposites to this aspect of faith are timidity, cowardice, fear, wavering, and a shabby, mean and calculating mentality.

3. Emotionally, faith is an attitude of serenity and lucidity. Its opposite here is worry, the state of being troubled by many things. It is said that someone who has faith loses the "five terrors," i.e., he ceases to worry about the necessities of life, about loss of reputation, death, unhappy rebirth and the impression he may make on an audience. It is fairly obvious that the burden of life must be greatly lightened by belief in karma, emptiness, or not-self. Even an unpleasant fate can be accepted more easily when it is understood as a dispensation of justice, when vexations are explained as an inevitable retribution, when law seems to rule instead of blind chance, when even apparent loss is bound to turn into true gain. And if there is no self, what and whom do we worry about? If there is only one vast emptiness, what is there to disturb our radiance?

4. Socially, and that is more difficult to understand, faith involves trust and confidence in the Buddha and the Sangha. Its opposite here is the state of being submerged in cares about one's sensory social environment, cares which spring from either social pressure or social isolation. The break with the normal social environment is, of course, complete only in the case of the monk who, as the formula goes, "in faith forsakes his home." To a lesser extent it must be carried out by every practitioner of the Dharma, who must "live apart" from his society, in spirit if not in fact.

The company of others and the help we expect from them are usually a mainstay of our sense of security. By going for refuge to the Buddha and the Sangha one turns from the visible and tangible to the invisible and elusive. By placing one's reliance on spiritual forces one gains the strength to disregard public opinion and social discouragement. Some measure of defiant contempt for the world and its ways is inseparable from a spiritual life. The spiritual man does not "belong" to his visible environment, in which he is bound to feel rather a stranger. He belongs to the community of the saints, to the family of the Buddha. Buddhism substitutes a spiritual for the natural environment, with the Buddha for the father, the Prajnaparamita for the mother, the fellow-seekers for brothers and sisters, relatives and friends. It is with these more invisible forces that one must learn to establish satisfactory social relations. In carrying out this task, faith requires a considerable capacity for renunciation.

This concludes our survey of the four factors which go into the making of faith. Like other spiritual qualities, faith is somewhat paradoxical in that in one sense it is a gift which one cannot obtain by merely wanting to, and in another sense it is a virtue that can be cultivated. The capacity for faith varies with the constitution of the individual and his social circumstances. It is usual to classify types of personality according to whether they are dominated by greed, hatred or confusion. Those who walk in greed are said to be more susceptible to faith than the other two, because of the kinship which exists between faith and greed. To quote Buddhaghosa (Visuddhimagga III,75): "As on the unwholesome plane greed clings and takes no offense, so faith on the wholesome plane. As greed searches for objects of sense-desire, so faith for the qualities of morality, etc. As greed does not let go that which is harmful, so faith does not let go that which is beneficial."

As regards social conditions, there are ages of faith and ages of unbelief. The present age rather fosters unbelief. It puts a premium on intellectual smartness, so that faith is easily held to indicate nothing but a weak head or a lack of intellectual integrity. It multiplies the distractions from the sensory world to such an extent that the calm of the invisible world is harder to reach than ever. It exposes the citizen to so great a variety of conflicting viewpoints that he finds it hard to make a choice. The prestige of science, the concern with a high standard of living, and the disappearance of all institutions of uncontested authority are the chief foes of faith in our present-day society. It is largely a matter of temperament whether we believe that matters will improve in the near future.

As a virtue, faith is strengthened and built up by self-discipline, and not by discussing opinions. Intellectual difficulties are by no means the most powerful among the obstacles to faith. Doubts are inevitable, but how one deals with them depends on one's character. The first of our four "articles of faith" well illustrates this situation. There are many sound reasons for accepting the rebirth doctrine. This is not the place to expound them, and I must be content to refer the reader to the very impressive "East-West Anthology" on Reincarnation which J. Head and S.L. Cranston have published in 1961 (New York, The Julian Press Inc.). Yet, although belief in rebirth is perfectly rational and does not conflict with any known fact, the range of the average person's vision is so limited that he has no access to the decisive evidence, which is direct and immediate experience.

The rebirth doctrine assumes at least two things: (1) that behind the natural causality which links together events in the world of sense there are other, invisible chains of a moral causality, which assures that all good acts are rewarded, all bad actions punished; and (2) that this chain of moral sequences is not interrupted by death, but continues from rebirth to rebirth. To the average person these two assumptions cannot be proved absolutely, conclusively and beyond the possibility of a doubt. However plausible they may seem on rational grounds, Buddhism teaches that they become a matter of direct experience only after the "superknowledges" (abhijna, abhiñña) have been developed.

The fourth "superknowledge" is the recollection of one's own previous rebirths, and the fifth the knowledge of the rebirths of other people, by which one "sees that whatever happens to them happens in accordance with their deeds." There are many well-authenticated cases of persons spontaneously remembering certain details of one or the other of their own previous lives, and these people obviously have an additional reason for belief in rebirth which is lacking in those who cannot recall ever having lived before. Full certitude on the issue is, however, given to those only who can, on the basis of the fourth jhana and by taking definite prescribed and disciplined steps on emerging from that jhana, "recall their manifold former lives," according to the well-known formula: "There I was, that was my name, that was my family, that was my caste, such was my food, this was the happiness, this the suffering which I experienced, this was the duration of my life-span. Deceased there I was born elsewhere and there had this name, etc."

When a monk has practiced properly and successfully, "these things become as clear to him as if lit up by a lamp" (Visuddhimagga, xiii, 23).

Until that time comes, we cannot claim that we fully know the doctrine of karma and rebirth to be true. We take it partly on faith. And this faith of ours is maintained less by our dialectical skill as by the virtues of patience and courage. For we must be willing to wait patiently until we are spiritually ripe for the emergence of the super-knowledges, however far off that might seem to be. And secondly, we must be willing to take risks. Life nowhere offers a one hundred per cent security, and for our convictions least of all. Employed in gaining wealth a merchant must risk his property. Employed in taking life, a soldier must risk his own life. Employed in saving his soul, the spiritual man must risk his own soul. The stake automatically increases with the prospect of gain. Of course, we may be mistaken. I sometimes wonder what I would think if, on dying, I would not, as I now fondly imagine, wake up on the Bardo plane, but find myself confronted with Acheron and the three-headed Cerberus, or, worse still, were ill-treated with fire and brimstone in a Christian hell. The experience would, I admit, be rather disconcerting. All that I can say in the face of such uncertainty is that I am willing to take the consequences, and that I hope that my fund of boldness, audacity and good humor will not run out.

One has the choice to magnify intellectual doubts, or to minimize them. It seems not unreasonable that one should blame the difficulties of the teaching on one's own distance from the truth, one's own intellectual and moral imperfections. How can one expect to remember one's past lives, if at present one cannot even recall hour by hour what one did during one single day a mere month ago? If one hesitates to accept, as not immediately obvious, the doctrine that this world is the result of ignorance and of the craving of non-existent individuals for non-existent objects - is this not perhaps due to the very denseness of one's own ignorance, for which one can collect plenty of proofs all day long? Doubts are effectively overcome when one purifies one's own life, so as to become more worthy of knowledge. It is a condition of all learning that one accepts a great deal on trust, that one gives the teacher the benefit of the doubt. Otherwise one can learn nothing at all, and remains shut out from all truth. To have faith means to take a deep breath, to tear oneself away from the daily cares and concerns, and to turn resolutely to a wider and more abiding reality. At first we are, by ourselves, too stupid and inexperienced to see the tracks which lead to salvation. So we must put our trust in the Sages of the past, and listen intently to their words, dimmed by distance and the noise of the present day, but still just audible.

One last word about tolerance, without which faith remains raw and unsure of itself. It is a perpetual trial to our faith that we should constantly meet with people who believe differently. We are easily tempted to wish this irritant removed, to coerce others, if only by argument, and to annihilate them, if only by dubbing them fools. Intolerance for people of other faiths, though often mistaken for ardor, betrays nothing so much as doubts within oneself. We can, of course, always console ourselves by assuming that the others, in their own way, believe what we do, and that in the end it all comes to the same thing. But that does not always sound very convincing, and what we must, I am afraid, learn to do is to bear with their presence.

2. Vigor

Next to faith, vigor (Skr.: virya; Pali: viriya). Little need be said about the need for being energetic if one wants to achieve something. Without vigor, without strenuous effort, without perseverance, one obviously cannot make much progress. Everybody knows what "vigor" is, although a generation which made the fortune of the discoverers of "night-starvation" might wish that it had more of it.

The fact that faith and vigor are virtues does not, however, imply that they are good all through, and that, regardless of the consequences, they should be strengthened at all times. Excess is to be deprecated, even in virtues. All the five virtues must be regarded as one whole. Their balance and harmony is almost as important as the virtues themselves.2 They support each other to some extent, but they also stand in each other's way. The one must sometimes be used to correct the excess of the other. In this way, concentration must come to the rescue of the latent faults of vigor. When vigor and energy have it all their own way, tranquillity is in danger. We all know people with a large dash of adrenalin in their blood, who are always busy, perhaps even "madly efficient," but not particularly restful. Vigor by itself leads to excitement, and has to be controlled by a development of concentrated calm.

Similarly, faith alone, without wisdom, can easily become mere credulity. Wisdom alone can teach what is worth believing. This can be illustrated by Don Quixote, who in literature is perhaps the purest embodiment of faith, and whose actions demonstrate that too much faith, by itself, is not necessarily a good thing. Cervantes' novel gives a fine and detailed description of all the chief attributes of faith. Don Quixote vigorously, fearlessly, without complaining, and even serenely endures all tribulations because he wants to help others, all of them equally, according to their needs. When he dashes into the middle of the boiling lake, he reaches the very height of self-abandonment of which faith as such is capable. "And just when he does not know what will happen to him, he finds himself among flowery fields beautiful beyond those of Elysium." His faith has conquered the senses, it transmutes the data of common-sense experience, and the barber's basin becomes Mambrino's helmet. And yet, when we consider the intellectual basis of his faith, we find that it consists in nothing more than a belief in the truth and veracity of the Romances which describe the fictitious and not particularly edifying doings of the knight-errants of the past. This is the reason why his adventures form a sorry sight, why he is a caricature even of a knight of the Middle Ages, why, shorn of all common-sense, faith in this case becomes slightly pathological.

Mr. Blyth claims that "the Don Quixote of the First Part is Zen incarnate," that "the man who surpasses Hakuin, Rinzai, Eno, Daruma and Shakyamuni himself is Don Quixote de la Mancha, Knight Errant." Zen, it seems, like all good things, can be abused. It is not very probable that, when the cloak of "Zen" is thrown over them, all donkeys do become tigers, all absurdities profundities. Irrationalism is not without its attractions, but can be overdone. To suggest that one scripture, one conviction, one faith is as good as another, smacks rather more of the spiritual nihilism of our present age, than of the wisdom of Sēng-t'san. I admit that I have always liked Don Quixote for saying that the "perfection" of madness does not consist in going "mad for some actual reason or other" but "in running mad without the least constraint or necessity." But still I cannot help feeling that there is some difference, intangible perhaps, but nevertheless real, between the perfection of madness and the perfection of wisdom. Don Quixote's faith was a rather puerile one, because he had no judgment, and his vision was defective. Blyth himself admits in the end that Don Quixote "lacks the Confucian virtue of Prudence, the balance of the powers of the mind" (p.210). I am not so sure about prudence, but the "balance of the powers of the mind" is certainly not only a Confucian, but also a Buddhist virtue, and a very essential one. Buddhaghosa, whom I am expounding here, leaves us in no doubt on this matter.6 What distinguishes a bhikkhu from a knight-errant is that he is essentially sober and calm, that his view of the world is sweetly rational, that he avoids violence in the pursuit of his aims, and that his estimate of his own role in the world does not greatly exceed his actual size in relation to the universe.

3. Mindfulness

A Buddhist owes his soberness to the cultivation of the third virtue of mindfulness (Skr.: smriti, Pali: sati). Whereas faith and vigor, when driven to excess, must be restrained by their counterparts, i.e., wisdom and tranquil concentration, the virtue of mindfulness does not share this disability. "Mindfulness should be strong everywhere. For it protects the mind from excitedness, into which it might fall since faith, vigor and wisdom may excite us; and from indolence, into which it might fall since concentration favors indolence. Therefore, mindfulness is desirable everywhere, like a seasoning of salt in all sauces, like the prime minister in all state functions. Hence it is said: 'The Lord has declared mindfulness to be useful everywhere, for the mind finds refuge in mindfulness and mindfulness is its protector. Without mindfulness there can be no exertion or restraint of the mind.' "

Although traces of it are not altogether absent in other religious and philosophical disciplines, in Buddhism alone mindfulness occupies a central position. If one were asked what distinguishes Buddhism from all other systems of thought, one would have to answer that it is the dharma-theory and the stress laid on mindfulness. Mindfulness is not only the seventh of the steps of the holy eightfold path, the third of the five virtues, and the first of the seven limbs of enlightenment. On occasions it is almost equated with Buddhism itself. So we read at the beginning of the Satipatthana Sutta that "the four applications of mindfulness are the one and only way (ekayano maggo) that leads beings to purity, to the transcending of sorrow and lamentation, to the appeasement of pain and sadness, to entrance upon the right method and to the realization of Nirvana."

What then is "mindfulness"? The Abhidharma, guided by the etymology of the Sanskrit term (smriti from smri, "to remember"), defines it as an act of remembering which prevents ideas from "floating away," and which fights forgetfulness, carelessness and distraction. This definition by itself, though correct, does not really make the function of this virtue very clear to us today.

The theoretical assumptions which underlie the various practices summed up in the word "mindfulness" are too much taken for granted. What one assumes is that the mind consists of two disparate parts - a depth which is calm and quiet, and a surface which is disturbed. The surface layer is in perpetual agitation and turmoil.

The center, at the bottom of the mind, beyond both the conscious and the unconscious mind as modern psychologists understand it, is quite still. The depth is, however, usually overlaid to such an extent that people remain incredulous when told of a submerged spot of stillness in their inmost hearts. In most cases the surface is so turbulent that the calm of the depth can be realized only in rare intervals.

Mindfulness and concentration are the two virtues which are concerned with the development of inward calm. The principal enemies of spiritual quietude are: (1) the senses; (2) the movements of the body; (3) the passions, wants and desires; and (4) discursive thinking. They have the power to be enemies when: (1) they are not subjected to any discipline; and (2) when the ego identifies itself with what takes place on the surface of the mind, participating heartily in it, and the illusion arises that these activities are "my" doings, "my" concerns and the sphere in which "I" live and have my being. When thus busy with worldly things, we have neither strength nor freedom. In order to conquer these enemies of spiritual quietude we must: (1) withdraw the senses from their objects, as the tortoise draws in its limbs; (2) keep watch on our muscular movements; (3) cease wanting anything, and dissociate all wants from the ego; and (4) cut off discursive thinking.

By an effort of the imagination one must try to see oneself at rest, floating freely, with no force exerted on one's spiritual self. The practice of mindfulness then is a series of efforts which aim at maintaining this isolation. Mindfulness is the name given to the measures which we take to protect the patch of inner calm, which may at first not seem very large. One, as it were, draws a line round this domain and at its boundaries keeps watch on trespassers. The expectation is that conscious attention will disintegrate the power of the enemies, diminish their number, and dissociate them from the ego. However diverse in nature the numerous exercises which come under the heading of mindfulness may seem to be, they all have in common this one purpose, that of guarding the incipient and growing calm in one's heart.

1. First, as regards the sensory stimuli, there is the "restraint of the senses," also called the "guarding of the doors of the senses." For two reasons sense stimulation may disturb inner calm: (1) because it gives an occasion for undesirable states, like greed, hate, etc., to invade and flood the mind; (2) because attention to the sensory world, however necessary and apparently innocuous, distracts from the object of wisdom, which is the emptiness of dharmas. One cannot grasp what is

meant by "restraint of the sense dominants," if one regards it as quite a natural thing that the mind should dwell on sense-linked objects. This is, indeed, most unnatural. In its natural purity thought abides in the calm contemplation of emptiness. The mind which sees, hears, etc., is a fallen mind.

The capacity of sense-experience to compel the mind to act in a certain way is greatly diminished if each sensory stimulus is examined at the point where it passes the threshold of consciousness. Attention, normally passive, involuntary and compulsive, is subjected to voluntary control. In the process of imposing some control on the senses one will be surprised to find how keen they are to function, how eager to find suitable objects with which to feed one's impulses and instincts, one's hopes and fears, one's interests and appetites, satisfactions and grievances. It is not so bad that one should see things, hear sounds, etc., but it is a threat to spiritual health when one gets interested and entranced, when one takes up what is seen and heard and seizes on it as a sign of what matters.

The practice of mindfulness is not confined to taking note of what enters the mind by way of the sense-organs. One also tries to determine what is allowed to enter, and to generally reduce the number of sensory impacts by restraining the use of the physical organ, for instance, when one walks with eyes directed only a few feet or yards ahead. In addition, by an effort of the will one refuses to co-operate with one's habitual impulses in building up a mere casual observation into a thing of moment to which one returns again and again. Finally the intruder is weakened and worn down by appropriate reflections. He is kept out of the heart and devalued - as trivial, as already passed, as nothing in particular, and by thinking that "this does not concern me at all, this means nothing to me, it is only a waste when salvation and Nirvana are considered."

2. Secondly, as regards the muscular movements of the body - an unquiet body is a concomitant of a disturbed mind, both its cause and symptom. It is important to mindfulness that one should consciously notice the position and movement of the body when walking, eating, speaking, etc., and suppress and correct those movements which are uncontrolled, hasty

and uncoordinated. This practice can, it is true, not be carried out at all times. In London traffic, for instance, the unhurried and unflurried demeanor of the mindful has little survival value. Where, however, it can be applied, we come to cherish this exercise which pulls us together, sometimes to an amazing extent in an amazingly short time. Insignificant as it may seem, compared with the splendors of Buddhist art and metaphysics, this training is their indispensable foundation stone. It is by his dignified and self-possessed deportment that the bhikkhu is recognized. And, of course, we should not forget that the mindful attention to muscular movements includes the breathing practices, which are a most fruitful source of insight.

3. Where we have to face the disturbance of the passions and of stray thoughts in general, the defense of our inward calm becomes more difficult. Mindfulness itself turns into incipient concentration.

At this point one may ask whether the practice of the five cardinal virtues, from faith to wisdom, is at all likely to be furthered by writing articles about them. It is, of course, not an entirely useless undertaking to guard the traditional teaching from current misunderstandings, quite apart from the pleasure of putting fleas into peoples' ears, and fomenting discussions about the importance of faith, or the value of erudition. But what about the virtues themselves? Thomas a Kempis once said that he would rather feel compunction than know the definition of it. What matters to a Buddhist is that he should be strong in faith, vigor, mindfulness, concentration and wisdom, and what use to him is the knowledge of how they are defined? Detailed advice on how these virtues should be practiced, it is true, can never be given in articles written for the general reader. Such advice must always be addressed to one person at a time, must take their individual constitution into account, and can, therefore, be given only by word of mouth.

On the other hand, if mindfulness is a virtue, then the ability to recollect one's own virtues is also a feature of the Buddhist life. And how can one attend to the presence or absence of mental states in oneself if one is unable to recognize them for what they are? The Satipatthana Sutta recommends systematic meditation on the wholesome and unwholesome mental states which arise in the mind. To quote the Sutta, one knows, for instance: (1) when there is vigor that there is vigor; (2) when there is no vigor that there is no vigor; (3) how the vigor which did not exist came to be produced; and (4) how and under what conditions it will grow to greater perfection. Psychology is so vital to Buddhist instruction because one cannot know anything definite about the furniture of one's mind unless one is acquainted with the categories into which mental conditions can be analyzed.

A mindful man is well informed about his own mental condition. His capacity for introspection is highly developed. And his interest in his own mind will not really make him self-centered as long as he remembers that he has to deal with the rise and fall of impersonal processes. In addition, in the case of the higher mental states, rational clarity is imperative if constant self-deception and wasteful groping in the dark are to be avoided. In a new country a map is helpful so that one may know where one is. The manuals of mystical theology written by the practicing contemplatives of the Catholic Church are also rich in descriptions of the sublimer virtues.

But this is not all. Where the Buddhist virtues are described for a lay audience one must not omit to mention the all-important fact that the upper ranges of these virtues demand a reformation of the conduct of life which is greater than almost any layman is willing to undertake.

The higher mindfulness, and nearly the whole range of concentration and wisdom, presuppose a degree of withdrawal from the world which is incompatible with the life of an ordinary citizen. Those who are unwilling to achieve a radical seclusion from the world can practice these virtues only in a very rudimentary form. It is quite idle to pretend that they do not involve a complete break with the established habits of life and thought. Unless we make the sacrifices involved in withdrawing from the world, we are bound to remain strangers to the fullness of mindfulness, concentration and wisdom.

But if the monastic life is a necessary condition for these virtues, why talk about them at all? Partly because it is salutary, though painful, that we should see their absence in us, and partly because they constitute the subjective counterpart of the scriptures which we read. The Suttas describe the world as it appears on a spiritual level on which concentration and wisdom have come to maturity. The understanding of the scriptures is furthered by an understanding of the subjective attitude which corresponds to them. And so, although we are forced to go beyond the range of our immediate experience, and although the description tends to become more intangible as it rises to loftier heights, we will now, leaving aside the higher ranges of mindfulness, try to explain the traditional definitions of concentration and wisdom, as they are handed down to us.

4. Concentration

Concentration (samadhi) continues the work of mindfulness. It deepens our capacity to regain the peaceful calm of our inner nature. But here we are at once faced with the difficulty that in Buddhist psychology "concentration" occurs twice: (1) as a factor essential to all thought; and (2) as a special, and rather rare, virtue.

1. In its simplest form, concentration is the narrowing of the field of attention in a manner and for a time determined by the will. The mind is made one-pointed, does not waver, does not scatter itself, and it becomes steady like the flame of a lamp in the absence of wind. Without a certain degree of one-pointedness no mental activity at all can take place. Each mental act lasts, strictly speaking, for one moment only, and is at once followed by another. The function of concentration is to provide some stability in this perpetual flux, by enabling the mind to stand in, or on, the same object, without distraction, for more than one moment. In addition it is a synthetic quality (sam-a-dhi = syn-thesis), that binds together a number of mental states which arise at the same time, "as water binds the lather of soap."

Buddhaghosa stresses the fact that intellectual concentration is also found in unwholesome thoughts. The mind must be undistracted so that the murderer's knife does not miss, the theft does not miscarry. A mind of single intent is capable of doing what it does more effectively, be it good or bad. The higher degrees of this kind of concentration owe much to the presence of the "hunting instinct," and can best be observed in a stoat following a rabbit. Intellectual concentration is a quality which is ethically and spiritually neutral. Many scientific workers have an unusually high capacity for concentrated thought. Anyone acquainted with the "scientific humanists" who inhabit our big cities will, however, agree that their intellectual achievements are not conducive to either peace of mind or spiritual progress. When Sir Isaac Newton boiled his watch instead of the egg his landlady had given him, he thereby showed the intensity with which he focussed his mind on his intellectual task. But the result of his intellectual labors has been to cast a dark shadow over the spiritual radiance of the universe, and ever since, the celestial harmonies have become nearly inaudible. As H.W. Longfellow, in his poem on "The Arsenal at Springfield," has put it:

> Is it, O man, with such discordant noises,
> With such accursed instruments as these,
> Thou drownest Nature's sweet and kindly voices,
> And jarrest the celestial harmonies?

2. How then does concentration as a spiritual virtue differ from concentration as a condition of the intellect? Spiritual or transic concentration results less from intellectual effort than from a rebirth of the whole personality, including the body, the emotions, and the will. It cannot possibly be achieved without some discipline over the body, since we must be able to endure the prescribed posture, practice the prescribed breathing exercises, and so on. It is further built on a change of outlook which we can well describe as "ethical." Tradition is quite unambiguous on this point. Before spiritual concentration can be even approached, we must have stilled or suppressed five vices, which are known as the "five hindrances": sense desire, ill will, sloth and torpor, excitedness and sense of guilt, and doubt. Where these hindrances are present, where concentrated

thought is fused with greed, the desire to excel, to get a good job, etc., there concentration as a spiritual virtue is not found.

In this sense physical ease and self-purification are the first two distinctive features of spiritual concentration. The third is the shift in attention from the sensory world to another subtler realm. The methods by which this shift is effected are traditionally known as the four trances (jhana) and the four formless attainments.

They are essentially a training in increasing introversion, achieved by progressively diminishing the impact of the outer stimuli. As a result of their successful withdrawal and renunciation the spiritually concentrated release the inward calm which dwells in their hearts. This concentration cannot be won, however, unless no attention is given to sensory data, and everything sensory is viewed as equally unimportant. Subjectively it is marked by a soft, tranquil and pacified passivity, objectively by the abstraction into an unearthly world of experience which lifts one above the world, and bestows a certainty greater than anything the senses may teach. The experience is so satisfying that it burns up the world, and only its cold ashes are found when one returns to it.

5. Wisdom

And so we come to wisdom (Skr.: prajna; Pali pañña), the highest virtue of all.

"Wisdom is based on concentration, because of the saying: 'One who is concentrated knows, sees what really is.'" Is concentration then an indispensable pre-condition of wisdom? The answer lies in distinguishing three stages of wisdom, according to whether it operates on the level of: (1) learning about what tradition has to say concerning the psychological and ontological categories which form the subject-matter of wisdom; (2) discursive reflection on the basic facts of life; and (3) meditational development. The third alone requires the aid of transic concentration, whereas without it there can be proficiency in the first two. And the wisdom which consists of learning and reflection should not be despised.

The main stream of Buddhist tradition has always greatly esteemed learning. Our attitude to the apple of knowledge differs from that of many Christians. On the whole, we regard it as rather more nourishing than baneful. The wisdom, which is the fifth and crowning virtue, is not the wisdom that can be found in the untutored child of nature, the corny sage of the backwoods, or the self-made philosopher of the suburbs. It can operate only after a great deal of traditional information has been absorbed, a great deal of sound learning acquired. The required skill in metaphysical and psychological analysis would be impossible without a good knowledge of the material on which this skill ought to be exercised. From this point of view learning is perhaps less to be regretted than its absence.

The second stage, after learning, is reflection, which is an operation of the intellect. Even the relative beginner can greatly increase his wisdom by discursive meditations on the basic facts of life. Finally, it is on the level of mental development (bhavana) that this meditational technique reaches its maturity, and then it does, indeed, require the aid of mindfulness and concentration.

"Wisdom" is, of course, only a very approximate equivalent of prajna. To the average person nowadays "wisdom" seems to denote a compound made up of such qualities as sagacity, prudence, a well-developed sense of values, serenity, and sovereignty over the world won by the understanding of the mode of its operation. The Buddhist conception of "wisdom" is not unlike this, but more precise. It is best clarified by first giving its connotations, and then its actual definition.

As for the connotations, we read in the Dhammasangani:14 "On that occasion the dominant15 of wisdom is wisdom, understanding,16 search, research, search for dharma;17 discernment, discrimination, differentiation, erudition, expert skill, subtlety, clarity,18 reflection, investigation,19 amplitude,20 sagacity,21 a guide (to true welfare and to the marks as they truly are), insight, comprehension, a goad (which urges the mind to move back on the right track); wisdom, wisdom as virtue, wisdom as strength (because ignorance cannot dislodge it), the sword of wisdom (which cuts through the defilements), the lofty (and overtowering) height of wisdom, the light,22 luster and splendor of wisdom, the treasure23 of wisdom, absence of delusion, search for dharmas, right view." From mere cleverness wisdom is distinguished by its spiritual purpose, and we are told expressly24 that it is designed "to cut off the defilements."

Now to the actual definition: "Wisdom penetrates25 into dharmas as they are in themselves. It disperses the darkness of delusion, which covers up the own-being of dharmas."26

What then does wisdom meditate about? Wisdom may be held to concern itself with three possible topics: (1) true reality; (2) the meaning of life; (3) the conduct of life. Buddhist tradition assumes that the second and third depend on the first. In its essence wisdom is the strength of mind which permits contact with the true reality, which is also called the realm of dharmas. Delusion, folly, confusion, ignorance and self-deception are the opposites of wisdom.

It is because ignorance, and not sin, is the root evil that wisdom is regarded as the highest virtue. A holiness which is devoid of wisdom is not considered impossible, but it cannot be gained by the path of knowledge, to which alone these descriptions apply. The paths of faith, of love, of works, etc., have each their own several laws.

As the unfaltering penetration into the true nature of objects, wisdom is the capacity to meditate in certain ways about the dharmic constituents of the universe. The rules of that meditation have been laid down in the scriptures, particularly in the Abhidharma, and a superb description can be found in the latter part of Buddhaghosa's Path of Purification. Mindfulness and concentration were, as we saw, based on the assumption of a duality in the mind - between its calm depth and its excited surface. Wisdom similarly assumes a duality between the surface and depth of all things. Objects are not what they appear to be. Their true reality, in which they stand out as dharmas, is opposed to their appearance to commonsense, and much strength of wisdom is required to go beyond the deceptive appearance and to penetrate to the reality of dharmas themselves.

1. The Five Faculties

(a) From the Milindapañha

The king said: "Is it through wise attention that people become exempt from further rebirth?" - "Yes, that is due to wise attention, and also to wisdom, and the other wholesome dharmas." - "But is not wise attention the same as wisdom?" - "No, Your Majesty. Attention is one thing, and wisdom another. Sheep and goats, oxen and buffaloes, camels and asses have attention, but wisdom they have not." - "Well put, Venerable Nagasena."

The king said: "What is the mark of attention, and what is the mark of wisdom?" - "Consideration is the mark of attention, cutting off that of wisdom." - "How is that? Give me a simile." - "You know barley-reapers, I suppose?" - "Yes, I do." - "How then do they reap the barley?" - "With the left hand they seize a bunch of barley, in the right hand they hold a sickle, and they cut the barley off with that sickle." - "Just so, Your Majesty, the yogin seizes his mental processes with his attention, and by his wisdom he cuts off the defilements." - "Well put, Venerable Nagasena."

The king said: "When you just spoke of 'the other wholesome dharmas,' which ones did you mean?" - "I meant morality, faith, vigor, mindfulness and concentration." - "And what is the mark of morality?" - "Morality has the mark of providing a basis for all wholesome dharmas, whatever they may be. When based on morality, all the wholesome dharmas will not dwindle away." - "Give me an illustration." - "As all plants and animals which increase, grow, and prosper, do so with the earth as their support, with the earth as their basis, just so the yogin, with morality as his support, with morality as his basis, develops the five cardinal virtues, i.e., the cardinal virtues of faith, vigor, mindfulness, concentration, and wisdom."

"Give me a further illustration."

"As the builder of a city when constructing a town first of all clears the site, removes all stumps and thorns, and levels it; and only after that he lays out and marks off the roads and cross-roads, and so builds the city, even so the yogin develops the five cardinal virtues with morality as his support, with morality as his basis."

The king said: "What is the mark of faith?" - "Faith makes serene, and it leaps forward." - "And how does faith make serene?" - "When faith arises it arrests the five hindrances, and the heart becomes free from them, clear, serene and undisturbed." - "Give me an illustration." - "A universal monarch might on his way, together with his fourfold army, cross over a small stream. Stirred up by the elephants and horses, by the chariots and infantry, the water would become disturbed, agitated and muddy.

Having crossed over, the universal monarch would order his men to bring some water for him to drink. But the king would possess a miraculous water-clearing gem, and his men, in obedience to his command, would throw it into the stream. Then at once all fragments of vegetation would float away, the mud would settle at the bottom, the stream would become clear, serene and undisturbed, and fit to be drunk by the universal monarch. Here the stream corresponds to the heart, the monarch's men to the yogin, the fragments of vegetation and the mud to the defilements, and the miraculous water-clearing gem to faith."

"And how does faith leap forward?" - "When the yogin sees that the hearts of others have been set free, he leaps forward, by way of aspiration, to the various fruits of the holy life, and he makes efforts to attain the yet unattained, to find the yet unfound, to realize the yet unrealized." - "Give me an illustration." - "Suppose that a great cloud were to burst over a hill-slope.

The water then would flow down the slope, would first fill all the hill's clefts, fissures, and gullies, and would then run into the river below, making its banks overflow on both sides. Now suppose further that a great crowd of people had come along, and unable to size up either the width or the depth of the river, should stand frightened and hesitating on the bank. But then some man would come along, who, conscious of his own strength and power, would firmly tie on his own loin-cloth and jump across the river. And the great crowd of people, seeing him on the other side, would cross likewise. Even so the yogin, when he has seen that the hearts of others have been set free, leaps forward, by aspiration, to the various fruits of the holy life, and he makes efforts to attain the yet unattained, to find the yet unfound, to realize the yet unrealized. And this is what the Lord has said in the Samyutta Nikaya:

By faith the flood is crossed,
By wakefulness the sea;
By vigor ill is passed;
By wisdom cleansed is he."

"Well put, Nagasena!"

The king asked: "And what is the mark of vigor?" - "Vigor props up, and, when propped up by vigor, all the wholesome dharmas do not dwindle away." - "Give me a simile." - "If a man's house were falling down, he would prop it up with a new piece of wood, and, so supported, that house would not collapse."

The king asked: "And what is the mark of mindfulness?"- "Calling to mind and taking up."

"How is calling to mind a mark of mindfulness?" - "When mindfulness arises, one calls to mind the dharmas which participate in what is wholesome and unwholesome, blamable and blameless, inferior and sublime, dark and light, i.e., these are the four applications of mindfulness, these the four right efforts, these the four roads to psychic power, these the five cardinal virtues, these the five powers, these the seven limbs of enlightenment, this is the holy eightfold path; this is calm, this insight, this knowledge and this emancipation. Thereafter the yogin tends those dharmas which should be tended, and he does not tend those which should not be tended; he partakes of those dharmas which should be followed, and he does not partake of those which should not be followed. It is in this sense that calling to mind is a mark of mindfulness." - "Give me a simile." - "It is like the treasurer of a universal monarch, who each morning and evening reminds his royal master of his magnificent assets: 'So many elephants you have, so many horses, so many chariots, so much infantry, so many gold coins, so much bullion, so much property; may Your Majesty bear this in mind.' In this way he calls to mind his master's wealth."

"And how does mindfulness take up?" - "When mindfulness arises, the outcome of beneficial and harmful dharmas is examined in this way: 'These dharmas are beneficial, these harmful; these dharmas are helpful, these unhelpful.' Thereafter the yogin removes the harmful dharmas, and takes up the beneficial ones; he removes the unhelpful dharmas, and takes up the helpful ones. It is in this sense that mindfulness takes up." - "Give me a comparison." - "It is like the invaluable adviser of a universal monarch who knows what is beneficial and what is harmful to his royal master, what is helpful and what is unhelpful. Thereafter what is harmful and unhelpful can be removed, what is beneficial and helpful can be taken up."

The king asked: "And what is the mark of concentration?"- "It stands at the head. Whatever wholesome dharmas there may be, they all are headed by concentration, they bend towards concentration, lead to concentration, incline to concentration."- "Give me a comparison." - "It is as with a building with a pointed roof: whatever rafters there are, they all converge on the top, bend towards the top, meet at the top, and the top occupies the most prominent place. So with concentration in relation to the other wholesome dharmas." - "Give me a further comparison." - "If a king were to enter battle with his fourfold army, then all his troops - the elephants, cavalry, chariots and infantry - would be headed by him, and would be ranged around him. Such is the position of concentration in relation to the other wholesome dharmas."

The king then asked: "What then is the mark of wisdom?"- "Cutting off is, as I said before, one mark of wisdom. In addition it illuminates." - "And how does wisdom illuminate?" - "When wisdom arises, it dispels the darkness of ignorance, generates the illumination of knowledge, sheds the light of cognition, and makes the holy truths stand out clearly. Thereafter the yogin, with his correct wisdom, can see impermanence, ill, and not-self." - "Give me a comparison." - "It is like a lamp which a man would take into a dark house. It would dispel the darkness, would illuminate, shed light, and make the forms in the house stands out clearly." - "Well put, Venerable Nagasena." - Milindapañha, pp. 51-62; translated by Edward Conze

(b) From the Akshayamati Sutra

The five faculties are faith, vigor, mindfulness, concentration, and wisdom. Here what is faith? By this faith one has faith in four dharmas. Which four? He accepts the right view which assumes renewed becoming in the world of birth-and-death; he puts his trust in the ripening of karma, and knows that he will experience the fruit of any karma, that he may have done; even to save his life he does not do any evil deed. He has faith in the mode of life of a Bodhisattva, and, having taken up this discipline, he does not long for any other vehicle.

He believes when he hears all the doctrines which are characterized by the true, clear, and profound knowledge of conditioned co-production, by such terms as lack of self, absence of a being, absence of a soul, absence of a person; and by emptiness, the signless and the wishless. He follows none of the false doctrines, and believes in all the qualities (dharmas) of a Buddha, his powers, grounds of self-confidence, and all the rest; and when in his faith he has left behind all doubts, he brings about in himself those qualities of a Buddha.

This is known as the virtue of faith. His vigor consists of his bringing about (in himself) the dharmas in which he has faith. His mindfulness consists in his preventing the qualities which he brings about by vigor from being destroyed by forgetfulness. His concentration consists in his fixing his one-pointed attention on these very same qualities. With the faculty of wisdom he contemplates those dharmas on which he has fixed his one-pointed attention, and penetrates to their reality.

The cognition of those dharmas which arises in himself and which has no outside condition is called the virtue of wisdom. Thus these five virtues, together, are sufficient to bring forth all the qualities of a Buddha. - Akshayamati Sutra (quoted in Shikshasamuccaya); translated by Edward Conze

2. The Restraint of the Senses

(a) From Ashvaghosha's Saundaranandakavya

By taking your stand on mindfulness you must hold back from the sense-objects your senses, unsteady by nature. Fire, snakes, and lightning are less inimical to us than our own senses, so much more dangerous. For they assail us all the time. Even the most vicious enemies can attack only some people at some times, and not at others, but everybody is always and everywhere weighed down by his senses. And people do not go to hell because some enemy has knocked them down and cast them into it; it is because they have been knocked down by their unsteady senses that they are helplessly dragged there. Those attacked by external enemies may, or may not, suffer injury to their souls; but those who are weighed down by the senses suffer in body and soul alike. For the five senses are rather like arrows which have been smeared with the poison of fancies, have cares for their feathers, and happiness for their points, and fly about in the space provided by the range of the sense-objects; shot off by Kama, the God of Love, they hit men in their very hearts as a hunter hits a deer, and if men do not know how to ward off these arrows, they will be their undoing; when they come near us we should stand firm in self-control, be agile and steadfast, and ward them off with the great armor of mindfulness. As a man who has subdued his enemies can everywhere live and sleep at ease and free from care, so can he who has pacified his senses. For the senses constantly ask for more by way of worldly objects, and normally behave like voracious dogs who can never have enough. This disorderly mob of the senses can never reach satiety, not by any amount of sense-objects; they are rather like the sea, which one can go on indefinitely replenishing with water.

In this world the senses cannot be prevented from being active, each in its own sphere. But they should not be allowed to grasp either the general features of an object, or its particularities. When you have beheld a sight-object with your eyes, you must merely determine the basic element (which it represents, e.g., it is a sight-object), and should not under any circumstances fancy it as, say, a "woman" or a "man." But if now and then you have inadvertently grasped something as a "woman" or a "man," you should not follow that up by determining the hairs, teeth, etc., as lovely. Nothing should be subtracted from the datum, nothing added to it; it should be seen as it really is, as what it is like in real truth.

If you thus try to look continually for the true reality in that which the senses present to you, covetousness and aversion will soon be left without a foothold. Coveting ruins those living beings who are bent on sensuous enjoyment by means of pleasing forms, like an enemy with a friendly face who speaks loving words, but plans dark deeds. But what is called "aversion" is a kind of anger directed towards certain objects, and anyone who is deluded enough to pursue it is bound to suffer for it either in this or a future life. Afflicted by their likes and dislikes, as by excessive heat or cold, men will never find either happiness or the highest good as long as they put their trust in the unsteady senses. - Saundaranandakavya, xiii, 30-56; translated by Edward Conze

(b) From the Prajnaparamita

The Lord: When he practices the perfection of meditation for the sake of other beings his mind becomes undistracted. For he reflects that "even worldly meditation is hard to accomplish with distracted thoughts, how much more so is full enlightenment. Therefore, I must remain undistracted until I have won full enlightenment."...

Moreover, Subhuti, a Bodhisattva, beginning with the first thought of enlightenment, practices the perfection of meditation. His mental activities are associated with the knowledge of all modes when he enters into meditation.

When he has seen forms with his eye, he does not seize upon them as signs of realities which concern him, nor is he interested in the accessory details. He sets himself to restrain that which, if he does not restrain his organ of sight, might give him occasion for covetousness, sadness or other evil and unwholesome dharmas to reach his heart. He watches over the organ of sight. And the same with the other five sense-organs-ear, nose, tongue, body and mind.

Whether he walks or stands, sits or lies down, talks or remains silent, his concentration does not leave him. He does not fidget with his hands or feet, or twitch his face; he is not incoherent in his speech, confused in his senses, exalted or uplifted, fickle or idle, agitated in body or mind. Calm is his body, calm is his voice, calm is his mind. His demeanor shows contentment, both in private and public... He is frugal, easy to feed, easy to serve, of good life and habits; though in a crowd he dwells apart; even and unchanged, in gain and loss; not elated, not cast down. Thus in happiness and suffering, in praise and blame, in fame and disrepute, in life or death, he is the same unchanged, neither elated nor cast down. And so with foe or friend, with what is pleasant or unpleasant, with holy or unholy men, with noises or music, with forms that are dear or undear, he remains the same, unchanged, neither elated nor cast down, neither gratified nor thwarted. And why? Because he sees all dharmas as empty of marks of their own, without true reality, incomplete and uncreated. - Prajnaparamita, ch. 68; translated by Edward Conze

(c) From the Visuddhimagga

This is the morality which consists in the restraint of the senses: "Here someone: (1) having seen a form with his eye, does not seize on its general appearance, or the (accessory) details of it. That which might, so long as he dwells unrestrained as to the (controlling) force of the eye, give occasion for covetous, sad, evil and unwholesome dharmas to flood him, that he sets himself to restrain; he guards the controlling force of the eye, and brings about its restraint. And likewise (2) when he has heard sounds with the ear, (3) smelled smells with the nose, (4) tasted tastes with the tongue, (5) touched touchables with the body, (6) cognized mind-objects (dharmas) with the mind." (M.i,180).

Having seen a form with his eye: when he has seen a form with the visual consciousness which is capable of seeing forms, and which in normal language is usually called the "eye," though it actually is its tool. For the Ancients have said: "The eye cannot see forms because it is without thought; thought cannot see forms because it is without eye. When the object knocks against the door (of sight) one sees with the thought which has eye-sensibility for its basis." In the expression "one sees with the eye," only accessory equipment is indicated, just as one may say, "one shoots with a bow" (and not "with an arrow"). Therefore, the meaning here is: "having seen form with visual consciousness."

He does not seize on its general appearance (lit. "the sign"): he does not seize on its appearance as man or woman, or its appearance as attractive, etc., which makes it into a basis for the defiling passions. But he stops at what is actually seen. He does not seize on the details of it: he does not seize on the variety of its accessory features, like the hands or feet, the smile, the laughter, the talk, the looking here, the looking away, etc., which are in common parlance called "details" (anubyanjana) because they manifest the defiling passions, by again and again (anu anu) tainting with them (byanjanato). But he seizes only on that which is really there, i.e., the impurity of the 32 parts of the body) like Mahatissa, the Elder, who lived on Mount Cetiya. Once that Elder went from Mount Cetiya to Anuradhapura, to gather alms. In a certain family the daughter-in-law had quarreled with her husband, and adorned and beautified like a heavenly maiden, she left Anuradhapura early in the morning, and went away to stay with some relatives. On the way she saw the Elder, and, as her mind was perverted, she gave a loud laugh. The Elder looked to see what was the matter; he acquired, at the sight of her teeth (-bones), the notion of repulsiveness (impurity), and thereby reached Arahatship... The husband who ran after her on same road, saw the Elder, and asked him whether he had by any chance seen a woman. The Elder replied:

"Whether what went along here

Was a man or a woman, I do not know.

But a collection of bones is moving

Now along this main road."

[That which might, etc.: that which might be the reason, or that non-restraint of the faculty of the eye which might be the cause, why in this person, when he dwells without having restrained the faculty of the eye with the gate of mindfulness, i.e., when he has left the door of the eye open, such dharmas as covetousness, etc., flood him, i.e., pursue and submerge him.

That he sets himself to restrain:] he sets himself to close this faculty of the eye with the gate of mindfulness. And one who sets himself to do that, of him it is said that he guards the controlling force of the eye, and brings about its restraint.

But it is not with reference to the faculty of the eye itself that there is restraint or non-restraint (i.e., it does not apply to the initial stage of the impact of stimulus on the eye), and it is not concerning the eye considered as a sensitive organ that mindfulness arises, or the lack of it. But it is at (the stage of the apperception of the object, with such and such a meaning and significance, and the volitional reaction to it, which is technically known as) the "impulsive moment," that there is lack of restraint, if and when immorality arises then, or lack of mindfulness, or lack of cognition, lack of patience or laziness. Nevertheless one speaks of the non-restraint of the sense of sight. And why? Because when the mind is in that condition, also the door (of the eye) is unguarded. The situation can be compared with that of a city: when its four gates are unguarded, then, although in the interior of the city the doors of the houses, the storerooms and private rooms are well guarded, nevertheless all the property in the city is actually unguarded and unprotected, and robbers can, once they have entered through the city gates, do whatever they like. In the same sense also the door (of the eye) is unguarded when, in consequence of the arising of immorality, etc., there is lack of restraint at the "impulsive moment."

But when morality, etc., arise at that moment, then the door (of sight) also is guarded. Just again as with the city: When the city-gates are well guarded, then, although in the interior the doors of the houses, etc., are unguarded, nevertheless all the property in the city is actually well guarded and well protected; for the city-gates being closed, robbers cannot enter. Just so also the door (of the eye) is guarded when morality, etc., arise at the "impulsive moment." The same explanation applies to: when he has heard sounds with the ear, etc. The restraint of the senses thus consists, in short, in the avoiding of the seizing of the general appearance, etc., of sight-objects, etc., which lead to one's being pursued by the defiling passions.

And it should be achieved through mindfulness. For it is effected by mindfulness, in so far as the sense-organs when they are governed by mindfulness, can no longer be influenced by convetousness, etc. Therefore, we should remember the "Fire Sermon" (S.iv,168) which says: "It were better, monks, if the eye were stroked with a heated iron bar, afire, ablaze, aflame, than that one should seize on either the general appearance or the details of the forms of which the eye is aware." The disciple should achieve a thorough restraint of the senses, in that, by unimpaired mindfulness, he prevents that seizing on the general appearance, etc., which makes the consciousness which proceeds through the door of the eye, etc., with forms, etc., for its range (province), liable to be flooded (influenced) by covetousness, etc.

And one should become like Cittagutta, the Elder, who lived in the great Kurandaka Cave. In that cave there was a delightful painting which showed the seven Buddhas leaving for the homeless life. One day numerous monks were wandering about in the cave, going from lodging to lodging. They noticed the painting and said: "What a delightful painting, Venerable Bhikkhu!" The Elder replied: "For more than sixty years, brethren, I have lived in this cave, and I have never known whether there is a painting here or whether there is not. Today only I have learned it from you people, who use your eyes." For all that time during which the Elder had lived there, he had never lifted up his eyes and looked more closely at the cave. At the entrance to the cave there was a large ironwood tree. To that also the Elder had never looked up; but he knew that it was in flower when each year he saw the filaments which had fallen down on the ground.

All the sons of good family who have their own welfare at heart should, therefore, remember:

"Let not the eye wander like forest ape,

Or trembling wood deer, or affrighted child.

The eyes should be cast downwards; they should look
The distance of a yoke; he shall not serve
His thought's dominion, like a restless ape."

Visuddhimagga, I, 42, 53-59, 100, 104-5, 109; translated by Edward Conze

3. The Control of the Mind

The Sutta on the Composition of Ideas:27

[If, whilst attending to a certain sign, there arise, with reference to it, in the disciple evil and unwholesome ideas, connected with greed, hate or delusion, then the disciple:]

I. should, by means of this sign (= cause, occasion) attend to another sign which is more wholesome;

II. or he should investigate the peril of these ideas: "Unwholesome truly are these ideas! Blameworthy are these ideas! Of painful result are these ideas!";

III. or he should pay no attention to these ideas;

IV. or he should attend to the composition of the factors which effect these ideas;

V. or, with teeth clenched and tongue pressed against the gums, he should by means of sheer mental effort hold back, crush and burn out the (offending) thought.

In doing so, these evil and unwholesome ideas, bound up with greed, hate or delusion, will be forsaken and disappear; from their forsaking thought will become inwardly settled and calm, composed and concentrated. This is called the effort to overcome.

The Commentary says:

I. Unwholesome ideas may arise with reference to beings-be they desirable, undesirable, or unconsidered - or to things, such as one's possessions, or things which annoy, like stumps or thorns. The wholesome counter-ideas which drive them out arise from the following practices, which are directly opposed to them:

Greed about beings: Meditation about the repulsiveness of the body.

Greed about things: Attention to their impermanence.

Hate for beings: The development of friendliness.

Hate for things: Attention to the elements: which of the physical elements composing the thing am I angry with?

Delusion about beings and things:

1. When he has, in his general bewilderment, neglected his duties to a teacher, he wakes himself up by doing some tiresome work, such as carrying water.
2. When he has been hazy in attending to the teacher's explanation of the doctrine, he wakes himself up by doing some tiresome work.
3. He removes his doubts by questioning authorities.
4. At the right time he listens respectfully to the Dharma.
5. He acquires the skill in distinguishing between correct and faulty conclusions, and knows that "this is the reason for that, this is not the reason."

These are the direct and correct antidotes to the faulty ideas.

II. He investigates them with the power of wisdom, and rejects them like a snake's carcass.

III. He should not remember those ideas, not attend to them, but become one who is otherwise engaged. He should be like someone who, not wanting to see a certain sight-object, just closes his eyes; when these ideas arise in his mind, he should take hold of his basic subject of meditation, and become engaged in that. It may help him to break the spell of intruding thoughts and to occupy his mind otherwise, if he recites with great faith a passage from the Scriptures, or reads out a passage in praise of the Buddha or Dharma; or he may sort out his belongings, and enumerate them one by one: "these are the scissors," "this is the needle," etc.; or he should do some sewing; or he should do some good work for a given period of time. And after that he should return to his basic subject of meditation.

IV. He should analyze the conditions for these ideas and ask himself: "What is their cause, what their condition, what the reason for their having arisen?"

V. He should put forth great vigor, and with a wholesome thought he should hold back an unwholesome one. - Majjhima Nikaya, No. 20, and Papañcasudani (Summary); translated by Edward Conze

4. The Buddha's Sayings on the Faculties

From the Samyutta Nikaya (Indriya Samyutta)

(a) At their Best

There are these five faculties, monks: the faculty of faith, the faculty of vigor, the faculty of mindfulness, the faculty of concentration and the faculty of wisdom.

Where can the faculty of faith be seen (at its best)? In the four characteristic qualities of a stream-winner.

Where can the faculty of vigor be seen (at its best)? In the four right efforts.

Where can the faculty of mindfulness be seen (at its best)? In the four foundations of mindfulness.

Where can the faculty of concentration be seen (at its best)? In the four meditative absorptions.

Where can the faculty of wisdom be seen (at its best)? In the Four Noble Truths. - Sutta 8 (PTS, iv,196); translated by Nyanaponika Mahathera

(b) The Measure of Achievement

By accomplishment and perfection in the five faculties one is an arahant. If the faculties are weaker, one is a non-returner; if they are still weaker, one is a once-returner, or a stream-winner, or a Dhamma-devotee (dhammanusarin), or a faith-devotee (saddhanusarin).

Thus, monks, through the difference of faculties, there is difference of result; and the difference of results makes for the difference of individuals. - Sutta 13; translated by Nyanaponika Mahathera

Thus, monks, he who practices the five faculties to their perfection, wins to perfection (of arahantship). He who practices them partially, wins a partial result. Not barren (of results),

I say, are the five faculties. - Sutta 14; translated by Nyanaponika Mahathera

But he who is entirely, in any degree and respect, without these five faculties, stands outside, in the class of ordinary men (puthujjana). - Sutta 18 (iv,200-202); translated by Nyanaponika Mahathera

(c) Rooted in Experience

Thus I have heard. On one occasion when the Exalted One lived in the Eastern Cottage at Savatthi, he addressed the Venerable Sariputta as follows: "Do you believe, Sariputta, that the faculty of faith, if cultivated and regularly practiced, leads to the Deathless, is bound for the Deathless, ends in the Deathless; that the faculty of vigor... the faculty of mindfulness... the faculty of concentration... the faculty of wisdom, if cultivated and regularly practiced, leads to the Deathless, is bound for the Deathless, ends in the Deathless?"

"Herein, O Lord, I do not follow the Exalted One out of faith. Those by whom this is unknown, unseen, uncognized, unrealized and unexperienced by wisdom, they will herein follow others out of faith. But those by whom this is known, seen, cognized, realized and experienced by wisdom, they have no uncertainty, no doubt about it that these five faculties, if cultivated and regularly practiced, lead to the Deathless, are bound for the Deathless, end in the Deathless. By me, O Lord, it has been known, seen, cognized, realized and experienced by wisdom and I have no uncertainty, no doubt about it that the faculty of faith... the faculty of vigor... the faculty of mindfulness... the faculty of concentration... the faculty of wisdom, if cultivated and regularly practiced, leads to the Deathless, is bound for the Deathless, ends in the Deathless."

"Well said, Sariputta, well said," spoke the Lord (and he repeated in approval the words of the Venerable Sariputta). - Sutta 44 (iv,220); translated by Nyanaponika Mahathera

(d) Wisdom, the Crowning Virtue - 1

It is through cultivating and regularly practicing one faculty that a canker-free bhikkhu makes known his knowledge (of final attainment):33 "Ceased has rebirth, fulfilled is the holy life, the task is done, nothing further remains after this." Which is the one faculty? The faculty of wisdom.

In a noble disciple endowed with wisdom, faith that goes along with it, is firmly established; vigor that goes along with it, is firmly established; mindfulness that goes along with it, is firmly established; concentration that goes along with it, is firmly established. This, monks, is the one faculty through the cultivating and regularly practicing of which, a canker-free bhikkhu makes known his knowledge (of final attainment): "Ceased has rebirth, fulfilled is the holy life, the task is done, nothing further remains after this." - Sutta 45 (iv,222); translated by Nyanaponika Mahathera

(e) Wisdom, the Crowning Virtue - II

Just as among all heartwood fragrances that of the red sandalwood is deemed best, so, monks, among states that partake of enlightenment the faculty of wisdom is deemed best, namely, for the purpose of enlightenment.

Which, monks, are the states partaking of enlightenment? The faculty of faith is a state partaking of enlightenment and it leads to enlightenment. The faculty of vigor... the faculty of mindfulness... the faculty of concentration... the faculty of wisdom is a state partaking of enlightenment and it leads to enlightenment.

And among them, the faculty of wisdom is deemed best, namely, for the purpose of enlightenment. - Sutta 55 (iv,231); translated by Nyanaponika Mahathera

(f) The Acme of Faith

Thus I have heard. On one occasion, the Exalted One dwelt among the Anga people, at Apana, a town of the Angas. There the Exalted One addressed the Venerable Sariputta as follows:

"A noble disciple, Sariputta, who has single-minded confidence in the Perfect One, can he have uncertainty or doubt concerning the Perfect One's dispensation?"

"A noble disciple, Lord, who has single-minded confidence in the Perfect One, cannot have uncertainty or doubt concerning the Perfect One's dispensation.

"Of a noble disciple endowed with faith it can be expected, Lord, that he will live employing his vigor to the overcoming of unsalutary states and the acquisition of salutary states, energetic, with strenuous exertion, unremittingly applying himself to things salutary. This vigor of his, O Lord, is his faculty of vigor.

"Of a noble disciple who is endowed with faith and employs his vigor, it can be expected, Lord, that he will be mindful, equipped with the highest mindfulness and circumspection, and that he remembers well and keeps in mind what has been done and said long ago. This mindfulness of his, Lord, is his faculty of mindfulness.

"Of a noble disciple who is endowed with faith, employing his vigor, keeping his mindfulness alert, it can be expected, Lord, that making the highest relinquishment (Nibbana) his object, he will obtain concentration, will obtain unification of mind. This concentration of his, Lord, is his faculty of concentration.

"Of a noble disciple endowed with faith, vigor and mindfulness, and whose mind is concentrated, it can be expected, Lord, that he will know this: 'Without a conceivable beginning and end is this round of existence; no first beginning can be perceived of beings hastening and hurrying on (through this round of rebirths), enveloped in ignorance and ensnared by craving. The entire fading away and cessation of this very ignorance which is a mass of darkness, this is the state of peace, this is the state sublime, namely, the quiescence of all formations, the relinquishment of all substrata of existence, the extinction of craving, dispassion, cessation, Nibbana.' This wisdom of his, Lord, is the faculty of wisdom.

"The noble disciple who has faith, after thus striving again and again, after thus applying mindfulness again and again, after thus concentrating his mind again and again, is now fully convinced: 'These teachings which before I had only heard, I now dwell in their personal experience, and having penetrated them with wisdom, I now see them (myself).' This faith of his, Lord, is his faculty of faith."

"Well said, Sariputta, well said," spoke the Exalted One (and he repeated in approval the words of the Venerable Sariputta).

Sutta 50 (iv,225ff.); translated by Nyanaponika Mahathera

5. The Balance of the Faculties

[According to the Visuddhimagga, the balance of the faculties (indriya-samatta) is one of the ten kinds of skill in absorption (appana-kosalla), and it is one of the seven things that lead to the arising of the enlightenment factor "investigation of (material and mental) phenomena" (dhammavicaya-sambojjhanga).]

Imparting balance to the faculties is the equalizing of the controlling faculties of faith, vigor, mindfulness, concentration and wisdom. For if the faith faculty is strong and the others weak, then the vigor faculty cannot perform its function of exerting, the mindfulness faculty its function of attending to the object, the concentration faculty its function of excluding distraction, the wisdom faculty its function of seeing. So the (excessive) strength of the faith faculty should be reduced by reflecting on the phenomenal nature (of faith and its objects), and by not paying attention to what has caused the excessive strength of the faith faculty. Then if the vigor faculty is too strong, the faith faculty cannot perform its function of convincing, nor can the rest of the faculties perform their several functions. So in that case the excessive strength of the vigor faculty should be reduced by cultivating (the enlightenment factors of) tranquillity, concentration and equanimity. So, too, with the other factors, for it should be understood that when any one of them is too strong the others cannot perform their several functions.

However, what is particularly recommended is the balancing of faith with wisdom, and concentration with vigor. For one who is strong in faith and weak in wisdom places his confidence foolishly in an unworthy object. One strong in wisdom and weak in faith errs on the side of cunning and is as hard to cure as a sickness caused by medicine. But with the balancing of the two, faith and wisdom, a man has confidence only in a deserving object.

If there is too much of concentration and too little of vigor, the mind will be overpowered by indolence to which concentration inclines. But if vigor is too strong and concentration too weak, the mind will be overpowered by agitation to which vigor inclines. But concentration coupled with vigor cannot lapse into indolence, and vigor coupled with concentration cannot lapse into agitation. So these two should be balanced; for absorption comes with the balancing of the two.

Again (concentration and faith should be balanced). One working on concentration needs strong faith, since it is with such faith and confidence that he reaches absorption.

As to (the balancing of) concentration and wisdom, one working on concentration (i.e., who practices tranquillity; samatha) needs strong one-pointedness of mind, since that is how he reaches full absorption; and one working on insight (vipassana) needs strong wisdom, since that is how he reaches penetration of (the phenomena's) characteristics; but with the balancing of the two he reaches full absorption as well.

Strong mindfulness, however, is needed in all instances; for mindfulness protects the mind from lapsing into agitation through faith, vigor and wisdom, which tend to agitation, and from lapsing into indolence through concentration, which tends to indolence. So it is as desirable in all instances as a seasoning of salt in all curries, as a prime minister in all the king's business.

Hence it is said (in the commentaries): "It was declared by the Exalted One that 'mindfulness, indeed, is of universal use.' Why? Because the mind has mindfulness as its refuge, and mindfulness is manifested as protection, and there is no exertion and restraint of the mind without mindfulness." - Visuddhimagga, (pp.129-30), Adapted from Bhikkhu Ñanamoli's translation: The Path of Purification, pp.135-36

ALL IS SUFFERING!

"All existance is suffering!" is the main doctrine of Buddhism. Mahayana too regards existance as sorrowful. In all forms of being there are grief and pain, longing and dissappointment. Life for a time may appear to be happy, and things one has grown fond of seem lasting, but what is loved has to perish as well as the person loving it. Parting and suffering are the inevitable course anyone must take.

There are 8 different types of suffering that Buddhism defined: "Suffering of birth - No one comes into life smiling, we call come with tears. Through growing up, we experience the pain of growing new teeth, puberty, and the pain of finding our own identiy in life. Life is full of sorrows and happiness seemed not to last a long time.

"Suffering of old age - We all grow old, it is the inevitable course of life. With old age, we grow frail and weak. Unable to help ourselves and bear the pain of growing old.

"Suffering of illness - Even the strongest man becomes ill. With illness we experience pain, whether psychological or physical. No one can claim that they have never been sick. The suffering of illness is a part of life.

"Suffering of death - Everyone must die. With death, we experience the pain of the body. We twitch and turn, as our last breath are released. Even the most powerful, successful, or riches person must die leaving their love ones behind to feel the pain of their departure. Death is the unavoidable consequence of life.

"Suffering of unfullfilled desires - We all want something in life, whether for ourselves or others. When our desires are unfullfilled, we suffer pain. The pain of not having what we want is great. To a child, the pain of not being able to have a toy is just as great as an adult not being able to have wealth, or a successful career, or love.

"Suffering of being in the company of dislikes ones - We all like to spend time with the ones we love. But that is not true many times. When we are in the company of those we fear, those we hate, it is like having a needle to our eyes. This is another part of living. "Suffering of separation from those we love - We all like to be with those we love. But separation is a part of life. When we lose those we love to death, to war, to life's circumstances, we all suffer pains. It is an unavoidable part of life.

"Suffering of health - Many would ask: "Why would being healthy is also suffering?". It is that when we are healthy, we dwell in running our lives with envy, lust, greed, passion and waste our time not knowing that death is just a breath away. We are like those who play in a house of fire not knowing that it is burning around us. Many healthy people cause their own suffering with drugs, alcohol, and other addictions when they regard themselves as immortal, not knowing that death is near.

We all see and hear suffering around us, even to ourselves. But does not understand the reality of it. Ignorance in our views cause us to look for illusory happiness that does not last forever. Even the happiest person would suffer death. The healthiest person will also suffer illness, and the least wanting person the suffering of loss. The Buddha's teachings of suffering is to lead all to see that life is but a illusory existence. We should not drown in depressing conceit in light of life's suffering, but take bold actions to end it and find the enternal happiness in our existence. We must seek the absolute truth to find our eternal self again. For our existence are that of illusions which is not as immutable as we think, but very mutable. Everything changes as the world turns. No matter how we try, no one can hinder death, or life. As the words of a famous Romantic poets "Pershy Bysshe Shelley" puts it:

Mutability

We are as clouds that veil the midnight moon;

How restlessly they speed; and gleam and quiver.

Streaking the darkness radiantly!-Yet soon!

Night closes round and they are lost forever:

Or like forgotten lyres whose dissonance strings,

Give various response to each varying blast,

To whose frail frame no second motion brings,
One mood or modulation like the last.
We rest - a dream has power to poison sleep;
We rise - one wandering thought pollutes the day;
We feel, conceive or reason, laugh or weep
Embrace fond woe, or cast our cares away:
It is the same ! - for, be it joy or sorrow,
The path of its departure still is free;
Man's yesterday may ne'er be like his morrow
Nought may endure but mutability.

BUDDHIST DEFINITION OF KARMAN

The Buddhist 'soul,' a series of physico-psychical states, would come to an end at death, when the physical organism dissolves, but for the strength of the actions which are to be enjoyed in a future life by a new physico-psychical apparatus, a continuation of the first one.

Action, in Sanskrit, karman, is one of the Indian words that the theosophists and the neo Buddhists have made known in the West. We must feel grateful for it. For we can say shortly 'doctrine of Karman,' meaning all the speculations concerned with action, and especially the dogma of the ripening of action.

The doctrine of Karman is more than the belief in the reward of good actions and the punishment of bad ones, here below or in another life; such a belief is a very common one and has nothing specifically Indian.

The doctrine of Karman presupposes the belief in transmigration and is primarily a rationalistic and moral explanation of the variety of the conditions of living beings through many consecutive existences.

By a rationalistic and moral explanation, we mean an explanation which is founded on the principle of causality understood as follows: "The good deed is rewarded, the evil deed is punished"; an explanation which leaves no place or very little place for any theological, mystical or superstitious agency:

it is in the very nature of a good deed to produce reward; reward is automatically produced, that is independently of any exterior factor, out of the very potentiality of the good deed.

The deep reason of the origin and of the spread of this doctrine was, without doubt, a sentiment of justice. It is not just that crime should remain unpunished and virtue unrewarded. Unmerited suffering and unmerited pleasure offend us for the same reason. Hence a certitude, a sort of scientific certitude, first that sin is certain to turn into pain and a good deed into pleasure, just as for the modern physicist motion turns into heat, and, second, that pain and pleasure are respectively the product of sin and of virtue.

It may be said without exaggeration that this certitude has been, for centuries, the strongest and most popular feeling of India. Even to-day, in the castes which practise child marriage, young widows are looked upon as criminal: "What a sinner you have been to lose your husband so soon!"

With the Buddhists, the doctrine of Karman is, as a rule 1, strictly understood, and is almost everything. In the case of the non-Buddhists, with the possible exception of the 'religions of devotion' (bhakti), it is no less important, although it is not understood strictly 2.

We propose to examine the history of Karman, and the part of Buddhism in this history. The conclusion of this inquiry will be (1) that the Buddhists did not discover Karman, but (2) that they were among the first to give a reasonable and moral definition of Karman. Moreover the Buddhists alone were successful in drawing from the doctrine of Karman all its consequences: human destiny, cosmogony and theogony are, in Buddhism, built on Karman.

There were, at the time of kyamuni, (1) unbelievers, deniers of soul, transmigration and action, (2) believers in transmigration and in destiny, (3) believers in transmigration who foreshadowed the doctrine of action, (4) believers in transmigration and in action.

We have, but briefly, studied the development of philosophical analysis which, for a long time, had been destroying the old religious and cosmical notions of the ?ryas. This analysis created an esoteric theology-literally a gnosis-took a pantheistic or monistic direction, and finally made prominent the idea of the universal Self.

But that is only one of the branches of the philosophical evolution, the 'orthodox' branch, or the Vedic or Brahmanic branch properly so called. In contrast with pantheists and mystics, there were materialists and positivists-many more, as it seems, in old India than later.

Our sources, which are both Brahmanic and Buddhistic, agree on the whole 1. Brahmanic sources lay much stress on the impiety of the 'would-be philosophers,' 'philosophasters' (pa??itam?nika) who do not believe in the Veda and in Sacrifice. Buddhists, who themselves broke with sacerdotalism and theology, are especially preoccupied with the negation of soul and future life.

The common name for the 'unbelievers' is lok?yata, mundane,' and n?stika, 'negator,' 'denier,' people who say: na asti, 'it is not'; that is, when a priest or a mendicant wants an alms: "There is nothing for you"; and also: "There is no such thing as a gift, a sacrifice, an offering, a result of good or evil deeds"; "there is no mother, no father": parents are not entitled to any respect; "no ascetic or Brahman has discovered truth or can ascertain the reality of another life": the sacerdotal tradition and the revelations of the holy men, leaders of ascetic orders, are alike falsehoods and vain pretences to extort money.

The unbelievers had probably a sort of philosophy. When we get more precise information concerning them, that is some centuries after the time of Buddha, we are told that the N?stikas were strong materialists, in the modern meaning of the word. Man is made of material elements; psychical phenomena are to be explained by the special possibilities of these elements when combined in a certain mixture: just as a mixture of rice and water develops an intoxicating power, in the same way consciousness arises in the living body.

However it may be with the ancient N?stikas, the old Buddhist texts report their views as follows 1:

Man is composed of four elements. When Man dies, the earthy element returns and relapses into the earth; the watery element returns into the water; the fiery element returns into the fire; the windy element returns into the wind; the senses pass into space. Four men, with the corpse as a fifth, go to the cemetery, murmuring prayers. But the bones are bleached in the flame, and the offerings of the living perish in the ashes of his pyre. Wise and fool alike, when the body dissolves, are cut off, perish, do not exist any longer.

Thus spoke Ajita of the garment of hair.

Therefore, as says Pur??a Kassapa:

There is no guilt for the man who mutilates or causes another to mutilate, who kills, takes what is not given, breaks into houses, commits dacoity, or robbery, or adultery; and so on. . . . Should he make all living creatures one heap, one mass of flesh, there would be no guilt. . . . Were he to go along the Ganges giving alms, and ordering gifts to be given. . . there would be no merit. . . .

Such were the strange sermons of the unbelieving ascetics; for ascetics had an absolute right of preaching the truth. As says the King Aj?ta?atru: "How should such a one as I am, think of giving dissatisfaction to any ascetic or Brahman in my realm?" In India, thought was free; opinion was no crime; but evildoers were summarily dealt with.

Side by side with the thorough N?stikas, a few philosophers, while believing in soul and transmigration, denied action and reward.

There are eighty-four hundred thousand periods during which both fools and wise alike, wandering in transmigration, will at last make an end of pain. . . . The happiness and pain, measured out, as it were, with a measure, cannot be altered in the course of transmigration; there can be neither increase nor decrease thereof. Just as a ball of string will stretch just as far as it can unwind, just so both fools and wise alike are wandering in transmigration exactly for the allotted term.

There is no cause, either ultimate or remote, for the depravity or rectitude of beings; they become depraved or pure without reason and without cause. There is no such thing as power or energy or human strength or human vigour. Beings are bent this way or that by their fate, by their individual nature.

Nor were the Brahmans very clear concerning the power which predetermines transmigration. It is true that references to Karman are not wanting:

The spirit, at death, takes upon itself another new form, a form of Fathers or of Gandharvas, of divine or human nature, or of any other kind of being. . . . As he acted and as he walked, so he becomes. He who does good becomes a good being, he who does bad becomes a bad being; he becomes pure by pure action, evil by evil action.

Elsewhere we meet a formula which is distinctly Buddhistic in tone and in meaning.

Man's nature depends on desire. As his desire, so is his aspiration; as his aspiration, so is the course of action which he pursues; whatever be the course of action he pursues, he passes to a corresponding state of being.

But, according to an important passage in the same book, the doctrine of Karman is a new doctrine, a doctrine to be kept secret. In the course of a philosophical tournament-such tournaments are not a rarity from the oldest times down to Akbar-J?ratk?rava ?rtabh?ga questions Y?jñavalkya on the destiny of the dead, and the celebrated Brahman answers: "Give me your hand, my friend; we two alone must be privy to this; not a word on that subject where people are listening." And the narrator dryly summarizes the debate they had privately: "What they said, they said regarding action; by pure action, man becomes pure."

To sum up, references to Karman are not numerous in the old Brahman literature, the Brahmanas or Upanisads. In the view of the authors of these books, sacrifice and esoteric wisdom are much more important than Karman. But it is only natural that liturgical treatises (Brahmanas) should consider sacrifice as the best means of improving future life; and, as concerns the philosophico-mystical treatises (Upanisads), they deal chiefly with the merging of the individual Self in the great Self; the common idea is that this great aim can be realized by the possession of a mystic wisdom; and accordingly the Upanisads are little concerned with the problem of action and reward. Therefore we are not justified in arguing, from the relative silence of the old texts, that the doctrine of Karman was not already widely known.

The best reason we have for believing that the doctrine of Karman was not new, but was widely known at the time of ??kyamuni, is to be found in the very teaching of ??kyamuni and in the history of the church.

Many, among the ascetics who joined the primitive brotherhood, were believers in Karman. The Jailas, the 'ascetics with matted hair,' were to be admitted without the noviciate or probation of three months imposed on others, "because they believe in Karman." The Master, for this reason, made an exception to the rule which wisely secured a thorough preparation for full admission to the Order 1.

But our point is that the teaching of ??kyamuni on Karman is in no way an improvisation, and clearly obtains a success which it could not have obtained if it had been new. ??kyamuni taught a path to deliverance, because many people were anxious to get deliverance.

The same holds good for Karman. Human destiny, free will, the efficacy of penance for destroying sin,-together with such questions as 'Is the soul the body?', 'Is the universe infinite?'-were the topics of lively discussions among hermits and mendicants; while the laymen, who actually fed all these troops of spiritual men, took great interest in these philosophumena and were disposed to admit the doctrine of Karman. This doctrine, as well as the doctrine of transmigration which it so happily completes, was already deeply rooted in the popular feeling.

As far as we can surmise-there are many more conjectures than ascertained facts in this old history-??kyamuni was the first or one of the first to give a reasonable and moral definition of Karman.

That appears from the comparison between the Buddhists and the Jains, a powerful mendicant order which originated or was reorganized a few years before yamuni.

The Jains are, in many respects, very much like the Buddhists, so much like that the different origin of the two sects was for a long time denied. They are good atheists-they even object to the common Indian saying, devo varati, they believe that Karman is the governing force in human destiny.

But they cherish the most materialistic idea of Karman. They are of opinion that bodily and verbal actions are important, that they create a subtle matter that envelops the soul and produces retribution-whereas mental action is weak, inefficacious.

Buddhism, on the contrary, teaches that there is no Karman without consciousness and even premeditation.

Karman is twofold: (1) volition (cetan?), or mental or spiritual action (m?nasa), and (2) what is born from volition, what is done by volition, 'what a person does after having willed,' namely bodily and verbal action 1.

By giving gold, while intending to give a stone, a gift of gold is indeed made; but, as it has not been premeditated or willed, the act is as if it were not done. It is not 'appropriated'; it is not 'stored up' (upacita); it will bear no fruit. In the same way, if a man kills his mother when striking at what is believed to be a pumpkin, there is no matricide, there is no murder, there is only destruction of a fruit.

The Jains criticize this doctrine strongly, and would believe that the unintentional murderer of his mother is a hideous criminal. The man who commits murder, or who harms in any way a living being, without intent, is none the less guilty, just as a man who touches fire is burned.

But this would lead to palpable absurdities. The embryo and the mother would be guilty of making each other suffer. The murdered man himself would be guilty, for he is the object and therefore the origin of the action of murder.

Further the comparison of the fire is not a happy one: a man would not be guilty of murder if he got another person to commit it, for we are not burnt when we touch fire by means of another. Again unconscious sin would be more heavy than conscious sin: a man who touches hot iron without knowing that it is hot, is likely to be more deeply burnt than the man who knows.

This contrast of the Buddhist doctrine with the Jain doctrine draws our attention to this fact that the views of ??kyamuni, which seem to us reasonable indeed, but rather evident, were bold and new, and of far-reaching consequences.

To take the risk of acquitting the unintentional murderer was in fact to break with the immemorial conception of sin. We do not mean that, in the oldest times, a moral conception of duty and sin did not exist; but sin was also looked upon as a sort of contagious fluid, a sort and the most dangerous sort of impurity. One becomes sinful, hateful to gods and men, not only by sinful acts, but also by kinship or any sort of contact.

A consequence of this materialistic conception is that sin is to be dispelled by physical contrivances, is to be burnt out by penances (tapas), by the heat penance-standing between the four penitential fires, with the sun above-when the sin is as it were 'extracted' from the body along with the perspiration. Or the sin is to be washed away by baths, especially by baths in the holy water of the Ganges.

These old and always living speculations have been somewhat spiritualized in some Indian religions, but Buddhism alone radically ignores or cancels them. We must consider this definition, "Karman is volition, and bodily or verbal action which follows volition," as one of the steps in the history of the Indian thought.

Volition is all important. Our future depends on our present volition, and our present state depends on our past volition.

All that we are is the result of what we have thought; it is founded on our thoughts; it is made up of our thoughts. If a man speaks or acts with an evil thought, pain follows him, as the wheel follows the foot of the ox that draws the wagon.

We are what we think, we are what we will.

While emphasizing the all-importance of volition, Buddhism does not minimize the importance of bodily and verbal action, the action that a person does after having willed. To forsake the secular life and actually join the Buddhist Brotherhood is an entirely different thing from resolving to do so. To kill a man is more hideous than to resolve to kill a man. It is true that, in the case of a Rishi, endowed with magical power, the resolve to kill actually kills; but in the case of ordinary mortals murder supposes a will strong and persistent.

A point of the later scholasticism is worth mentioning. While a pure volition only leaves traces in the series of thoughts, bodily and verbal actions-which are corporeal and material-create a thing of a particular nature, semi-material and semi-spiritual, which is called 'action,' although it is really a result of action. Scholastics name it avijñapti. Once produced by a voluntary verbal or bodily action (vijñapti), the avijñapti exists and develops of its own accord, without the agency of thought, whether a man is waking, sleeping or absorbed in contemplation.

The idea which gave rise to the conception of avijñapti is clear enough. A man who has taken the vows of the religious life by a solemn declaration (vijñapti)-a verbal action-is not a man like others.

He has engaged himself to avoid certain actions, killing, stealing, etc., during his life-time. He is not always pondering over this engagement during sleep or at any other time; nevertheless as long as he has not formally given up his vows or committed an action contrary to his vows, he remains a man who has taken the vows, literally 'who is restrained; his avoidance of sinful actions is another thing than the casual avoidance of sinful actions by a man who has taken no vows.

An action, to be 'complete' and really 'fruitful,' apt to 'ripen,' must consist of three parts: (1) the preparation, that is the first volition and all the contrivances necessary to the so-called 'principal action.' For instance, a butcher arises, takes some money, goes to the market, buys a goat, has the knife in his hand; (2) the principal action: the killing of the goat, the actual death-dealing blow; (3) the 'back' of the principal action: the cutting up and selling of the meat, etc.

The Buddhist theory of confession is based upon these considerations. The moral benefit or merit (pu?ya) of a gift is totally or almost totally lost for the giver if he regrets his generosity; in the same way a sin is not done, it is only half done, if one regrets one's sin. Confession, as it is practised by the Buddhist monks, is not a sacramental rite; it is an expression of repentance, an affirmation: "I will not do it again," and also the accomplishment of one of the vows of a monk: "I will not tell lies." Confession does not destroy sin; but it is the intention of concealing sin that makes sin 'complete.'

According to the Buddhists, the only action (karman) is volition and intentional word and deed; further action, to be complete, must be 'prepared'-not casual or impulsive-and 'backed up,' approved of afterwards, not counteracted by repentance.

It must be added that Buddhists lay all the stress on the morality of actions, and in this was a marked progress.

Morality, of course, was not unknown in ancient India; but, to say the least, the ideas were somewhat confused by ritual prejudice. In Buddhism, all the intricate fabric of the rites of purification and of sacrifice falls to the ground. Whereas it was thought that Indra, King of the gods, had obtained his sovereignty through a hundred sacrifices (hence his name, ?atakratu), Buddhists believe that sacrifice is of no avail, that sacrificial murder is a murder. Whereas austerities and purifications of many kinds were deemed necessary, Buddhists condemn them as so many superstitions (??lavrata). In the same way they abandon the most pious among the pious works of yore, gifts to the dead, funeral rites: the monks took no care of the funeral of kyamuni himself.

Morality alone makes the value of an act.

The fact has often been emphasized that the Buddhist rule of morality is, or seems to be, a purely negative one: to avoid the ten sins. "Do not kill, do not take what is not given, do not indulge in illicit love,"-three bodily sins. "Do not use mischievous, rude, mendacious, foolish language,"-four verbal sins. "Do not cherish lust, hatred, wrong doctrines, especially the doctrine that there is annihilation at death,"-three mental sins. A layman has to accept this tenfold discipline or restraint (sa?vara) to be admitted as a 'devotee' (up?saka). Monks take a more strict discipline: for instance, they renounce not only illicit love, but also marriage; but the negative character of their morality (bhik?ut?) is the same as it is for laymen.

Are we to conclude that positive morality, altruism or love, is foreign to the Buddhist ideal of conduct? As is well known, scholars disagree.

It may be first observed that Indian philosophers have been from of old keen enough to understand that man has always in view his own interest, even when he seems to be the most generous and disinterested. They have discovered La Rochefoucauld long ago. "It is for the sake of Self that Man loves cattle, wife, sons or riches," says the Upanisad. And kyamuni comforts the king Prasenajit and his wife the queen Mallik? ('Jessamine'); this loving pair ashamed at discovering that each of them preferred his or her Self to anybody else: "I do not see," says ??kyamuni, "any living being in the three worlds who does not prefer his own Self to anything."

Self-love, self-love well understood, governs all the actions of a Buddhist, whether monk or layman.

The monk has arrived at a stage in the spiritual career when a purely egoist behaviour is necessary. The monk has not to practise good actions,-such actions he has done in heaps in former births,-he has only to avoid evil actions, to avoid any occasion of an evil action, to extinguish desire. His ideal is absence of desire, absence of action. The monk has broken natural and social bonds; he has no obligation towards his former wife, his former children.

The case is quite different as concerns the layman. The layman has to acquire merit, he has to do positive acts of morality, good acts. "A good act is the act that benefits one's neighbour; a bad act, the act that harms one's neighbour."

Such a dogmatical definition of good and evil is scarce, and as a rule the morality of acts is to be known by their fruits: "A good act is an act that ripens into a pleasurable existence; a bad act, an act that begets suffering." Proofs are innumerable that Buddhists recommend good acts of every description. A man who does not commit any sin will be reborn as a man, not as an inhabitant of hell, an animal or a ghost; but if this sinless person is wanting in positive meritorious actions, especially in giving, he will be reborn as a poor man. Whereas a generous man, who has indulged in some sin, will, it is true, pay for this sin by rebirth in an inferior state (hell, etc.); but he will also, after being released from the ties of sin, enjoy on this earth, as a rich man, or in heaven, as a god, the fruit of his gifts.

Among meritorious actions, giving is the most fruitful. It may be interesting to state the principles of the valuation of the merit of giving.

One must take into account:

1. The qualities of the giver, faith, morality learning, and his intention in giving: 'I give in order to receive in my turn,' 'I give because I have received,' 'I give because my parents and grand-parents were wont to give. . . .'

2. The manner of giving: with respect, with the right hand, at the opportune moment.

3. The qualities of the object given, excellence in colour, smell, and so on. There is nevertheless an episode parallel to the widow's mite.

4. The qualities of the person who receives, that is, as Indians say, the 'field' (k?etra) on which the gift is poured. Much depends, in Buddhism and in Brahmanism, on the fertility of the field. Our sources distinguish (a) the excellence in relation to the kind of existence: a gift to a wicked man has a hundred times the value of a gift to an animal; (b) the excellence due to suffering: gifts to the poor and to the sick are especially productive of fruit; (c) the excellence due to services received: our parents are our benefactors and have a right to our gifts; the preacher, who teaches us the Buddhist doctrine, gives us a second birth, better than the first; (d) last not least, the excellence due to qualities, morality, knowledge, in a word to sanctity.

Buddhists are not as jealous as the Brahmans, and kyamuni extols the gifts made to the ascetics of the rival sects. But a

Buddhist monk is evidently a better 'field' than a heretic. A gift to a Buddha, small as it may be, is very good indeed.

The gift given by a man who does not care for reward, who gives in order to free himself from greed, who understands fully the Buddhist doctrine,-that is, who knows the unsubstantiality (nairtmya) of the giver, of the gift and of the receiver,-that is the best gift.

The confusion of 'good' (kuala) and 'meritorious,' 'bearing a pleasant fruit' , which seems to be one of the consequences of the doctrine of Karman as understood by the Buddhists, leads to some results that are not perfectly sound. For instance, a man will abandon secular life in order to be reborn as a god and to enjoy pleasures incomparably greater than the pleasures of human life. The story of Nanda is a good illustration of this case: once this relative of kyamuni realizes that his wife cannot vie with the celestial damsels-just as the female apes cannot vie with his wife-he becomes a monk, for he will obtain, through actual continence, sensual pleasures of the highest degree.

An action is good when it does not aim at immediate (aihika) ends, when it is made in order to obtain reward in a future life; it is bad when it aims at an immediate end, viz. pleasure in this life. This rule, practically a golden rule, is possibly a little too empirical. But to appreciate it without prejudices, we must remember, first, that a system of morals is not to be estimated from the details of casuistry, and, second, that the true Buddhist is the man who does not care for merit or reward, but who strives for Nirvna.

2

Buddhistic Teachings

These are the basic teachings and concepts in Buddhism.

Karma: Actions have consequences; so our lives are conditioned by our past actions.

Rebirth: Consciousness continues after death, and finds expression in a future life.

Liberation from Karma: By following the Buddha's path one escapes the cycle of craving and suffering.

The Four Noble Truths: These are the essentials of Buddhism.

Enlightenment: The highest goal of life is to reach Enlightenment; a state of being that goes beyond suffering.

Dharma: The teachings and hence the way to nirvana.

The Core of Buddhist Teaching: At the heart of the Buddha's teaching lie The Four Noble Truths and The Eightfold Path which lead the Buddhist towards the path of Enlightenment.

Facing the Truth: The Buddha taught that the human tendency is to avoid the difficult truths of life and this in turn leads to suffering. By enabling the mind to be at peace through meditation a human being can confront reality and overcome hatred and craving.

Buddhism and Slavery

Slavery would seem to be incompatible with a fundamental idea of Buddhism; that of freeing oneself of attachments: Thus the ideal community of the selfless arahants form an ideal, or a standard on which ethical and moral judgement of lay societies are based.

Thus such violations of human rights as slavery, torture, etc. could only be a movement in the opposite direction to the ideal, for these violations all result from strong attachment to the self of the violators of human rights.

Wayne R. Husted, Damien V. Keown, Charles S. Prebish, Buddhism and Human Rights, 1998

Buddhist teachings don't explicitly forbid slavery, but the eightfold path says that engaging in trade in living beings is not a right form of livelihood. This appears to ban Buddhists from engaging in the slave trade.

...a lay follower should not engage in five types of business. Which five? Business in weapons, business in living beings, business in meat, business in intoxicants, and business in poison. Eightfold path

Other texts seem incompatible with many aspects of slavery itself. For example, this quotation requires Buddhists to ensure that their workers and servants are properly treated:

In five ways should a master minister to his servants and employees:

by assigning them work according to their ability,

by supplying them with food and with wages,

by tending them in sickness,

by sharing with them any delicacies,

by granting them leave at times.

Sigalovada Sutta

Despite these texts there's no doubt that slavery was part of some Buddhist cultures, although many of these slaves were servants, rather than slaves of the sort traded across the Atlantic. Richard Gombrich has argued that the Buddha did not intend to do away with slavery: Though it could well be argued that the Buddha made life in the world more worth living, that surely was an unintended consequence of his teaching. To present him as a sort of socialist is a serious anachronism.

He never preached against social inequality, only declared its irrelevance to salvation. He neither tried to abolish the caste system nor to do away with slavery.

While a famous sermon, the Sumanna-phala Sutta, stresses the practical benefits for a slave in leaving his servitude and joining the Order, in fact runaway slaves were not allowed to join the Order.

Moreover, though in ancient India there was no caste or other form of social ranking within the Order itself, the Order soon came to own (lay) slaves.

Richard F. Gombrich, Theravada Buddhism: A Social History from Ancient Benares to Modern Colombo, 1988

In fact the restrictions placed on monks required them to have some form of servant in monastic communities. So for example if monks were to obey the rule barring the cooking and storing of food, they would need somebody to do it for them. Some Buddhist commentaries warn that slaves are not allowed, unless they are called "called monastery servants (aramika) or legalisers (kappiya-karaka)".

Gombrich also notes that:

> *at one point the Vinaya commentary says in so many words that kings gave slaves to monasteries, and that they could not be ordained unless they had first been freed. Inscriptions record that people gave money for the specific purpose of maintaining monastic slaves-and offered the resulting merit to all living beings. Richard F. Gombrich, Theravada Buddhism: A Social History from Ancient Benares to Modern Colombo, 1988*

If granting endowments to maintain slaves at monasteries was considered meritorious, freeing them from slavery was considered even more meritorious. Thus the device of offering slaves to monasteries provided a two-fold way for the acquisition of merits. Rahula, Walpola (1956), History of Buddhism in Ceylon: the Anuradhapura Period, Colombo. Quoted in Gombrich

Some kings in Ceylon offered themselves to the monastic community "as slaves and then redeemed themselves, thus combining a symbolic gesture of total humility with extreme munificence".

In 9th century China Buddhist institutions are reputed to have employed 150,000 slaves, who were taken over by the Taoist Emperor Wu-tsung in 845 as part of his action against the Buddhist community.

In some parts of South East Asia Buddhist locations were a sanctuary for those fleeing more oppressive forms of slavery:

Where Buddhist monastic orders had claimed political retreats from state military power, their estates and temple complexes became sanctuaries where peasants sought the exemption from state conscription and corvee that 'slavery' to a privileged individual or institution provided. Gwyn Campbell, The Structure of Slavery in Indian Ocean Africa and Asia, 2004

Pagoda Slaves

In some Buddhist cultures a male slave would become free if their owner allowed them to become a Buddhist monk.

In Kampuchea a person could be made a 'Pagoda Slave' if they were found guilty of certain crimes-as could members of their family up to seven degrees removed. Pagoda slaves did domestic and maintenance work on temple sites. While pagoda slaves might have a relatively easy life for a slave they ranked very low on the social ladder and had an extra disadvantage:

Pagoda slaves, who were supposed to belong only to Buddha, could not be redeemed. Gwyn Campbell, The Structure of Slavery in Indian Ocean Africa and Asia, 2004

Because pagoda slaves could not be redeemed their children inherited slave status. Pagoda slaves were found mostly in what are now Burma and Thailand.

Pagoda slaves weren't only 'criminals' or the descendants of slaves; people could be given to monasteries for slave use.

Among Buddhist reformers of slavery was King Thibaw of Burma, a former monk. He paid 40,000 rupees in 1883 to buy the freedom of many slaves; 1,000 of those he freed are said to have become Buddhist monks and novices.

Slavery and Karma

Some writers think that slavery is justified by the doctrine of karma. They argue that people are born into slavery or become slaves because of their bad actions in a previous life. The way for a slave to progress towards salvation was to obey his or her owner, and do so willingly and without any bad feelings.

PURE LAND BUDDHISM

Pure Land Buddhism: Pure Land Buddhism offers a way to enlightenment for people who can't handle the subtleties of meditation, endure long rituals, or just live especially good lives.

The essential practice in Pure Land Buddhism is the chanting of the name of Amitabha Buddha with total concentration, trusting that one will be reborn in the Pure Land, a place where it is much easier for a being to work towards enlightenment.

Pure Land Buddhism adds mystical elements to the basic Buddhist teachings which make those teachings easier (and more comforting) to work with.

These elements include faith and trust and a personal relationship with Amitabha Buddha, who is regarded by Pure Land Buddhists as a sort of saviour; and belief in the Pure Land, a place which provides a stepping stone towards enlightenment and liberation. Pure Land Buddhism is particularly popular in China and Japan.

History: Pure Land Buddhism as a school of Buddhist thinking began in India around the 2nd century BCE.

It spread to China where there was a strong cult of Amitabha by the 2nd century CE, and then spread to Japan around the 6th century CE. Pure Land Buddhism received a major boost to its popularity in the 12th century with the simplifications made by Honen.

A century later Shinran (1173-1262), a disciple of Honen, brought a new understanding of the Pure Land ideas, and this became the foundation of the Shin (true) sect. Pure Land Buddhism took off in Japan when the monk Honen (1133-1212) simplified the teachings and practices of the sect so that anyone could cope with them. He eliminated the intellectual difficulties and complex meditation practices used by other schools of Buddhism. Honen taught that rebirth in the Pure Land was certain for anyone who recited the name with complete trust and sincerity. Honen said that all that was needed was...

saying "Namu Amida Butsu" with a conviction that by saying it one will certainly attain birth in the Pure Land.

The result was a form of Buddhism accessible to anyone, even if they were illiterate or stupid.

Honen didn't simplify Buddhism through a patronising attitude to inferior people. He believed that most people, and he included himself, could not achieve liberation through any of their own activities. The only way to achieve Buddhahood was through the help of Amitabha.

The Shin Sect

A century after Honan, one of his disciples, Shinran (1173-1262) brought a new understanding of the Pure Land ideas. Shinran taught that what truly mattered was not the chanting of the name but faith. Chanting on its own had no value at all. Those who follow the Shin school say that liberation is the consequence of a person achieving genuine faith in Amitabha Buddha and his vow to save all beings who trusted in him.

AMITABHA

Amitabha in context: The Pure Land sect emphasises the important role played in liberation by Amitabha (which means Immeasurable Light) who is also called Amitayus (which means Immeasurable Life).

People who sincerely call on Amitabha for help will be reborn in Sukhavati-The Pure Land or The Western Paradise-where there are no distractions and where they can continue to work towards liberation under the most favourable conditions. The nature of Amitabha is not entirely clear. Encyclopedia Britannica describes him as "the great saviour deity worshiped principally by members of the Pure Land sect in Japan." Another writer says "Amitabha is neither a God who punishes and rewards, gives mercy or imposes tests, nor a divinity that we can petition or beg for special favours". The mystical view of Amitabha regards him as an eternal Buddha, and believes that he manifested himself in human history as Gautama, or "The Buddha".

Amitabha translates as "Amito-fo" in Chinese and "Amida" in Japanese.

The Story of Amitabha

Once there was a king who was so deeply moved by the suffering of beings in the world that he gave up his throne and became a monk named Dharmakara.

Dharmakara was heavily influenced by the 81st Buddha and vowed to become a Buddha himself, with the aim of creating a Buddha-land that would be free of all limitations.

He meditated at length on other Buddha-lands and set down what he learned in 48 vows. Eventually he achieved enlightenment and became Amitabha Buddha and established his Buddha-land of Sukhavati.

His most important vow was the 18th, which said: "If I were to become a Buddha, and people, hearing my Name, have faith and joy and recite it for even ten times, but are not born into my Pure Land, may I not gain enlightenment."

Since he did gain enlightenment, it follows that those who do have faith and joy and who recite his name will be born into the Pure Land.

PURE LAND ESSENTIALS

Nembutsu: This means concentration on Buddha and his virtues, or recitation of the Buddha's name.

No special way of reciting the name is laid down. It can be done silently or aloud, alone or in a group and with or without musical accompaniment. The important thing is to chant the name single-mindedly, while sincerely wishing to be reborn in the Pure Land.

Scripture: The Pure Land scriptures include The Infinite Life Sutra, The Contemplation Sutra and The Amitabha Sutra.

Chanting: Chanting the name of Amitabha Buddha does not do anything at all to help the person to the Pure Land. Chanting is nothing more than an expression of gratitude to Amitabha Buddha and an expression of the chanter's faith. But it's not possible to do away with the chanting: Shinran wrote "the True Faith is necessarily accompanied by the utterance of the Name".

Faith: Shin Buddhists say that faith in Amitabha Buddha is not something that the believer should take the credit for since it's not something that the believer does for themselves. Their faith is a gift from Amitabha Buddha.

And in keeping with this style of humility, Shin Buddhists don't accept the idea that beings can earn merit for themselves by their own acts; neither good deeds, nor performing rituals help. This has huge moral implications in that it implies (and Shinran quite explicitly said) that a sinner with faith will be made welcome in the Pure Land-even more welcome than a good man who has faith and pride.

Popularity: The sect's teachings brought it huge popularity in Japan, since here was a form of Buddhism that didn't require a person to be clever, or a monk, and that was open to the outcasts of society.

It remains a popular group in Buddhism-and the reasons that made it popular 700 years ago are exactly the same ones that make it popular today.

UNDERSTANDING PURE LAND

Is this a new understanding of Buddhism?

On the surface Pure Land Buddhism seems to have moved a very long way from the basic Buddhist ideas, and it's important to see how it might actually fit in. The way to do this is to tackle each issue and see what's really going on.

Amitabha Buddha is treated as if he were God: On the surface, yes. But perhaps chanting Amitabha Buddha's name is not praying to an external deity, but really a way of calling out one's own essential Buddha nature. However some of Shinran's writings do speak of Amitabha Buddha in language that a westerner would regard as describing God. The Pure Land appears to be a supernatural place: On the surface, yes.

But perhaps the Pure Land is really a poetic metaphor for a higher state of consciousness. Chanting the name can then be seen as a meditative practice that enables the follower to alter their state of mind. (This argument is quite hard to sustain in the face of the importance given to chanting the name in faith at the moment of death-when some supernatural event is clearly expected by most followers. And the chanting is not regarded solely as a meditative practice by most followers. However gaps between populist and sophisticated understanding of religious concepts are common in all faiths.) There is no reliance on the self to achieve enlightenment. On the surface, yes. But in fact this is just a further move in the direction that Mahayana Buddhism has already taken to allow assistance in the journey to liberation. And the being still has much work to do when they arrive in the Pure Land. (Shinran however taught that arriving in the Pure Land was actually the final liberation-the Pure Land was nirvana.)

TIBETAN BUDDHISM

Tibetan Buddhism is a religion in exile, forced from its homeland when Tibet was conquered by the Chinese. At one time it was thought that 1 in 6 Tibetan men were Buddhist monks. The best known face of Tibetan Buddhism is the Dalai Lama, who has lived in exile in India since he fled Chinese occupation of his country in 1959. Tibetan Buddhism combines the essential teachings of Mahayana Buddhism with Tantric and Shamanic, and material from an ancient Tibetan religion called Bon. Although Tibetan Buddhism is often thought to be identical with Vajrayana Buddhism, they are not identical-Vajrayana is taught in Tibetan Buddhism together with the other vehicles.

History: Buddhism became a major presence in Tibet towards the end of the 8th century CE. It was brought from India at the invitation of the Tibetan king, Trisong Detsen, who invited two Buddhist masters to Tibet and had important Buddhist texts translated into Tibetan.

First to come was Shantarakshita, abbot of Nalanda in India, who built the first monastery in Tibet. He was followed by Padmasambhava, who came to use his wisdom and power to overcome "spiritual" forces that were stopping work on the new monastery.

Groups within Tibetan Buddhism

- Nyingmapa: Founded by Padmasambhava, this is oldest sect, noted in the West for the teachings of the Tibetan Book of the Dead.
- Kagyupa: Founded by Tilopa [988-1069), the Kagyupa tradition is headed by the Karmapa Lama. Important Kagyupa teachers include Naropa, Marpa, and Milarepa.
- Sakyapa: Created by Gonchok Gyelpo (1034-1102) and his son Gunga Nyingpo (1092-1158).
- Gelugpa: (The Virtuous School) Founded by Tsong Khapa Lobsang Drakpa (also called Je Rinpoche) (1357-1419), this tradition is headed by the Dalai Lama.

Special Features of Tibetan Buddhism

- the status of the teacher or "Lama"
- preoccupation with the relationship between life and death
- important role of rituals and initiations
- rich visual symbolism
- elements of earlier Tibetan faiths
- mantras and meditation practice

Tibetan Buddhist practice features a number of rituals, and spiritual practices such as the use of mantras and yogic techniques. Supernatural beings are prominent in Tibetan Buddhism. Buddhas and bodhisattvas abound, gods and spirits taken from earlier Tibetan religions continue to be taken seriously. Bodhisattvas are portrayed as both benevolent godlike figures and wrathful deities. This metaphysical context has allowed Tibetan Buddhism to develop a strong artistic tradition, and paintings and other graphics are used as aids to understanding at all levels of society.

Visual aids to understanding are very common in Tibetan Buddhism-pictures, structures of various sorts and public prayer wheels and flags provide an ever-present reminder of the spiritual domain in the physical world.

Tibetan Buddhism is strong in both monastic communities and among lay people.

The lay version has a strong emphasis on outwardly religious activities rather than the inner spiritual life: there is much ritual practice at temples, pilgrimage is popular-often including many prostrations, and prayers are repeated over and over-with the use of personal or public prayer wheels and flags. There are many festivals, and funerals are very important ceremonies.

Lay people provide physical support to the monasteries as well as relying on the monks to organise the rituals.

ASPECTS OF FAITH

Lamas

A lama is a teacher. They are often a senior member of a monastic community-a monk or a nun-but lay people and married people can also be lamas. They are very often reincarnations of previous lamas.

As well as being learned in Buddhist texts and philosophy, lamas often have particular skills in ritual.

The Dalai Lama

Dalai is a Mongol word meaning ocean, and refers to the depth of the Dalai Lama's wisdom.

The first Dalai Lama to bear the title was the 3rd Dalai Lama, Sonam Gyatso. (The two previous incarnations were named "Dalai Lama" after their deaths.)

The current Dalai Lama (2002), Tenzin Gyatso, was born in Amdo, Tibet in 1935 and is the fourteenth Dalai Lama.

The Karmapa Lama

Karmapa means "one who performs the activity of a Buddha". The current incarnation (2002) is the 17th Karmapa. Two individuals have been declared the 17th Karmapa; Orgyen Trinley Dorje is generally and officially recognised as the official 17th Karmapa, however a rival Buddhist group give their allegiance to Trinlay Thaye Dorje.

Tantra: Tibetan Buddhism was much influenced by Tantra, and this has brought in a wealth of complex rituals and symbols and techniques. Tantra originated in India and appears in both the Hindu and Buddhist traditions. It brings Tibetan Buddhism a magical element and a rich portfolio of heavenly beings. It also brings a wide variety of spiritual techniques such as mantras, mandalas, ceremonies, and many varieties of yoga.

Rituals: Rituals and simple spiritual practices such as mantras are popular with lay Tibetan Buddhists. They include prostrations, making offerings to statues of Buddhas or bodhisattvas, attending public teachings and ceremonies.

Tibetan temple ceremonies are often noisy and visually striking, with brass instruments, cymbals and gongs, and musical and impressive chanting by formally dressed monks. It takes place in strikingly designed temples and monasteries.

Advanced Practices: Tibetan Buddhism also involves many advanced rituals. These are only possible for those who have reached a sophisticated understanding of spiritual practice.

There are also advanced spiritual techniques. These include elaborate visualisations and demanding meditations. It's said that senior Tibetan yoga adepts can achieve much greater control over the body than other human beings, and are able to control their body temperature, heart rate and other normally automatic functions.

Living and Dying: Tibetan Buddhism emphasises awareness of death and impermanence. Everything is always dying-the cells of our bodies are dying even while we live, reminding us of our own impermanence. And all the living things around us are dying, too.

This awareness should not produce sadness or despair, nor should it cause a Buddhist to start a frantic pursuit of the impermanent pleasures of life. Instead, it should lead the Buddhist to see the value of every moment of existence, and be diligent in their meditation and other religious practice. Awareness of death, combined with the understanding of the impermanence of everything, leads the Buddhist to realise that only spiritual things have any lasting value.

Preparing for Death: Tibetan Buddhists use visualisation meditations and other exercises to imagine death and prepare for the bardo. They work towards a holistic understanding and acceptance of death as an inevitable part of their journey.

Another way of preparing for death is to take part in helping those who have died through their experience in the bardo. This not only aids the dead, but enables the living practitioner to gain a real experience of the bardo, before they themselves enter it.

Even those who cannot gain the spiritual awareness to have a consciousness of the bardo are helped by achieving a greater experience of the impermanence of everything.

Tibetan Book of the Dead: This is one of the great texts of Tibetan Buddhism, and a big seller in the west. The English title is not a translation of the Tibetan title-the book's true name is Great Liberation through hearing during the intermediate state, commonly known in Tibet as Liberation through hearing.

The book deals with the experiences of a person as they pass between death and rebirth.

Bardo

Bardo is the state between death and rebirth. The different schools of Tibetan Buddhism have different understandings of this state which is regarded as lasting for 49 days.

The experience of a person during bardo depends on their spiritual training during life. An untrained person is thought to be confused as to where they are, and may not realise that they have died. People are often unwilling to give up attachment to their previous life-and their negative emotions-may cause their rebirth to be less good than it would otherwise have been.

In traditional Tibetan Buddhism, the dead person is helped through bardo by a lama who reads prayers and performs rituals from the Book of the Dead, advising the deceased to break free from attachment to their past life and their dead body. In some schools of Tibetan Buddhism, the lama will actively help the dead person to transfer their consciousness from their body, in preparation for rebirth.

Many Tibetan Buddhists believe that it is possible for those left behind to assist the dead person on their journey by doing spiritual work that increases the merits of the deceased and thus helps them to a better rebirth.

During the 49 day period the dead can see clearly into the minds of those left behind, which allows the living to help the dead by thinking good thoughts, meditating on Buddha and other virtuous beings, and engaging in spiritual practices.

3

Buddhists Ethics

Essentially, according to Buddhist teachings, the ethical and moral principles are governed by examining whether a certain action, whether connected to body or speech is likely to be harmful to one's self or to others and thereby avoiding any actions which are likely to be harmful. In Buddhism, there is much talk of a skilled mind. A mind that is skilful avoids actions that are likely to cause suffering or remorse.

Moral conduct for Buddhists differs according to whether it applies to the laity or to the Sangha or clergy. A lay Buddhist should cultivate good conduct by training in what are known as the "Five Precepts". These are not like, say, the ten commandments, which, if broken, entail punishment by God. The five precepts are training rules, which, if one were to break any of them, one should be aware of the breech and examine how such a breech may be avoided in the future. The resultant of an action (often referred to as Karma) depends on the intention more than the action itself. It entails less feelings of guilt than its Judeo-Christian counterpart. Buddhism places a great emphasis on 'mind' and it is mental anguish such as remorse, anxiety, guilt etc. which is to be avoided in order to cultivate a calm and peaceful mind. The five precepts are:

(1) To undertake the training to avoid taking the life of beings. This precept applies to all living beings not just humans. All beings have a right to their lives and that right should be respected.

(2) To undertake the training to avoid taking things not given. This precept goes further than mere stealing.

One should avoid taking anything unless one can be sure that is intended that it is for you.

(3) To undertake the training to avoid sensual misconduct. This precept is often mistranslated or misinterpreted as relating only to sexual misconduct but it covers any overindulgence in any sensual pleasure such as gluttony as well as misconduct of a sexual nature.

(4) To undertake the training to refrain from false speech. As well as avoiding lying and deceiving, this precept covers slander as well as speech which is not beneficial to the welfare of others.

(5) To undertake the training to abstain from substances which cause intoxication and heedlessness. This precept is in a special category as it does not infer any intrinsic evil in, say, alcohol itself but indulgence in such a substance could be the cause of breaking the other four precepts.

These are the basic precepts expected as a day to day training of any lay Buddhist. On special holy days, many Buddhists, especially those following the Theravada tradition, would observe three additional precepts with a strengthening of the third precept to be observing strict celibacy. The additional precepts are:

(6) To abstain from taking food at inappropriate times. This would mean following the tradition of Theravadin monks and not eating from noon one day until sunrise the next.

(7) To abstain from dancing, singing, music and entertainments as well as refraining from the use of perfumes, ornaments and other items used to adorn or beautify the person. Again, this and the next rule.

(8) To undertake the training to abstain from using high or luxurious beds are rules regularly adopted by members of the Sangha and are followed by the layperson on special occasions.

Laypersons following the Mahayana tradition, who have taken a Bodhisattva vow, will also follow a strictly vegetarian diet. This is not so much an additional precept but a strengthening of the first precept; To undertake the training to avoid taking the life of beings. The eating of meat would be considered a contribution to the taking of life, indirect though it may be.

The Buddhist clergy, known as the Sangha, are governed by 227 to 253 rules depending on the school or tradition for males or Bhikkhus and between 290 and 354 rules, depending on the school or tradition for females or Bhikkhunis. These rules, contained in the Vinaya or first collection of the Buddhist scriptures,, are divided into several groups, each entailing a penalty for their breech, depending on the seriousness of that breech. The first four rules for males and the first eight for females, known as Parajika or rules of defeat, entail expulsion from the Order immediately on their breech. The four applying to both sexes are: Sexual intercourse, killing a human being, stealing to the extent that it entails a gaol sentence and claiming miraculous or supernormal powers. Bhikkhunis' additional rules relate to various physical contacts with males with one relating to concealing from the order the defeat or parajika of another. Before his passing, the Buddha instructed that permission was granted for the abandonment or adjustment of minor rules should prevailing conditions demand such a change. These rules apply to all Sangha members irrespective of their Buddhist tradition.

The interpretation of the rules, however differs between the Mahayana and Theravada traditions. The Theravadins, especially those from Thailand, claim to observe these rules to the letter of the law, however, in many cases, the following is more in theory than in actual practice. The Mahayana Sangha interprets the rule not to take food at an inappropriate time as not meaning fasting from noon to sunrise but to refrain from eating between mealtimes. The fasting rule would be inappropriate, from a health angle, for the Sangha living in cold climates such as China, Korea and Japan. When one examines the reason that this rule was instituted initially, the conclusion may be reached that it is currently redundant. It was the practice in the Buddha's time for the monks to go to the village with their bowls to collect food. To avoid disturbing the villagers more than necessary, the Buddha ordered his monks to make this visit once a day, in the early morning. This would allow the villagers to be free to conduct their day to day affairs without being disturbed by the monks requiring food. Today, of course, people bring food to the monasteries or prepare it on the premises so the original reason no longer applies. As many of you would be aware, in some Theravadin countries, the monks still go on their early morning alms round, but this is more a matter of maintaining a tradition than out of necessity. Also, a rule prohibiting the handling of gold and silver, in other words-money, is considered by the Mahayana Sangha a handicap were it to be observed strictly in today's world. They interpret this rule as avoiding the accumulation of riches which leads to greed. Theravadin monks tend to split hairs on this rule as, although most will not touch coins, many carry credit cards and cheque books.

Let me now deal briefly with the Buddhist attitude to violence, war and peace. The Buddha said in the Dhammapada:

* Victory breeds hatred. The defeated live in pain. Happily the peaceful live giving up victory and defeat.(Dp.15,5) and
* Hatreds never cease by hatred in this world; through love alone they cease. This is an eternal law. (Dp.1,5)

The first precept refers to the training to abstain from harming living beings. Although history records conflicts involving the so-called Buddhist nations, these wars have been fought for economic or similar reasons. However, history does not record wars fought in the name of propagating Buddhism. Buddhism and, perhaps, Jainism are unique in this regard. His Holiness, the Dalai Lama has never suggested armed conflict to overcome the persecution and cruelty perpetrated by the Communist Chinese occupation forces. He has always advocated a peaceful and non-violent solution. Venerable Maha Ghosananda, the Supreme Patriarch of Cambodia has urged Cambodians to put aside their anger for the genocide of the Khmer Rouge and to unify to re-establish their nation. He has written: The suffering of Cambodia has been deep. From this suffering comes great compassion. Great compassion makes a peaceful heart. A peaceful heart makes a peaceful person. A peaceful person makes a peaceful family. A peaceful family makes a peaceful community. A peaceful community makes a peaceful nation. A peaceful nation makes a peaceful world.

Going back to the early history of Buddhism, Emperor Asoka, who, after a bloody but successful military campaign, ruled over more than two thirds of the Indian subcontinent, suffered great remorse for the suffering that he had caused, banned the killing of animals and exhorted his subjects to lead kind and tolerant lives. He also promoted tolerance towards all religions which he supported financially. The prevalent religions of that time were the sramanas or wandering ascetics, Brahmins, Ajivakas and Jains. He recommended that all religions desist from self praise and condemnation of others. His pronouncements were written on rocks at the periphery of his kingdom and on pillars along the main roads and where pilgrims gathered. He also established many hospitals for both humans and animals. Some of his important rock edicts stated:

1. Asoka ordered that banyan trees and mango groves be planted, rest houses built and wells dug every half mile along the main roads.
2. He ordered the end to killing of any animal for use in the royal kitchens.
3. He ordered the provision of medical facilities for humans and beasts.
4. He commanded obedience to parents, generosity to priests and ascetics and frugality in spending.
5. All officers must work for the welfare of the poor and the aged.
6. He recorded his intention to promote the welfare of all beings in order to repay his debt to all beings.
7. He honours men of all faiths.

Not all Buddhists follow the non-violent path, however. A Buddhist monk, Phra Kittiwutthi of the Phra Chittipalwon College in Thailand, is noted for his extreme right-wing views. He said that it was not a breech of the first precept to kill communists. He said that if Thailand were in danger of a communist takeover, he would take up arms to protect Buddhism. Sulak Sivaraksa, a Thai peace activist, reports in his book, "Seeds of Peace" that Phra Kittiwutthi has since modified his stance by declaring "to kill communism or communist ideology is not a sin". Sulak adds that the monk confessed that his nationalist feelings were more important than his Buddhist practice and that he would be willing to abandon his yellow robes to take up arms against communist invaders from Laos, Cambodia or Vietnam. By doing so, he said, he would be preserving the monarchy, the nation and the Buddhist religion. In contrast to the views of Phra Kittiwutthi, Sulak Sivaraksa reports that the Vietnamese monk, Thich Nhat Hanh is of the view that 'preserving Buddhism does not mean that we should sacrifice people's lives in order to safeguard the Buddhist hierarchy, monasteries or rituals. Even if Buddhism as such were extinguished, when human lives are preserved and when human dignity and freedom are cultivated towards peace and loving kindness, Buddhism can be reborn in the hearts of human beings.

In conclusion, I will briefly mention some other issues mentioned in the Syllabus.

The third precept on training in restraint of the senses includes sexuality. A Buddhist should be mindful of the possible effects on themselves and on others of improper sexual activity. This precept would include adultery because this also breeches the precept of not taking what does is not freely given. A relationship with someone who is committed to another is stealing. Similarly in cases of rape and child abuse, one is stealing the dignity and self respect of another. One is also the cause of mental pain, not to mention physical pain so one is causing harm to another living being. Therefore, such behaviour is breaking several precepts.

Marriage is not a sacrament in Buddhism as it is in other religions. Marriage is governed by civil law and a Buddhist is expected to observe the prevailing law in whatever country they live. In the Theravadin tradition, monks are prohibited by their Vinaya rules to encourage or perform a marriage ceremony. The rule states: Should a Bhikkhu engage to act as a go-between for a man's intentions to a woman or a woman's intentions to a man, whether about marriage or paramourage, even for a temporary arrangement, this entails initial and subsequent meeting of the Sangha.

In many Theravadin countries, the couple will, following their marriage in a civil ceremony, invite the monks to their home to perform a blessing ceremony. They will offer food and other requisites to the monks and invite their family and friends to participate. In the Mahayana tradition the same rule conveys an entirely different meaning. It reads: Should a Bhikkshu, seek to establish a conducive situation by means of which a man and a woman engage in sexual misconduct, either by himself, by order, or by means of messages, and as a result of his activities the man and woman should meet, he has committed an offence.

This rule does not preclude marriage but, rather, deals with the monk assuming the role of a procurer for immoral purposes. In Western countries, following the Christian precedent, many Mahayana monks become registered marriage celebrants so that, if called upon, a marriage ceremony can be performed in the temple. Generally, in countries where the law allows, Buddhists accept de-facto relationships. Promiscuity would be frowned upon as sexual misconduct but an ongoing relationship between two people, either within or outside of marriage would be considered moral conduct. As one of the essential Buddhist teachings is that everything is impermanent and subject to change, the irrevocable breakdown of a relationship between a couple would be understood in this light, so divorce would not be considered improper.

As far as bioethical questions are concerned, it is mainly a matter of the attitude of the different traditions or schools of Buddhism. This is tied to the concept of rebirth and when it occurs. According to the Theravadin tradition, rebirth occurs immediately upon death. The body of the deceased is no longer considered as a part of the former being, so such things as autopsies, organ transplants etcetera are allowable. In fact, many Theravadins, especially in Malaysia, encourage the donation of human organs as being the highest form of giving. Often, especially at Vesak, the celebration of the birth, enlightenment and passing away of the Buddha, blood donations are performed in the temple grounds. The Mahayana, on the other hand, believes that there is an intermediate state between incarnations, known as Antarabhava. Most people following this tradition try to avoid touching or moving the body for, at least eight hours after death. This, of course, means that the organs would by then be useless for transfer to another human being. The Buddhist work ethic and business and professional ethics would, ideally be closely tied to respect for the environment. It is well described in E. F. Schumacher's book "Small is Beautiful":

"While the materialist is mainly interested in goods, the Buddhist is mainly interested in liberation. But Buddhism is the Middle Way and therefore in no way antagonistic to physical well being. The keynote of Buddhist economics is simplicity and non-violence. From an economist's point of view, the marvel of the Buddhist way of life is the utter rationality of its pattern-amazingly small means leading to extraordinarily satisfying results."

Ken Jones in a paper called "Buddhism and Social Action" comments: "Schumacher outlines a 'Buddhist economics' in which production would be based on a middle range of material goods (and no more), and on the other a harmony with the natural environment and its resources.

The above principles suggest some kind of diverse and politically decentralised society, with co-operative management and ownership of productive wealth. It would be conceived on a human scale, whether in terms of size and complexity or organisation or of environmental planning, and would use modern technology selectively rather than being used by it in the service of selfish interests. In Schumacher's words, 'It is a question of finding the right path of development, the Middle Way, between materialist heedlessness and traditionalist immobility, in short, of finding Right Livelihood'".

Despite the theory surrounding Buddhist business practice, greed still seems to be the order of the day in many Buddhist countries. In Thailand, a monk in the north, Acharn Ponsektajadhammo, has been leading a campaign against the environmental vandalism of the timber industry. Tree felling in Northern Thailand has caused erosion, flooding and has economically ruined small farmers. For his environmental efforts, Acharn Ponsektajadhammo has had death threats and was recently arrested. In Japan, another country where the majority of the population is Buddhist, the killing of whales and dolphins is still prevalent. Animals seem to find no place in the group culture of Japanese society.

As may be seen from the foregoing, Buddhist ethical principles are very noble and in an ideal world their practice would lead to peace and harmony but, unfortunately, as the Buddha has taught, people are motivated by greed hatred and delusion-even Buddhists.

THE ETHICS OF BUDDHISM

It is well-known that Buddhism is the most ethical of "religions". An important part of the Noble Eightfold Path relates to the development of ethical conduct; for many a layperson Buddhist practice consists mainly in the "keeping of the precepts"; many Bhikkhus see in the Vinaya rules the essence of the religious life; and even many of the paramitas expected of those aspiring to Buddhahood are ethical in nature. Yet to present the teaching of the Buddha as being solely and exclusively concerned with ethics could serve as a detraction from the real objective of the Buddha-Dhamma, which is to serve as a path or vehicle leading to Enlightenment. While conforming to the norms of Buddhist ethics is essential for this purpose this alone will not guarantee the elimination of ignorance (avijja), which is the real meaning of Enlightenment.

The tendency of some exponents of the Dhamma to represent Buddhism as just another ethical system is misleading, especially when put before a newcomer to the Dhamma who may not be able to distinguish between Buddhist ethics and the precepts of other ethical teachers, and may conclude that Buddhism has nothing new to offer.

All religions inculcate some basic ethics, whether relating to individual or to social conduct. Indeed the advocacy of an ethical system does not need a religious framework, and some: of the great ethical teachers of the world (e.g. Socrates or Confucius) did not feel the need for one. The religion-surrogates of the modern world, like Humanism, rationalism, or Communism, have all evolved their own norms of ethics, however inadequate we may consider them to be. Wherein, then, lies the uniqueness of Buddhist ethics? This question could be answered in many ways, but here we shall look at it from the standpoint of three criteria.

First of all there are the ethical rules themselves. When we consider what actions are considered "good" and what are deemed to be "bad", it might appear that there is a great deal of agreement between the different ethical Systems. Such actions like killing, theft, sexual misconduct, and falsehood seem to be condemned universally. The differences emerge when we examine the question more closely, e.g. when we investigate the rationale for these rules, whether they are absolute or are relative to some other end, and so on. The rule against killing could be taken as an example. Many ethical systems proscribe only the killing of humans (i.e. murder), but Buddhism applies the rule to all sentient existence. Furthermore even in the case of humans, exceptions are sometimes allowed, e.g. for "holy" or "just" war. Buddhism admits of no such exemptions. In Buddhism the ethical quality of actions depends on the mental factors associated with their commission or even contemplation, and on the impact they have on the well-being of others. If action is committed with greed, aversion or delusion it is unwholesome (akusala), but the degree of moral reprehensibility (and karmic consequence) depends on a whole host of factors. Even an "accidental" killing could have adverse consequences if it was caused through negligence and unmindfulness, which is a kind of "Delusion" (moha). What has been said of the rule regarding killing, may also be extended to the other ethical precepts as well. Furthermore Buddhist ethics does not stop at the Five Precepts (panca siila), which provides only the very minimum for the proper conduct of lay persons.

The second criterion that could be adduced for the evaluation of ethical Systems relates to the motivation for adhering to the ethical rules of the system, religious or secular. In Buddhism the goal of ethical conduct is self-control, self-understanding, and self-development. It is an essential prerequisite for the training of the mind, the elimination of ignorance and the attainment of Enlightenment. Theistic religions usually require the adherence to their ethical precepts as a means to the union with God, whether in an abstract metaphysical sense or more directly as entry into a kingdom ruled by God, or even the enjoyment of pleasures in a heavenly paradise. In such a system the most important rule, precept or commandment is not usually an ethical one, but belief in, love of, submission and obedience to, and veneration of God. This is thus placed at the head of the Judeo-Christian decalogue, with the ethical rules coming subsequently. When we look at "secular" ethics, such as those embodied in legal systems, the objective is usually the avoidance of social conflict, the regularization of property rights, and the like. Of course, some secular laws (e.g. those relating to the so-called "victimless crimes") are more directly "moral" in nature, but these too usually are indirect social objectives. The pursuit of Buddhist ethics too leads to social harmony, but this harmony is achieved through individual perfection, rather than through the compulsory observance of legalistic rules. But because of the non-compulsive nature of Buddhist ethics, they are not intended to replace the laws of society, but neither are those of other ethical systems erected on religious and philosophical foundations.

The third aspect of the question relates to the way in which "good" and "bad" conduct results in appropriate consequences. This is the question of the "policing of the rules". Here two approaches may be distinguished. One is where some kind of trial and punishment (or reward) is instituted individually for each person. The supreme judicial authority could be God to the theist; or simply the normal judicial processes of society in the case of the secularist and the materialist. The second approach relies on the workings of an impersonal law (like the Law of Karma in its Buddhist and Hindu-Jam forms).

The legal model of trial-and-punishment is best suited to the enforcement of the laws of society, such as are necessary for the preservation of the authority of the State and the well-being of society. When this model is used to evaluate personal moral conduct and behaviour, as in the theory of divine judgement, several curious features arise. One that could be mentioned is the doctrine of the "forgiveness of sins". According to this doctrine the exercise of divine grace could wipe out "sins" and negate the principle that actions bring their own reward. In such a system the ultimate factor which determines the destiny of an individual is not the scrupulous observance of the ethical rules of the system, but the element of blind faith in its dogmas.

In Buddhism the operation of the law of kamma (karma) is all-pervasive and universal. Its exact modus operandi is not detailed, and may not be immediately obvious. Unlike in some other versions of the karmic hypothesis, in Buddhism there is no mechanical equivalence between action and result (vipaka). As mentioned above the karmic quality of an act depends on a whole host of circumstances. In the accumulation of kammas, good and bad, the fruiting of some may be postponed or delayed while that of others could be immediate. What is certain is that the law of kamma makes divine authority, divine grace, etc. redundant.

Thus in spite of superficial similarities, Buddhist ethics differs from other ethical systems when analysed in detail. In the Noble Eightfold Path the elements corresponding to morality and ethics are Right Speech, Right Action and Right Livelihood. These three together constitute siila. The cultivation of siila normally proceeds alongside progress in the other two great constituents of the Path, namely mental training (bhavana) and wisdom-insight (panna). Because of the mutually supportive nature of the three components of morality, mental development and wisdom, it is difficult to argue about the relative importance of these three components. Nonetheless it has long been the generally accepted view that panna is both the threshold as well as the culmination of Buddhist practice, with the other two components of sla and bhavana being the chief means to the realization of this great objective. The distinction between ends and means is very important in the understanding of the true place of ethics in Buddhism. For the ordinary person (putujjana) ethical conduct may appear to be an end in itself, but for the adept (sekha) it is a means to the realization of a greater end. Because of the Buddha's custom of proclaiming the Dhamma according the varied capacities of his listeners, there are diverse references to the importance of siila in the Buddha's discourses which at first sight might appear to be inconsistent or even contradictory. This apparent inconsistency, however, disappears when the actual context is considered. By way of illustration we can consider two places in the Pali Cannon of Buddhism which seem to attach different degrees of importance to morality (siila) in the Buddha's system.

"The first of these comes from the Brahmajala Sutta. This is the first discourse in the Sutta Pitaka (the section dealing with Buddhist doctrines), and this exalted position accorded to it reflects its importance to the early Buddhists, perhaps to the Buddha himself. This discourse was occasioned by a report brought to the Buddha of derisive commuents made on him, his Doctrine and the Sangha by a wandering teacher called Suppiya, and the equally unfounded praise bestowed on him by Brahmadatta a follower of Suppiya. This had led to conflict between teacher and pupil, and disquiet amongst the followers of the Buddha. The Buddha commences the discourse by advising his followers to consider all statements made about him, whether favourable or unfavourable, in an objective manner, with equanimity and even-handedness, and then to reject what was wrong, whether it be unfounded blame or unfounded praise, and to point out these errors in a calm and reasoned manner.

The Buddha anticipated that much of the praise heaped on him would be for the wrong reasons: "It is in respect only of trifling things (appamattaka.m) or matters of little value (oramattaka.m), or mere morality (siilamattaka.m) that an unconverted man (putujjana) when praising the Buddha would speak". What is interesting from our point of view is that the Buddha considers the mere keeping of ethical rules to be a matter not worthy of any real praise. In this sutta the Buddha groups ethical rules into three categories. The first of these (the cula siila) contains the basic ethical precepts (like the "killing of living things") which are usually included amongst the Five Precepts laid down for the guidance of lay persons. The other two categories (the majjhima and maha siilas) contain, ethical rules of lesser importance or those specially laid down for monks. As against these "moralities", none of which is deserving of real praise, the Buddha describes those things that are deserving of real praise. These are the "things profound difficult to realize, hard to understand, tranquillising, sweet, not to be grasped by mere logic, subtle, comprehensible only to the wise". More specifically they turn out to be the realization of Right View (samma di.t.ti), and the refutation of wrong views, in which connection the Buddha outlines the famous list of sixty-two schools of thought, ranging from theism to materialism, which then as now, were the main contenders with the Dhamma. Even though the Brahmajala was mainly concerned with what was praiseworthy in a Buddha, it does provide a clear statement of the principle that wisdom-insight (panna) ranks above siila and bhavana in the accomplishments necessary for the realization of the Buddhist goal of Nibbana.

The second extract from the Dhama which we shall consider seems to paint a slightly different picture. This is probably the best known stanza in the Dhamapada, itself the best-known of the Buddhist books. This Stanza (No.183) with its usual translation is as follows:

Sabbapapassa akara.na.m, kusalassa upasamapda,

sacittapariyodapana.m eta.m Buddhana sasana.m

Not to do any evil, to do good,

To purify one's mind, this is the teaching of the Buddhas.]

The ethical import of this Stanza is obvious. It seems to claim that the Buddha's teaching is threefold: avoid unethical conduct, cultivate good deeds, and train one's mind. There is no question of the ethical purport of the first two postulates. "Training the mind" could also be interpreted as an ethical postulate, especially when we consider the Buddhist view that evil thoughts generated by an unguarded mind are karmically effective. The last phrase of this Stanza is usually taken to mean that the three ethical postulates constitute the whole (or at least the most important part) of the Dhamma. However it could be taken to mean that these ethical principles are part of the teachings of the Buddha, and not necessarily the part that constitutes the Buddha's unique discovery.

In the Commentary to the Dhammapada it is stated that this and the two following Stanzas constituted the admonition (ovadagata) delivered by the previous legendary Buddhas to bhikkhus on the uposatha days.

In the explanation of the meaning of the terms in this Stanza, the Commentator says that "to do good" really means the "generation and development of skillful acts from ordination until the realization of the path of Arahat-hood", while "purifying the mind" means the elimination of the five "hindrances" which are obstacles to the realization of jhanic states during meditation.

All this is in keeping with the general purpose of these stanzas, which was to serve as exhortations to Bhikkhus on the uposatha day, and not to serve as a summary of the Buddha-Dhamma.

The uniqueness of Buddhist ethics lies in its many outstanding qualities. It is all-embracing and comprehensive without being impractical or impossible to follow. It is free from taboos relating to diet, dress, behaviour etc. which very often pass as ethical principles. It serves the needs of the worldling as well as those of the recluse. It is useful to the rich and to the poor; to the powerful as well as to the powerless. To conform to Buddhist ethics one need not have to be a "buddhist"; and it serves as a norm to measure the ethical standard of other teachings. But Buddhist ethics is only the threshold for those who wish to pursue the Buddha's path to Enlightenment and the end of all ill.

BUDDHIST ETHICS AND SOCIAL CRITICISM

Buddhism arose in India during a period of intense intellectual and social ferment. It was a period during which the authority of the Vedas had been placed in doubt, the concept of god as a supreme being and creator was in question, the hereditary restrictions on caste mobility were under attack, and the efficacy of Brahminical rituals was being challenged. The authors of the Upanishads had opened the door for various heterodox currents to emerge in society, and amongst the most significant of these were the Lokayatas who polemicized against religious charlatans, and the Nyayavadis whose rational epistemology created the foundation for intense philosophical debate and encouraged the investigation of the real world based on reason and logic, freed from the burden of superstition and irrational adherence to burdensome rituals. Various ideological sects competed for the attention and acceptance of the ruling elites and the public. The most important amongst these were the Jains and the Buddhists. Although each of the various sects made original and interesting contributions to philosophy, it was the early Buddhists who attempted to provide a unified philosophical system where ethical conduct and social criticism lay at the very core of their ideological system.

Although today, Buddhism is viewed as a religion by many of its followers, the early Buddhists sects were either strongly atheistic or agnostic. The atheists believed that rather than "God having created man in his own image" it was man who had created "God" in his image. In their view, the liberation of humanity was contingent upon humanity shedding the delusion that "God" existed.

Other parables from surviving Buddhist texts indicate agnosticism. For instance, there is a suggestion that Buddhist followers ought not to waste their time on unsolvable metaphysical questions such as "does god exist". The search to identify the "one true god" or to speculate on the nature of god was seen as an exercise in futility.

But the most frequently cited argument against god by the Buddhists was that if an omnipotent and omniscient being such as "God" truly existed, and who was also all good, there could not be the kind of dukkha (suffering) that was so widespread in the real world.

These shlokas (verses) from the Bhuridatta Jataka illustrates this point:

If the creator of the entire world they call "God" be the lord of every being, why does he order such misfortune, and not create concord?

If the creator of the entire world they call "God" be the lord of every being, why let prevail deceit, lies and ignorance, why create such inequity and injustice?

If the creator of the entire world they call "God" be the lord of every being, then an evil master is he, knowing what's right did let wrong prevail!

Unlike religions that ascribed earthly miseries to human sinfulness that brought upon the wrath of a vengeful god who needed to be feared, Buddhism saw the root of human suffering in ignorance that could only be ended through the acquisition of wisdom. Rather than expect some supernatural entity to end human suffering, the Buddhists argued that it was in human hands to end their sorrows through conduct and action driven by knowledge and correct understanding of human nature and the physical world. Hence, the aspiration for knowledge (jigyasa) was seen as the answer to blind faith. Although the Buddhists were not alone in developing this view, the elaboration of this point of view became pivotal to early Buddhist philosophy.

Central to Buddhist philosophy was an understanding of human nature and what caused dukkha-i.e. human suffering. They saw human personality as constituting five attributes, i.e. body, feeling, perception, disposition and consciousness, and used this framework to develop their understanding of human suffering. Citing examples of conditions that led to human suffering, such as aging, sickness and death, or association with the unpleasant, (or separation from the pleasant), or the inability to get what one wished-they concluded that suffering was a condition of stress and conflict inherent within human existence and interaction with the world. They also connected suffering to the very impermanence of things. They observed how people lamented over the loss of a loved one, or experienced sorrow when something or someone that had once given them happiness became separated from them. They noted that even human pleasures were not immune from suffering because they didn't last forever, and the loss of pleasure inevitably left people feeling deprived. Seeing as how clinging to things (that were necessarily impermanent) was one of the primary causes of dukkha, they cautioned against excessive attachment. At the same time, they recognized a recurring and more general type of existential unease and anxiety (anicchha) that arises from the very transience of life, and our inability to control or comprehend all worldly phenomenon, which they characterized as viparinama-dukkha.

But the Buddhists did not see dukkha only emanating from the difficulties of an individual. They also saw suffering emerge on a much larger scale from hostile social conditions such as poverty, war, and social oppression which they described as dukkha-dukkha.

As a formula (char-mulya) for addressing these different types of suffering, the Buddhists advocated a four-fold scheme of (a) recognizing the problem i.e. suffering (dukkha); (b) identifying the cause of the suffering-such as craving stemming from ignorance (samudaya); (c) establishing the goal of ending the problem (nirodha)-i.e. the cessation of suffering (nirvana); (d) conducting life in a manner that was consistent with the cessation of suffering-following the right path or engaging in the right practice (marga).

Followers were thus goaded into developing both a sense of personal ethics and a social conscience:

> *"He who has understanding and great wisdom does not think of harming himself or another, nor of harming both alike. He rather thinks of his own welfare, of that of others, of that of both, and of the welfare of the whole world. In that way one shows understanding and great wisdom." Anguttara Nikaya-(Gradual Sayings)*

> *"By protecting oneself (e.g., morally), one protects others; by protecting others, one protects oneself." Samyukta Nikaya (Kindred Sayings)*

Human actions (kamma, kaama, or karma) in the Buddhist framework were to be judged based on both the intention or motive (chetanaa) and the consequences (vipaaka) of the action. Altruistic actions which helped in the establishment and promotion of a just society were encouraged in the dharmaniyama (moral duty code).

{The discourses, or suttas in the Digha Nikaya, illustrate how there was deep concern with the creation of social conditions favourable to the cultivation of Buddhist values and the expansion of social equity and justice. These views undoubtedly influenced the creation of a "welfare state" during the reign of emperor, Ashoka (B.C. 274-236)}

In their theories of causality Buddhists challenged the view that human destiny was unaffected by the ethics or morality of human actions. They countered the doctrine of amoral causation (akriyavaada) whose adherents argued that there was no merit in doing good and no demerit for doing evil. (An extreme expression of such thinking was seen in philosophers who denied all morality and saw no crime in the killing of any person.)

Realizing that such a world-view could lead to the rejection of moral distinctions and personal responsibility for ones actions, they argued strenuously against such beliefs. They also argued against the theory of Makkali Ghosha (or Ghoshala) who believed that human fate was predetermined, and therefore denied that human actions had any bearing on the results of things (ahetuvaada) and maintained that human intention and effort were essentially powerless in changing human destiny, and therefore advocated fatalism (niyati).

They also countered philosophers from the school of "absolute skepticism" who doubted everything and never committed themselves to any specific position in doctrinal debates.

Philosophers from this school such as Sanjaya Belarthaputra (who was known as a theorist of endless equivocation or an equivocationist (amraavikkhepavaadin)) were criticized in the Brahmajaala Sutta (or Sutra) as "eel-wrigglers" who were incapable of taking a definitive stance on the vital philosophical questions of the day. Such skepticism was seen as emanating from both the fear of being in error and the lack of knowledge (or inability) to provide reasonable answers to question put forward for discussion. Such all-pervading doubt coupled with a cynical skepticism (vichikicchaa) was viewed as a serious mental hindrance, a fetter in the path to wisdom.

Other theories that contradicted the notion that human actions mattered were theories of accidentalism (ahetu-apachayavaada), theistic determinism (ishvaranimmaanavaada) and past-action determinism (purvaketavaada or purvekatahetu). All of these were opposed by the Buddhists. Accidentalism was an indeterminist theory which held that whatever was experienced was uncaused and unconditioned by human intervention. Theistic determinism was a determinist theory, which held that whatever was experienced was due to God's will or by plan of a "Supreme-Being". Past-action determinism was also a determinist theory, but it held the belief that whatever was experienced, whether pleasurable or painful or indifferent was entirely due to ones past actions (from a previous life), and ones present actions had no relevance.

The danger in each of these theories was highlighted in these words: "Thus for those who fall back on these three erroneous views as essential dogma, there is neither the will to do what is ought to be done, or not to do what is ought not to be done, nor necessity to do this deed or abstain from that deed. No moral improvement or intellectual culture can be expected from them."

Some of the theories in circulation at that time built on a germ of truth but generalized to the point of absurdity. For instance the accidentalists were correct only to the extent that certain things did indeed appear to happen by random chance or accident. But they failed to recognize that sometimes what may have seemed to be accidental was more due to inadequate understanding or improper or incomplete perception, and that other activities had a clearly discernible cause. To deal with the extreme generalizations of such theorists, they introduced a middle standpoint for their epistemology and ethics.

They thus rejected the theory admitting that everything exists (sabba atthii ti) and in permanence-i.e. the extreme of eternalism (sassatavaada), and its opposite which advocated that nothing actually exists (sabba natthii ti) i.e. nihilism (the denial of all reality in real-world phenomenon) or the extreme of annihilationalism (ucchedavaada). Related to their critique of the eternalist and nihilist philosophies was their rejection of both hedonism and self-mortification (attakilamathaanuyoga) which they viewed as painful, fruitless, unprofitable and ignoble.

Buddhist texts also expressed suspicion about claims by heretical teachers of being constantly "all-knowing" and "all-seeing" and in possession of "all-embracing knowledge-and-vision." Such claims were countered with arguments relating to the actual behaviour of such charlatans in different situations. For instance, they wondered why such "all-knowing" and "all-seeing" spiritual teachers lost their way in an unfamiliar place or why they were unable to escape from trouble while countering a fierce animal such as dog, elephant, horse or bull. Moreover, if they were really omniscient, they wouldn't need to ask for people's names, clans, or the name of a village or market town or make enquiries about anything. That they did such things indicated that their knowledge was evidently limited just like that of any average worldly person (puthujjana).

Unlike religions that were based on revealed truth or the sanctity of every word in a holy textbook, the Buddhist belief system prescribed reasoning based on investigation as the means of determining ones dhamma, (or dharma as in Hindu practise). In a parable in the Kaalaama Sutta, followers of Budhism are advised not to accept any moral codes on the following ten grounds: (1) Vedic authority (anussava), (2) tradition (paramparaa), (3) hearsay or report (itikiraa), (4) textual authority (pittakasampadaa), (5) apparent agreebility of the view (sama o no garu), (6) authority of the holder of the view (takkahetu), (7) apparent logicality of the view (nayahetu), (8) the fact that the view is an accepted standpoint (aakaaraparivitakka), (9) inadequate reflection on reasons (bhabbaruupataa), or (10) the fact that the view agrees with one's own.

In this manner, the Buddhism developed a very sophisticated philosophical system in which social ethics were integrated with rational investigation of human nature, social organization and the physical world. Buddhist ideas and concepts left a powerful impression on other Indian philosophical and religious belief systems, and over time, many commonalities developed amongst the competing ideologies.

However, there were also certain problems with the Buddhist world view which prevented its complete acceptance by intellectuals committed to the scientific method. For instance, although the Buddhists rejected the theory of past action determinism, they did posit the existence of a soul which survived a person's death and carried with it the merits and demerits of a person's past lives. Presumably this concept was essential to the Buddhist goal of encouraging right conduct but it was rejected by those who considered the soul as inseparable from the body and did not believe that the soul survived death. Those who rejected the concept of transmigration of the soul naturally couldn't accept the idea that human destiny had anything to do with merits and demerits accumulated in previous incarnations of the "soul". In their view, morality and ethics were entirely social constructs and had to be dealt with accordingly. The realists (such as the Nyayavadis) who shared the Buddhist concern for morals and ethics in society argued that while morals and ethics ought to be encouraged, they could only be enforced through societal laws and judicial codes.

Another problem facing the Buddhists was that in many ways, their views were too advanced for their times. Society had not yet developed to the point where education was universal, and knowledge of the real world sufficient to prevent superstitions and irrational beliefs from being completely abandoned by the masses. In an era where society had only limited control over nature, it was inevitable that sections of society would continue with beliefs in deities and supernatural phenomenon in the hope that they may be spared from natural disasters or that their crops might withstand attacks from pests and disease. Thus although the Buddhists had a very important and salutatory effect on Indian society, the most advanced Buddhist concepts could be understood and practised by only a minority in society.

Over time, the spirit of inquiry and rational investigation that had spurred the early Buddhist scholars towards dialectical thinking and critical social analysis became more and more replaced by narrow and literalist interpretations of the earlier texts. For instance, advice against accepting something that appeared "logical" without personal verification was taken to mean that logic could be rejected. Advice against wasting ones time on unsolvable metaphysical questions was also taken too literally and many Buddhist scholars remained aloof from the metaphysical debates pursued by other philosophical schools such as those of the Jains and the Nyaya Vaisheshikas. What they didn't anticipate was that some of these debates might lead to useful advances in mathematics or deeper understanding of human thought processes and new insights on human memory and psychology. These led to valuable advances in the interpretation of moods and emotions-thus benefiting Indian art, literature and music.

In addition, later Buddhist monks lapsed into some of the very things that had been attacked by the early Buddhists such as indulgence in unnecessary and elaborate rituals, belief in supra-natural phenomenon, and alienation of the priests from the masses. Activities such as meditation which were encouraged as a means to gaining wisdom became ends in themselves, and were turned into idealistic fetishes. Although Buddhist monks dutifully delivered sermons on right conduct and right action, they often failed to engage in relevant and timely social criticism-and did not always connect the textual suggestions to concrete practice. Intra-Buddhist disputes developed around less significant details, even as some of the most important ideas that had initially shaped the philosophy were pushed into the background. As a result Buddhism as it was practised came to be associated with idealism and inaction. Whereas the early Buddhists saw no merit in worshipping god or its images, later Buddhism developed a pantheon of deities not very different from other Indian religions. Thus even as Buddhism had spread almost throughout Asia by the 5th-6th C AD, it gradually began to lose its distinct edge and liberating influence on much of Indian society. Within the Indian subcontinent, strains of Buddhism survived in Sri Lanka, Bengal, Bhutan, Sikkim, parts of Bihar and Nepal, and parts of Sindh, Punjab, Kashmir and Afghanistan. In parts of Orissa and adjoining regions (such as Chhattisgarh and Telengana), Tantric (and other) influences reshaped the practice of Buddhism. Yet, Buddhism continued to have an impact outside India and developed pockets of influence as far West as Syria, as well as in much of Central Asia (including what is now Uzbekistan, Tajikistan, Kyrgyzia, Kazakhstan) and Tibet. In the East, its influence was felt on virtually every nation including Burma, Thailand, Malaya and Indonesia, Laos, Cambodia, Vietnam, China, Korea and Japan.

As noted earlier, the vast literature of Buddhism (like much of Hindu or Jain literature) was not a literature of revelation and authority. Its essays on social ethics and moral responsibilities, its treatises on philosophy and science, its art and poetry were but pointers to a path to wisdom. This gave Buddhism both flexibility and adaptability. Owing to its non-hegemonic character and humanist appeal, Buddhism was adopted without coercion or force. It was also successfully fused with Hinduism in many parts of South East Asia just as elements of it had been integrated into Hindu practices in India. In China, it was integrated with Taoism and Confucian principles; in Japan with Shinto beliefs. For several centuries, within India and outside, several people followed multiple faiths and identified as both Buddhists and Hindus, or as both Buddhists and Tantrics, (or Buddhists and Taoists) and so on. During the Gupta period (and in other reigns), philosophers from various schools of thought received royal patronage and temple grants were conferred for the construction of Buddhist and Hindu monuments alike.

It is also important to recognize that the form of Buddhism that was embraced in each nation was often quite different. For instance, in Western and Central Asia, it was not the philosophical or intellectual aspects of Buddhism that were popularized, but rather, its personal moral codes. Buddhist prosletysers imbued their stories of the Buddha with examples of miraculous healing and super-natural compassion so as to win more followers.

While such tendencies were also to be seen as Buddhism travelled within India or outwards, in Burma, Sri Lanka and

Thailand, Buddhism developed organizational structures that appear to have been much more resilient. It was perhaps realized that the development of Buddhist virtue would require leadership and constant interaction with the community. In these nations, Buddhism did not degenerate into the extremes of mysticism or retreatism that became commonplace in certain parts of India (such as in the foothills of the Western Himalayas). Burmese and Thai monks maintained a practical and benevolent connection with the community, and thus retained a measure of respect within the community. This also appears to be the case in Japan. In Korea, the emphasis on gaining wisdom was taken very seriously, and Buddhist monks took the lead in promoting mass literacy. This propelled the growth of technologies associated with the production of paper, writing instruments, inks, and furniture. And unlike in India, (where due to Upanishadic influences, "inner" wisdom came to be favoured over outer wisdom), Buddhist concern for disseminating the writings of the Buddha had significant positive secular impact. In Korean (and other Eastern) Buddhism, there was the correct realization that a Buddhist mindset, or that a Buddhist society could not be constructed overnight. There was thus the emphasis on the (helical) upgradation of individuals and society towards greater "Buddhahood". This philosophical element was perhaps signficant in that it prevented the sort of philosophical stagnation that occurred in India, where followers too often sought immediate succuor, and thus not only became divorced from reality, but also lost sight of the strategic potential of the philosophy.

In addition, it ought to be noted that Buddhism in India also had to contend with strongly anarchic and ultra-democratic tendencies. Precisely because its philosophical structure emphasized the relative and changing nature of truth, different tendencies under the Buddhist mantle competed for leadership through argument and debate. Initially, this led to important advances in democratic practices within the Sanghas. But over time, it also led to clashes of egoes, hair-splitting and deadlock. While some Buddhist sects compromised and fused with other tendencies (even alien tendencies), others remained fiercely autonomous. To survive, Buddhism had to confront both the tendency to be co-opted, as well as the tendency to atomize.

However, the catastrophic demise of Buddhism in India was triggered by the onslaught of Islam which first obliterated the remnants of Buddhism in Central Asia, and then later in Afghanistan and India. By and large, Buddhism survived only in those countries that escaped invasions by Islamic conquerors. As a gentle faith that encouraged its followers to abjure violence, it was perhaps unable to protect itself from iconoclasts and proselytizers who intended to enforce a new religio-political order. Accustomed to centuries of peaceful co-existence, India's Buddhists had not anticipated the need to develop viable strategies for self-defence that could have combated the violence of India's Islamic conquerors who virtually obliterated Buddhism from the land of its birth.

Yet, it also appears that (in large part) later Buddhism had deviated considerably from the rational principles outlined in the early texts. Monasteries often became isolated from mainstream society, and monks who focused exclusively on meditative practices and idealistic or esoteric philosophical speculation contributed little to social progress. Some have even argued that the monastic orders had degenerated into sheer parasitism and were becoming a heavy social drain. Consequently, value judgements on the demise of Buddhism and the rise of Islam in India need to be made with a measure of caution.

Nevertheless, it must be acknowledged that the ascent of Islam was concomitant with the eclipse of Buddhism, and since the influence of Buddhism was greatly dependant on the existence of the monastic orders, the destruction of monasteries and their conversion to mosques and institutions of Quranic learning simply lead to mass conversions to Islam.

In the long term, this could have had the effect of stunting India's future intellectual development, since the destruction of important institutions of Buddhist learning also led to a notable decline in the opportunity (and social sanction) to study secular subjects such as logic and epistemology (which were also taught at Buddhist universities-such as Bhagalpur).

It might also be observed that the destruction of Buddhist centres of learning coincided with the destruction of extremely valuable textual materials-which could have been potentially rediscovered, and revived or reinterpreted by future generations of Indians so as to achieve a society that was more thoughtful and learned. Islamic texts did not offer anything comparable in terms of causality or epistemology. Nor did they offer the psychological, sociological, or moral insights that had been developed under the ambit of Buddhism. Nor was there any comparable stress on seeking knowledge or constantly updating ones understanding of nature and human society.

One can, therefore, only speculate as to the full consequences of this profound sociolgical and cultural loss (and discontinuity).

But East of India, Buddhism did survive, and in countries such Korea, Thailand and Burma, it continued to enjoy a loyal popular following. Philosophical innovations also took place, and as noted earlier, Buddhist scholars in China, Korea and Japan offered their own commentaries and somewhat individual interpretations of Buddhist concepts and formulations outlined in later (5-7th C.) Indian texts. And although the sacking of monasteries and centres of learning (such as Nalanda and Vikramshila in Bihar) led to records of the original Buddhist texts being permanently destroyed, it has been possible to reconstruct some of them from translations that survived outside India such as in Thailand and Tibet. Notwithstanding the virtual erasure of Buddhism in India, it is possible to infer from these reconstructed texts and other archaeological records (and surviving monuments and artifacts) that Buddhism had a very powerful impact in shaping the destiny of India, and in triggering a social and cultural renaissance that would take Indian and other Asian civilizations to a higher level of social, cultural and material development.

BUDDHIST ETHICS

PAI LU-TIEN, a famous Chinese poet, author, and statesman who lived in the thirteenth century of the Christian era, once went to see an eminent Buddhist monk whose saintly life was known far and near, and asked him if he would instruct him in the essentials of Buddhist doctrine. The monk assented and recited the following gatha:

"Commit no wrong, but good deeds do,
And let thy heart be pure,
All Buddhas teach this truth,
Which will for aye endure."

The statesman-poet was not at all satisfied with this simple moral teaching, for he expected to have something abstruse, recondite, and highly philosophical from the mouth of such a prominent and virtuous personality. Said the poet, "Every child is familiar with this Buddhist injunction. What I wish to learn from you is the highest and most fundamental teaching of your faith." But the monk retorted, "Every child may know of this gatha, but even a silvery-haired man fails to put it into practice." Thereupon, it is said, the poet reverentially bowed and went home meditatively.

If we are requested today to state what is the most fundamental in Buddhist ethics, we have to make the same assertion. There may be and in fact are many schools and denominations in Buddhism, each claiming to have transmitted the true spirit of Buddha; but they will be unanimous in declaring that the gatha aforementioned is one of the common grounds on which they all stand. "Sabba papassa akaranam" is heard in all Southern monasteries, and the lines "Chu wo mo tso, etc.," are seen everywhere in the Eastern lands of Buddhism. If Buddhism were called a sort of ethical culture society on account of this simple code of morality, its followers would make no objection to it, for the recognition of a personal God, or the conception of original sin, or belief in a risen Christ is not thought indispensable to Buddhist salvation. Let a man do what is good and avoid what is bad and have his heart as pure as he can of all egotistic impulses and desires, and he will be delivered from the clutches of ignorance and misery. What ever his dogmatic views on religion, he is one of the enlightened who are above bigotry, intolerance, vanity, conceit, pedantry, and prejudice. He must truly be said to be one whose spiritual insight has penetrated into the depths of existence. Now, the question is: What is good? What is evil? And how is the heart to be cleansed? I am not going to discuss here these great ethical and religious problems from a mere theoretical point of view. Buddhism has nothing to do with utilitarianism or intuitionalism or hedonism or what not. Buddhism is most practical in its announcement of what constitutes goodness. It dogmatically and concretely points out good deeds one by one. First, negatively, it enumerates ten deeds of goodness (kusalam) as most fundamental in Buddhist ethics; while, positively, it considers the six paramitas (virtues of perfection) or eightfold path as the route leading to a virtuous life.

The ten deeds of goodness are: (1) Not to kill any living being; (2) Not to take anything that does not belong to oneself; (3) Not to look at the other sex with an unclean heart; (4) Not to speak falsehood; (5) Not to calumniate; (6) Not to use vile language; (7) Not to make sensational utterances; (8) Not to be greedy; (9) Not to be out of temper; and lastly, (10) Not to be confused by false doctrines. Later Buddhists, however, make ten affirmative propositions out of those just mentioned, thus: It is good (1) to save any living being, (2) to practise charity, (3) to be clean-minded, (4) to speak truth, (5) to promote friendship, (6) to talk softly and gently, (7) to be straightforward in speech, (8) to be content with one's own possessions, (9) to be meek and humble, and (10) to think clearly and rightly.

The six paramitas or virtues of perfection are: (1) Charity, which includes the giving away of worldly possessions as well as the proclamation of the Good Law, (2) The observation of the moral precepts as formulated by Buddha, (3) Meekness, (4) Strenuosity, (5) Contemplation, (6) Spiritual enlightenment.

The eightfold path is: (1) Right view, (2) Right reflection, (3) Right speech, (4) Right deed, (5) Right livelihood, (6) Right striving, (7) Right understanding, (8) Right contemplation. In these various enumerations of Buddhist virtues, what is most unique are perhaps the virtues of strenuosity and those of contemplation and enlightenment. To be good Buddhists, we must never be indolent, whiling away our time to no purpose. Mere piety will not do, so long as there is some work to be accomplished for the sake of humanity and civilization. Love, again, must be accompanied with enlightenment, for the affection is very frequently wasted on account of its blindness. God-fearing is recommendable, but without contemplation we fail to recognize the purport of our own position in the system of the universe. Mere passion leads to fervour and violence if not properly guided by contemplation which brings enlightenment, revealing the reason of existence and purifying the heart of ignorance.

Ignorance, according to Buddhism, is the root of all evil, and therefore it advises us in strong terms to have ignorance completely destroyed. And it is only then that the all-illuminating light of enlightenment guides us gloriously to the destination of all beings, where we gain purity of heart, and whatever flows from this eternal fountain of purity is good.

It is evident, then, that by purity of heart is meant absence of ignorance and self-will. But it is not a negative condition, for the most essential postulate of Buddhism is that in each of us there abide the indwelling reason of the universe, which, when released from the temporal bondage of ignorance and self-will, becomes the master of itself by reducing everything to subjection and restoring it to its right place. In a pure heart, therefore, the universal reason manifests itself in its full glory and works its own destiny unmolested. What one with such a heart wills is what makes the bird sing and the flower smile, what has raised the mountain and makes the water flow. He is hungry and the universe wishes to eat; he is asleep and all the world hybernates. This sounds extraordinary, but the enlightened understand it perfectly well. We cannot make the blind see what we ourselves see. The blind may protest that we are deceiving them; but could we do otherwise, inasmuch as they are deprived of the sense we have, or they have not yet learned how to make use of it? It is declared by Buddhists, therefore, that to realize fully the sanctity of religious life one must have Buddha-wisdom awakened from its unconscious slumber in which it is indulging from time out of mind.

Analytically, purity of heart consists of sympathy and intelligence, and on this groundwork the structure of practical

Buddhism is founded. Sympathy is the tremulation of the spiritual cord which unites the hearts of all sentient beings; and it is intelligence that discovers the presence of the sacred cord in every one of us and keeps it from being entangled. The cord freely responds to cries of suffering. The heart contrives to effect all the possible means to relieve sentient beings from misery and ignorance. The ten deeds of goodness, the eightfold path, the six virtues of perfection, and many other good things all flow from this one source of pure-heartedness.

It is, then, of unqualified importance in the ethics of Buddhism to have one's heart perfectly cleansed and free from the dust of egotism which has been accumulating through the want of enlightenment. In this sense "blessed are the pure in heart"; they may not see God as he is superficially and superstitiously understood, but they will surely come into personal touch with the ultimate authority of conduct and also perceive that the author is not residing outside of their being but within themselves. We read in the Dharmapada:

"Manopubbangama dhamma, manosettha, manomaya;
Manasa, ce padutthana bhasati va karoti va,
Tato nam dukkham anveti, cakkara va vahato padam.
"Manopubbangama dhamma, manosettha, manomaya;
Manasa ce pasannena bhasati va karoti va,
Tato nam sukhara anveti, chaya va anapayinî."

In this respect Buddhism can be said to have a decidedly idealistic tendency, since it fully recognizes the paramountcy of ideas in the moral realm. But we must not lose sight of the fact that Buddhism is not a system of metaphysics, but a religion which is practical more than anything else. What it teaches is the profound spiritual experience of every enlightened man, while the philosopher and theorist will speculate on the facts and offer whatever interpretation they may please or feel compelled to give to account adequately for them.

Buddhism is often charged with passiveness and quietism, lacking the "push" of some other religions; and the backwardness of Asiatic nations in the general march of humanity is sometimes ascribed to the influence of Buddhism. Though I am not here entering upon any lengthy polemics, a few words may not be altogether inopportune to refute such an erroneous opinion as this.

If there is anything passive in Eastern culture, which is often no more than tolerance or indifference or self-restraint, it is not due to Buddhism but to the racial idiosyncrasy of Asiatic peoples. Buddhism teaches contemplation and tranquillity and at the same time strenuosity, indefatigable energy in following truth and in destroying ignorance. We see many admirable examples among its believers who have fully illustrated these virtues in their person. The history of Buddhism, while perfectly free from bloodshed and inhumanity, evidences how far its moral teachings have been carried out. Buddhist ethics is not certainly passive or negative, unless the absence of arrogance, aggressiveness, intolerance, bigotry, and fanaticism could be called so.

Religion in its social aspect is not omnipotent, nor is it absolute, as is imagined by some. It is, like many other things created by man, a human institution; it has been discovered, shaped, developed according to the inner necessity of mankind; and as long as he is imperfect and steering his course through innumerable obstacles, religion also must share his imperfection and adapt itself to ever-changing surroundings. Instead of imposing its ideals upon man tyrannically and absolutely, religion reconciles itself to his needs, going through all the necessary modifications. Therefore, one religion is diversely interpreted by different peoples among whom it may thrive. To suppose that religion could do anything it desires without regard to individual, national, racial peculiarities is far from the fact. The difference between Oriental and Occidental civilization is by no means due to the difference between Christianity and Buddhism. On the other hand, the difference between the two religions is due to the difference between the two great types of Civilization. Truth, be it religious or philosophical or scientific, is universal, and as such does not allow any modification or distortion. But it suffers modification in its practical application, for it is like a mathematical formula or figure. When conceived a priori, it is formal and not subject to any concrete individualization, which latter in fact is the condition of its particular forms.

In conclusion let me say most emphatically that the ethics of Buddhism is summed up in the purification of the heart, in keeping oneself unspotted even though living in the world; and from this eternal root must sprout such things of God as love, a heart of compassion, the virtue of strenuosity, humbleness of mind, longsuffering, forbearing one another, forgiving one another, and freedom from all evils. It is said that there were eighty-four thousand virtues of perfection practised by all Bodhisattvas, but they are no more than so many leaves and branches growing from the one stem of pure-heartedness.

4

Mahayana Buddhist Teachings

The Consciousness-Only School

The starting point of the Consciousness-Only School is that everything is created from the mind as is "consciousness-only". Everything, from birth and death to the cause of attaining nirvana, is based upon the coming into being and the ceasing to be of consciousness, that is, of distinctions in the mind. Consciousness-Only doctrine is characterized by its extensive and sophisticated inquiry into the characteristics of dharmas. For if we can distinguish what is real from what is unreal, if we can distinguish what is distinction-making consciousness and not mistake it for the originally clear, pure, bright enlightened mind, then we can quickly leave the former and dwell in the latter.

Ch'an Master Han-shan (AD 1546-1623) has said, "When Consciousness- Only was made known to them (i.e., those of the Hinayana vehicles), they knew that [all dharmas] had no existence independent from their own minds. If one does not see the mind with the mind, then no characteristic can be got at. Therefore, in developing the spiritual skill necessary for meditative inquiry, people are taught to look into what is apart from heart, mind, and consciousness and to seek for what is apart from the states of unreal (polluted) thinking."

The founder of the Consciousness-Only School was the Bodhisattva Maitreya, who transmitted its teaching to the Venerable Asanga. He and his brother Vasubandhu were responsible for its early spread in India. The school was influential in Jung-Gwo (i.e., China) primarily because of the efforts of Tripitaka Master Hsuan-Tsang.

Asanga (Bodhisattva)

Together with his teacher the Bodhisattva Maitreya, Asanga was the founder of the Yogacara, or Consciousness-Only, School of Mahayana Buddhism.

The oldest of three sons, all called Vasubandhu, born in Purusapura (Peshwar) who were members of the Kausika family of Indian brahmins. All three became Buddhist Bhikshus. Asanga's youngest brother was known as Virincivatsa, while the middle brother was known merely as Vasubandhu.

Asanga was a man who was endowed with the innate character of a Bodhisattva. He became a Bhikshu of the Sarvastivada School, but afterwards he practiced meditation and became free from desire. Though he investigated the doctrine of emptiness, he could not understand it. He was about to commit suicide. Pindola, an Arhat, who was then in Eastern Purvavideha, having perceived this, came to him from that region and expounded the doctrine of emptiness peculiar to the Hinayana.

He arranged his thoughts according to what he was taught and at once comprehended it. Though he had attained the doctrine of emptiness peculiar to the Hinayana, he, nevertheless, did not find comfort in it. Thinking that it would not be right to drop the matter altogether, he went up to the Tusita Heaven using the supernatural power peculiar to the Hinayana and inquired of Maitreya, the Bodhisattva, who expounded for him the doctrine of emptiness belonging to the Mahayana.

When he returned to Jambudvipa, he investi-gated according to the methods explained to him and soon became enlightened. While he was engaged in investigation, the earth began to quake (of its own accord) in six ways. Since he understood the doctrine of emptiness, he called himself "Asanga", which means "without attachment". He afterwards often went up to the Tusita Heaven in order to ask Maitreya about the doctrines of the Mahayana sutras.

The Bodhisattva explained them extensively for him. Whenever he acquired any new understanding, he would come back to Jambudvipa and teach it to others. Most of those hearing him did not believe him. Asanga, Teacher of the Dharma, then prayed, saying, "I now intend to bring all beings to believe fully in the doctrine of the Mahayana. I only pray that you, O Great Master, come down to Jambudvipa to expound the Mahayana so that all beings may become fully convinced of its truth." Maitreya, thereupon, in accordance with his prayer, came down to Jambudvipa at night, flooding it with great rays of light, had a large assembly of those connected with the Dharma called in a lecture hall, and began to recite the Saptadasabhumi-sutra.

After having recited a passage, he would explain its purport. The seventeen bhumis were finished during the nights of four months. Although all were together in one and the same hall listening to the discourse, it was, neverthe-less, only Asanga, Teacher of the Dharma,, who had access to the Bodhisattva Maitreya, while the others could merely hear him from afar. At night, all together heard the religious discourse by Maitreya, while in the daytime Asanga, Teacher of the Dharma, commented once again, for the sake of others, upon what had been taught by the Bodhisattva.

In this way all the people could hear and believe in the doctrine of the Mahayana. Maitreya, the Bodhisattva, taught Asanga, Teacher of the Dharma, to learn the "sunlight" samadhi. As he learned according to what he had been taught, he subsequently attained entry into that samadhi. After he attained entry into that samadhi, what he formerly could not understand all became intelligible. Whatever he heard or saw was never forgotten, his memory having become retentive, whereas he formerly could not fully understand the sutras of the Mahayana, such as the Avatamsaka, previously taught by the Buddha. Maitreya explained for him all these in the Tusita heaven; thus the Teacher of the Dharma became well-versed in them and remembered them all.

Afterwards in Jambudvipa he composed several upadesa on the sutras of the Mahayana, in which he expounded all the teachings of the Mahayana taught by the Buddha. (Paramartha, "The Life of Vasubandhu", J. Takakusu, tr. [with some editing], pp. 273-275)

Vasubandhu (Bodhisattva) (fl. 4th cent. AD)

The second of three sons, born in Purusapura (Peshwar), India, into the Kausika family of Indian Brahmins. All three sons were called Vasubandhu and all three became Buddhist Bhikshus. His older brother was known as Asanga and his younger brother as Virincivatsa. He is known simply as Vasubandhu. In his youth he adhered to the Hinayana teachings of the Sautrantika School and wrote the Abhidharmakosa, perhaps the most well-known of all treatises on the Abhidharma. He was converted to the Mahayana by his older brother the Bodhisattva Asanga. After his conversion, he wrote many celebrated works on the Consciousness-Only School of the Mahayana, including the Twenty Verses on Consciousness-Only and the Thirty Verses on Consciousness-Only.

Vasubandhu's Conversion

"Asanga, teacher of the Law [Dharma], saw that his younger brother was endowed with an intelligence surpassing that of others, his knowledge being deep and wide, and himself well-versed in esoteric and exoteric doctrines. He was afraid that the latter might compose a sastra and crush the Mahayana. He was living then in the land of the Hero (Purusa-pura) and sent a messenger to Vasubandhu in Ayodhya with the following message: "I am seriously ill at present. You had better attend to me quickly." Vasubandhu followed the messenger to his native land, saw his brother and inquired what was the cause of his illness.

He answered: "I have now a serious disease of the heart, which arose on account of you." Vasubandhu again asked: "Why do you say on account of me?" He answered: "You dot no believe in the Mahayana and are always attacking and discrediting it. For this wickedness you will be sure to sink forever in a miserable Life. I am now grieved and troubled for your sake to such an extent that my life will no long survive. On hearing this Vasubandhu was surprised and alarmed and asked his brother to expound the Mahayana for him. He then gave him a concise explanation of the essential principles of the Mahayana. Thereupon the Teacher of the Law (Vasubandhu), who was possessed of clear intelligence and especially of deep insight, became at once convinced that the truth of the Mahayana excelled even that of the Hinayana.

"He then fully investigated, under his brother, the principles of the Mahayana. Soon after he became as thoroughly acquainted with the whole as his brother was. When its meaning was already clear to him, he would meditate on it. From the beginning to the end everything was perfectly in accordance with the truth, there being nothing contradictory to it. For the first time he realized that the Hinayana was wrong and the Mahayana right. If there were no Mahayana, then (he thought) there would be no path (marga) and no fruition (phala) of the Tri-yana [Three Vehicles]. Since he formerly did harm by speaking ill of the Mahayana, in which he then had no faith, he was now afraid that he might fall into a miserable life on account of that wickedness. He deeply reproached himself and earnestly repented of his previous fault. He approached his brother and confessed his error, saying: 'I now desire to make a confession. I do not know by what means I can be pardoned for my former slander.' He said (further): 'I formerly did harm speaking ill (of the truth) by means of my tongue. I will now cut out my tongue in order to atone for my crime.' His brother answered: 'Even if you cut out your tongue a thousand times, you cannot wipe out your crime. If you really want to wipe out your crime, you must find some other means.' Thereupon he asked his brother to explain the means of wiping out the offence. The latter said: 'Your tongue was able to speak very skillfully and effectively against the Mahayana, and thus discredit it. If you want to wipe out your offence, you must now propound the Mahayana equally skillfully and effectively.'" (The Life of Vasubandhu, J. Takakusu, tr., pp. 290-292)

A eulogy says:

It is difficult to practice two teachings at once.
He brought forth the secret meanings of the Compassionate Sage.
In awesome Shastras like piled up clouds,
Explaining the untransmitted doctrine,
Revealing the Consciousness-Only,
complete in both the Nature and Appearance Schools.
An eternal Dharma lamp,
He lights a million generations.
(Vajra Bodhi Sea #20, p. 2)

Hsuan-Tsang (Tripitaka Master) (596-664)

Great enlightened master, translator, and founder of the Consciousness-Only School in China.

"This Bhikshu's contributions to Buddhism have been exceptionally great. It can be said that from ancient times to the present, there has never been anyone who can compare to this Dharma Master in his achievements. His worldly name was Ch'a. His father was an official, but a poor one. Why did he end up a poor official? It was because he didn't take bribes. He wasn't after the citizens' money nor that of the government. He wasn't like people today who hold office and always feel they are earning too little money so that on top of their government salary they force the citizens to give them their hard-earned money as well. Dharma Master Hsuan-Tsang's father didn't want money. He remained a poor official all his life. Even though he was poor, he had a virtuous nature and because of that he had two sons who left the home-life, lectured Sutras, and were adept cultivators of the Way.

"Dharma Master Hsuan-Tsang left the home-life at the age of thirteen and commenced his study of the Buddhadharma. During those early years of study, if there was a Dharma Master lecturing a Buddhist text, no matter who the Dharma Master was or how far away the lecture was being held, he was sure to go to listen, whether it was a Sutra lecture, a Shastra lecture or a Vinaya lecture. He went to listen to them all. Wind and rain couldn't keep him away from lectures on the Tripitaka, to the point that he even forgot to be hungry. He just ate the Dharma, taking the Buddhadharma as his food and drink. He did this for five years and then took the Complete Precepts.

"However, the principles lectured by the Dharma Masters he heard were all different. They all explained the same Sutras in very different ways--each with his own interpretation. And there was a big difference between the lectures of those with wisdom and those without wisdom. But Dharma Master Hsuan-Tsang had not yet really become enlightened, and he didn't have the Selective Dharma Eye, and so how could he know whose lectures to rely on? At that time he vowed to go to India, saying,

The Buddhadharma has been transmitted from India, and so there is certainly true and genuine Buddhadharma to be found in India.

Thereupon, he wrote a request for permission to go to India to seek the Dharma and presented it to the emperor. Emperor Tai Dzung of the Tang Dynasty did not grant his wish, but Dharma Master Hsuan-Tsang, who had already vowed to go, said, 'I would prefer to disobey the son of Heaven and have my head cut off than not to go and seek the Dharma.' And so he returned to the monastery and began to practice mountain-climbing. He piled chairs, tables, and benches together to simulate a mountain and practiced jumping from one piece of furniture to the next. This was his method of practicing mountain-climbing.

From morning till night he leaped from table to chair. Probably there weren't any big mountains--where he lived, and so he had to practice in the temple. All the young, old, and older novices wondered what he was up to, jumping on furniture all day long instead of reciting Sutras or cultivating. He didn't tell anyone that he was training to climb the Himalayas, and so most people thought he was goofing off. Eventually he trained his body so that it was very strong, and then when he was physically able, he started his trip through Siberia.

"On the day of his departure, when Emperor Tai-Dzung learned he intended to go even without imperial consent, the emperor asked him, 'I haven't given you permission and you still insist on going. When will you be back?'

"Dharma Master Hsuan-Tsang replied, 'Look at this pine tree. The needles are pointing toward the west. Wait until those needles turn around and face east. That is the time when I will return.' He didn't say how many years that would be. And so he set out. At that time there were no airplanes, steamboats, buses, or trains. There were boats, but they were made of wood and not too sturdy. Besides, since he didn't have imperial permission, he probably could not have gotten the use of a boat anyway. And so he travelled by land through many countries, from the Siberian area of the Russian border to India. He was gone for more than a decade. When he reached India, he didn't know the language at all. But bit-by-bit he studied Sanskrit and listened to many Dharma Masters lecture the Buddhadharma. Some people say this took him fourteen years. Others say it took nineteen. In general he went through a great deal of suffering and difficulty to study the Buddhadharma and then when he'd completed his studies, he returned to China.

"When his return was imminent, the needles on the pine tree turned to the east. As soon as the emperor saw that the pine needles were indeed pointing east, he knew that Dharma Master Hsuan-Tsang was coming back and he sent out a party of officials to the western gate to welcome him and escort him back. When they reached the gate, there indeed, was Dharma Master Hsuan-Tsang returning.

"Dharma Master Hsuan-Tsang then concentrated on translating the Sutras and other works that he had brought back with him. He translated from Sanskrit into Chinese. At the time when he was translating the Mahaprajnaparamita-sutra, within one single year, the peach trees blossomed six times. That was a sign of the auspiciousness of the Mahaprajnaparamita-sutra and its importance to all of us. The fact that it was being translated moved even the wood and plants to display their delight. "Dharma Master Hsuan-Tsang translated a great many sutras. While in India, he bowed to the Buddha's sarira and bones. He saw where the Buddha in a previous life had given up his eyes, and went to the place where the Buddha in a previous life had practiced the conduct of patience, and went to the place where the Buddha in a previous life had given up his life for the sake of a tiger. He also went to see the Bodhi tree under which the Buddha realized the Way. He went to all of those places celebrated in Buddhism. These pilgrimages are another indication of the extent of his true sincerity. While in India, whenever he met Dharma Masters, he never looked down on them, no matter how little they may have cultivated. He was extremely respectful. He wasn't the least bit arrogant or haughty. When he finished his studies, many Small vehicle Dharma Masters and masters of externalist ways came to debate with him, but none was able to defeat him.

Dharma Master Hsuan-Tsang is known as a Tripitaka Master (Tripitaka='Three Treasuries', 'Three Baskets'). The Tripitaka includes the Sutra Treasury, the Shastra Treasury, and the Vinaya Treasury. He was honoured with this title because he understood all three Treasuries without obstruction....

"As to his name, Sywan means 'esoteric and wonderful.' He was esoteric in the sense that none could really understand him. Dzang means 'awe-inspiring.' He was awe-inspiring in that he could do what others could not do. He was an outstanding person among his peers...." (HD 15-17)

The Master's name has also been transliterated as follows: Xuanzang, Sywan-Dzang, Yuan Chwang, etc.

TRANSFORMATION OF CONSCIOUSNESS INTO WISDOM

In the Chinese Consciousness-Only School of Buddhism, Buddhahood, characterized by the perfectly enlightened mind of True Suchness (bhutatathata) is understood as the final realization of a systematic and gradual path. Buddhahood is not a goal which is attained through the acquisition of a special conceptual understanding. Rather it is the end product of a fundamental internal transformation of all mental activity. In the language of Consciousness-Only, that process is referred to as the transformation of "consciousness" that has attachment to distinctions as its basic nature, into "wisdom" that is by its very nature totally free from attachment. "Wisdom", therefore, indicates a radically, qualitatively and totally different type of mental functioning.

The purpose of this paper is twofold: 1) to delineate briefly the stages of transformation, and 2) after transformation is complete and Buddhahood has been realized, to indicate how the immanent aspect of Buddhahood utilizes wisdom tofunction in the world. Below we shall try to give a sketch of the prescriptions given by the School to rid oneself of the basic obstacles on the pathway to Buddhahood and to indicate briefly the manner in which one functions in the world after those obstacles have been removed.

The System of the Eight Consciousnesses

The Consciousness-Only School describes the mind as a system of seven active consciousnesses (vijnana) which all develop out of the eighth, or storehouse, consciousness. The latter is passive and contains the potentials, or "seeds" (bija) for the development and activity of the first seven consciousnesses. The seventh consciousness contains the sense of self or of ego individuality with which it defiles the first six consciousnesses. The sixth consciousness is a perceptual and cognitive processing centre, while the first five consciousnesses are the perceptual awarenesses of eyes, ears, nose, tongue and body.

Although with the emanation of these consciousnesses out of the eighth formal division is made among them, the distinction is totally based upon mental distinction. The eight are still basically "one." To use a simple analogy, let us think of a room with seven light-bulbs. You flick the light switch and seven distinct lights shine. Turn the switch off and the lights disappear. Yet there is just one electric current, and its source is comparable to the storehouse consciousness, or, as it is understood in the transformation of consciousness, to the enlightened mind. The system of eight consciousnesses, and the mental dharmas (caittas) which arise out of them and are dependent upon them, was developed as an important part of a pragmatic psychology of mind. The system can be used to describe in a manner which is accurate and practical both mental functioning and the specific techniques employed on the Path to the enlightenment of Buddhahood.

It provides a way to account for mental processes without recourse to the notions of a real, permanent self (atman) or of real, permanent external (and internal) objects (dharma). All actual and potential realms of experience are shown to be contained within the transformations of consciousness and appear as manifestations of the distinction-making mind.

Nevertheless, because of our attachment to and belief in the reality of self and the reality of the "objects" (dharmas) which we perceive and understand to be the external world, the true nature of ourselves and the world is obscured so that we are unaware of it.

The Types of Attachment

The basic obstacles which arise from the distinction-making character of consciousness are the division of the world into 1) subject, or one who grasps onto distinctions (the grasper), and 2) object, those distinctions which are grasped (the grasped). This distinction occurs on various levels and is reflected in each of the eight consciousnesses.

The grasper corresponds to attachment to self and the grasped to attachment to dharmas. The former is often referred to as the obstacle of the afflictions and the latter as the obstacle of the knowable. These obstacles or attachments are of two types: 1) innate, and 2) distinguished or learned. The innate attachments are quite subtle and have existed from beginningless time as part of the human (or more generally, the sentient) condition.

The distinguished attachments, on the other hand, are coarser and arise from the distinction-making of our cognitive and perceptual processes. These attachments, the innate and distinguished attachments to self and the innate and distinguished attachments to dharmas, are the only obstacles to the realization of Buddhahood.

The Attachment to Self

The innate attachment to self is twofold. By taking the eighth consciousness, more specifically its "perceived portion," as its object, the seventh consciousness generates a continuous image of the eighth or storehouse consciousness as a real permanent self. Secondly, by taking the manifestation of the five aggregates (form, feeling, cognition, formation, and consciousness) as object, the sixth consciousness generates various non-continuous concepts of self.

The distinguished attachment to self belongs solely to the realm of the sixth consciousness and is much coarser in nature than the innate attachment of the seventh consciousness. The sixth consciousness either takes various aspects of the aggregates as object and conceives them to be the real self or independently generates self-concepts and takes them to be the real self. Such wrong conceptualization is often the result of misinformed religious or philosophical teaching.

The Attachment to Dharmas

The innate attachment to dharmas is also twofold. As the seventh consciousness takes the eighth consciousness as its object, it can also use it, more specifically its "perceived portion," to generate a continuous mental image of the eighth consciousness as dharmas.

Likewise, the sixth consciousness can take aspects of the aggregates and the perceptual faculties and their objects to be real dharmas; however, in contrast to the seventh consciousness, the functioning of the sixth consciousness in this manner is discontinuous.

The distinguished attachment to dharmas is exclusively an aspect of functioning of the sixth consciousness and is relatively coarse in its nature.

The sixth consciousness can either take concepts of the Hinayana Buddhist dharmas to be real or take the various objective categories or elements of non-Buddhist schools to be real. In other words, it mistakes its own concepts of an external reality for a real external reality.

The Five-stage Path of the Bodhisattva

Now that we have briefly outlined the nature of the obstacles to the realization of Buddhahood, we are in a position to discuss the Consciousness-Only School's prescriptions for their elimination. This is the gradual five-stage process known as the Path of the Bodhisattva. It begins with the birth of the intention to become fully enlightened (bodhicittotpada), which marks the entrance into the first stage, that of gathering provisions or Resources. It is followed by the stages of Application, Vision, Meditational Development, and culminates in the final stage which is Perfection, the perfect enlightenment of Buddhahood, the full realization of True Suchness.

The Stage of Resources

In the stage of developing his Resources, the Bodhisattva develops his deep faith in and understanding of the teachings of Consciousness-Only. During this period the Bodhisattva is merely able to subdue the rise in consciousness of the coarse, learned aspects of the grasper and the grasped, that is, of attachment to self and dharmas. In other words, he learns to see through and replace with dharmic analysis the learned conceptual analysis of perceiving and thinking about the world in terms of a real self and real objects. He does this by learning to prevent such concepts from arising and then snowballing into verbal and physical activities (the creation of karma). Thus he is able to utilize effectively the Consciousness-Only School's doctrinal framework in his everyday thinking and functioning in the world.

The Stage of Application

In the following stage, that of Application, concentration and insight are developed through preliminary meditational practices called the Four Aids to Penetration: Heat, Summit, Patience, and Highest Worldly Dharma. The Heat, Summit, and first two portions of the Patience Aid are practiced in meditations in which one enters into the first three dhyanas. The remainder of Patience and Highest Worldly Dharma Aids can only be practiced by entering into the fourth dhyana. During this gradual process not only is manifestation of the coarse, learned aspect of grasper and grasped subdued so that it no longer arises in consciousness, but the seeds of its manifestation, which are stored in the eighth consciousness, are completely destroyed. Since the seeds have been destroyed, they cannot sprout in dharmas; therefore, this coarse aspect of the attachment to self and dharmas can never again appear. It is the completion of this process that allows entrance into the third stage.

The Stage of the Path of Vision

Entrance onto the Path of Vision provides the first realexperience of True Suchness. It marks leaving the worldly flow and entering the flow of the Holy Ones. It corresponds to entrance onto the first of the "grounds" (bhumi) of the Path of the Bodhisattva, the Ground of Extreme Joy. It is at this point that the gradual transformation of consciousness into wisdom begins. This pure wisdom is the activity or functioning of True Suchness. The process of transformation is a gradual one and takes place as the Bodhisattva passes through the Ten Grounds of the Bodhisattva.

The Stage of the Path of Meditational Development

On the Path of Meditational Development (from dwelling on the first ground of the Bodhisattva through the final, tenth, ground) the wisdom, which first appeared on the Path of Vision, gradually eliminates the manifestations and the seeds of the manifestations of the innate attachments of grasper and grasped. In passing through the first seven grounds, the Bodhisattva eliminates all the seeds of the subtle, innate attachment to self of both sixth and seventh consciousnesses (obstacle of the afflictions; the grasper). The single exception is the very subtle seeds of what is known as the spontaneous aspect of the obstacle afflictions. The Bodhisattva must preserve those seeds all the way up to the moment of realizing Buddhahood because they are the primary cause of the Bodhisattva's continued rebirth and, therefore, necessary for continued progress on the Path of the Bodhisattva.

The subtle, innate attachment to dharmas, (the obstacle of the knowable); the grasped) is also eliminated in gradual stages as the Bodhisattva proceeds through the ten grounds. On the final, tenth ground, the last, extremely subtle attachments to all known dharmas and their seeds,together with the above-mentioned seeds of the spontaneous aspect of the affliction obstacle necessary for rebirth, are completely eliminated. Then there can no longer ever be any kind of attachment, coarse or subtle, to self or dharmas, grasper or grasped. The obstacle of the afflictions and the obstacle of the knowable are completely eliminated.

The Stage of Perfection

Having outlined briefly the Path to Buddhahood and the stages in which the various obstacles to that enlightenment are eliminated, we are now in a position to discuss in greater detail the types of wisdom in terms of how they are used on the Path. As we have already seen, the distinguished or learned aspects of attachment to self and dharmas, grasper and grasped, are destroyed at the moment of entrance onto the Path of Vision. Their elimination clears the way for the appearance of a pure wisdom that has two components. It is characterized as pure because of its complete lack of outflows (asraya), that is, the outward flowing of the mind and its attachment to various aspects of the conditioned world. Previous to this, the wisdom used as a guiding force in the meditational process was an impure, preliminary "applied" wisdom (prayogajnana) characterized by outflow. The first of the two components of the non-outflowing wisdom is called fundamental wisdom (mulajnana). It is characterized as non-distinction-making (nirvikalpa). In the process of its initial appearance, it naturally destroys the seeds of the distinguished attachment to self and dharmas. The destruction of the seeds and the appearance of the fundamental wisdom is a simultaneous and instantaneous process.

The second component of the non-outflowing wisdom is based on the first and for that reason is called subsequently attained wisdom (prsthalabdajnana). It is an expedient wisdom which operates in the world of distinctions. It analyzes the characteristics of dharmas, yet does not become attached to those characteristics as is the case with the preliminary "applied" wisdom, which has outflows. The subsequently attained wisdom reflects on the seeming characteristics of True Suchness and in this way is used to eliminate the seeds of learned attachment to self and dharmas. However, the mode of its functioning is gradual. It is employed in various meditational techniques to destroy the many separate aspects of the learned seeds.

The Functioning of Wisdom

Generally, wisdom functions in two ways. It acts to subdue the phenomenal activity of the mind (dharmas), and then, on a more fundamental level, it eliminates the seeds (bija), which are the source of that activity. Wisdom and distinction-making consciousness are like ice and water. As the water freezes, the ice appears; as the ice melts, the water appears. On the level of the phenomenal activity of the mind, the greater the attachment to distinctions, the weaker the functioning of wisdom; the stronger the functioning of wisdom, the less attachment to distinctions. For attachment to distinctions to be permanently eliminated, wisdom must operate with sufficient basis and power to supercede not only the manifestation of the distinctions but also their seeds, which are their basic cause. Another image often used to describe the process is that of light superceding darkness. If the light can not only fill the darkness but also fully and permanently penetrate the barriers to the light, then the darkness is permanently eliminated.

At the beginning of the Path, the power of wisdom is weak and the power of distinction-making consciousness is strong. In the first two stages of the path, those of Resources and Application, there is no manifestation of pure wisdom, wisdom characterized by complete lack of outflows. In order to clear the mind so that the seeds of pure wisdom can grow and finally become actualized, the Bodhisattva temporarily employs preliminary "applied" wisdom, which is characterized by outflows. That is, it tends to seek out the characteristics of mental objects, and by nature depends upon them for support. By treating True Suchness as a perceived characteristic of the mind, this provisional wisdom utilizes its own characterization of True Suchness as a support for meditation on the emptiness of the grasper and the grasped. In this way, the coarse aspects of the distinguished obstacles are eliminated and the other aspects of the distinguished and innate obstacles are subdued, that is, they are partially or fully prevented from rising into active awareness.

As an aid to this type of meditation, the Bodhisattva gradually decreases the extent of phenomenal activity produced by the seeds of the two obstacles by the use of resolution (adhimaksa), a special mental state, and of remorse (hri) and shame (apatrapa), both wholesome mental states. Resolution, remorse, and shame are all technical "dharmas," which are included in the One Hundred Dharmas of the Consciousness-Only School. Resolution is explained as that mental state which examines dharmas and comes to a decision about their natures. Employing resolution helps the Bodhisattva to see the conditioned, empty nature of all dharmas so that he will not become attached to them. Remorse and shame are the inner and outer recognition of one's own improper behavior and of a desire to change it.

With the successful completion of the first two stages, the balance shifts. The turning point is the entrance onto the Path of Vision. At that point wisdom no longer functions totally in dependence upon distinction-making consciousness. For the first time its non-outflow potential actually becomes operative as the basis for further progress on the Path. As we have already noted, the entrance onto the Path of Vision marks the initial experience of the nature of True Suchness. It is then fully realized as the Ten Grounds are passed through. With each step in the progressive elimination of the obstacles to Buddhahood, there is a corresponding step in the development of wisdom.

On the Path of Vision, fundamental wisdom instantaneously destroys the seeds of the distinguished attachment to grasper and grasped, while subsequently attained wisdom is used to eliminate gradually the various distinguished characteristics which are an obstruction to True Suchness. During this stage the preliminary "applied" wisdom does not operate.

On the first seven grounds of the Path of Meditational Development all three types of wisdom operate. The preliminary, "applied" wisdom, though characterized by outflows, functions because outflowing attachments are still present and practice is still intentional. That is, it involves an act of will, signifying a tension be-tween two competing aspects of mind. The subsequently attained wisdom is utilized in meditations with characteristics, whereas fundamental wisdom is employed in the meditations without characteristics.

Starting with the Eighth Ground and continuing to the realization of Buddhahood, outflows and the innate attachment to self are totally ended (except for that extremely subtle, spontaneous attachment necessary for rebirth). Because there is no longer any self, cultivation proceeds completely spontaneously. Since there is no longer any personal effort, the preliminary "applied" wisdom no longer functions (though its seeds are not totally eliminated until Buddhahood). All meditation is without characteristics and utilizes fundamental wisdom, while all actionsproceed spontaneously from the functioning of subsequently attained wisdom.

Development of the Four Types of Enlightened Wisdom

Fundamental wisdom and subsequently attained wisdom are classifications of wisdom, that is, the activity or functioning of True Suchness in terms of whether or not they act to distinguish the characteristics of dharmas. The Four Types of wisdom is another classification of the activity of True Suchness, in this instance, in terms of the functions which they inherit from the eight consciousnesses of which they are transformations.

'The first five perceptual consciousnesses are transformed into the Wisdom of Successful Performance; the sixth consciousness, the perceptual and cognitive processing centre, is transformed into the Wisdom of Wonderful Contemplation; the seventh consciousness, which ordinarily de-files the first six consciousnesses with self and self-related afflictions, is transformed into the Wisdom of Equality; and the eighth, the storehouse consciousness, is transformed into the Great Mirror Wisdom. Both the Wisdom of Equality and the Wisdom of Wonderful Contemplation first begin to function on the Path of Vision. As attachment to the distinctions of the sixth and seventh consciousnesses diminishes, the power of these two types of wisdom increases. The functioning of the Wisdom of Equality is occasionally interrupted up through the Seventh Ground of the Bodhisattva when there are outflows (innate attachments) in the sixth consciousness that evoke the outflowing functioning of the seventh consciousness as support. This occurs because the seventh consciousness's attachment to grasper and grasped has not yet been fully eliminated.

The Wisdom of Wonderful Contemplation has two aspects, corresponding to understanding of the emptiness of self and of the emptiness of dharmas. They both function as long as there is no outflowing functioning of the sixth consciousness, which would naturally interfere. This type of wisdom is not active during the course of meditation without characteristics. (Meditation without characteristics becomes predominant on the Sixth Ground and is the exclusive type of meditation from the Seventh Ground on.)

On the first seven grounds, the progress which takes place has to do with the transformation of the sixth and seventh consciousnesses into their respective wisdoms. During this period, meditations with characteristics, which employ the sixth consciousness, are gradually phased out and replaced by meditations without characteristics. At the entrance onto the Eighth Ground, all outflowing activity of the seventh and sixth consciousnesses is permanently ended and the functioning of the Wisdoms of Equality and of Wonderful Contemplation proceeds spontaneously and without effort.

Both the Great Mirror Wisdom and the Wisdom of Successful Performance begin to function only at the moment of the realization of Buddhahood. The eighth consciousness must continue to exist upto that point as a receptacle of the wholesome outflowing seeds which allow the Bodhisattva to be reborn and to continue progress on the Path from the Eighth Ground to entry into Buddhahood. By the moment of entry, the eighth consciousness has become so pure that it can no longer serve as support for the seeds of outflowing dharmas, no matter how fine. Although from the Eighth Ground, the eighth consciousness continues to act as the supporting basis for the extremely subtle spontaneous affliction that the Bodhisattva purposely preserves as the vehicle of his continued rebirth in the world, in every other sense the eighth consciousness is undefiled and no longer the cause of rebirth. From the latter point of view, the Eighth Ground marks the beginning of the laying of the groundwork for the Great Mirror Wisdom.

The activity of the Wisdom of Successful Performance must await the appearance of the Buddha's pure non-outflowing perceptual faculties, because the faculties of a Bodhisattva, even after the Eighth Ground, are based on a body which is the result of the subtle seeds of affliction and, therefore, could not provide the proper support.

This kind of wisdom is active only when attention is directed to the perceptual faculties. The groundwork for it is laid when the awareness of the faculty of pure form, an aspect of the perceiver portion of the eighth consciousness, no longer associates itself with the characteristics of perceived objects, that is, the dharmas arising from the perceived portion of the eighth consciousness. (This also marks the initial emergence of subsequently attained wisdom.)

The Four Types of Wisdom and Buddhahood

Having discussed when on the Path the Four Types of Wisdom arise, we can now describe their functioning after the full realization of True Suchness at Buddhahood. All seeds and all dharmas, the entire universe both potential and actual, are reflected without distortion in the Great Mirror Wisdom. Its awareness of True Suchness is the functioning of the fundamental component of this type of wisdom, while its awareness of the activity of seeds and dharmas (as an aspect of True Suchness) is the functioning of its subsequently attained component. The Great Mirror Wisdom is equated with that aspect of the functioning of the reward-body (svasambhogakaya) and pure land of the Buddha which has no purpose beyond what it is in itself.

The Wisdom of Equality understands the nature of the equality of self and other and of all beings. It appears as images of the Buddhas which are limitless. It is equated with that aspect of the reward-body (parasambhogakaya) of the Buddha that functions for the sake of others. More specifically, it is the mode of wisdom which the Buddha uses to teach the great Bodhisattvas.

It is also called the great transformation body (nisyandakaya). As is the case with the Great Mirror Wisdom, both components of wisdom function here to include both True Suchness and "worldly" aspects in their understanding.

The Wisdom of Wonderful Contemplation understands withoutdistortion the individual and universal characteristics of all dharmas in both their True Suchness and worldly aspects. According to Master Kuiji, it "examines the merits and abilities of all beings and rains the great rain of Dharma to destroy the great net of doubts and to benefit all sentient beings. " (59:32b)

The Wisdom of Successful Performance operates as the countless transformation bodies of the Buddhas and as the lands both with and without outflows in which they teach living beings. It is exclusively concerned with those dharmas that are the dharmas of perception, that is, the transformation bodies of the Buddha and the phenomena which the faculties of those bodies perceive. Therefore, only the subsequently attained component of wisdom functions in relation to it.

In other words, the Buddha employs the Wisdom of Successful Performance to appear in his ordinary earthly body (and other transformation bodies) and to function perceptually within that body. He sees, hears, smells, tastes, and touches without any obstruction or distortion of feeling not only in the ordinary range of perception but in an unlimited manner, universally in time and space.

With the Wisdom of Wonderful Contemplation he knows clearly, without distortion or obstruction, all dharmas which are the objects of his perception and all other dharmas which are exclusively the objects of cognitive processes. In this way he knows the mental and physical condition of all beings and speaks and acts accordingly in all the various ways necessary to teach them most effectively.

Summary

The Consciousness-Only School teaches that our true nature and the true nature of the world is Consciousness-Only, which is ultimately understood to be True Suchness. True Suchness is covered over by the distinction-making consciousnesses' attachments to grasper and grasped, self and dharmas. These attachments are systematically overcome on the Bodhisattva Path by the use of wisdom. One component of wisdom, fundamental wisdom, knows True Suchness as the real, underlying nature of distinction-making consciousness. As such, it eliminates confusion about principle (deviant views, their accompanying afflictions, and the seeds of both), radically undermining it. The other component, subsequently attained wisdom, works on the level of the distinctions themselves to eliminate attachment to them. Based on fundamental wisdom, it acts to eliminate confusion about phenomena, particularly the dharmas of greed and other primary afflictions. Upon the total realization of True Suchness at Buddhahood, the subsequently attained component, previously used as a tool for progress on the Bodhisattva Path, is the modality through which the Buddha operates in the world of distinctions made by sentient beings and through which he teaches them the Buddhadharma, a Path for the transformation of distinction-making consciousness into True Suchness and its Four Types of Wisdom.

5

Dhammapada: The Path of Real Religion

The Path of Dhamma

The Pairs Heedfulness

1. Mind precedes all mental states. Mind is their chief; they are all mind-wrought. If with an impure mind a person speaks or acts suffering follows him like the wheel that follows the foot of the ox.

2. Mind precedes all mental states. Mind is their chief; they are all mind-wrought. If with a pure mind a person speaks or acts happiness follows him like his never-departing shadow.

3. "He abused me, he struck me, he overpowered me, he robbed me." Those who harbor such thoughts do not still their hatred.

4. "He abused me, he struck me, he overpowered me, he robbed me." Those who do not harbor such thoughts still their hatred.

5. Hatred is never appeased by hatred in this world. By non-hatred alone is hatred appeased. This is a law eternal.

6. There are those who do not realize that one day we all must die. But those who do realize this settle their quarrels.

7. Just as a storm throws down a weak tree, so does Mara overpower the man who lives for the pursuit of pleasures, who is uncontrolled in his senses, immoderate in eating, indolent, and dissipated.

8. Just as a storm cannot prevail against a rocky mountain, so Mara can never overpower the man who lives meditating on the impurities, who is controlled in his senses, moderate in eating, and filled with faith and earnest effort.

9. Whoever being depraved, devoid of self-control and truthfulness, should don the monk's yellow robe, he surely is not worthy of the robe.

10. But whoever is purged of depravity, well-established in virtues and filled with self-control and truthfulness, he indeed is worthy of the yellow robe.

11. Those who mistake the unessential tu be essential and the essential to be unessential, dwelling in wrong thoughts, never arrive at the essential.

12. Those who know the essential to be essential and the unessential to be unessential, dwelling in right thoughts, do arrive at the essential.

13. Just as rain breaks through an ill-thatched house, so passion penetrates an undeveloped mind.

14. Just as rain does not break through a well-thatched house, so passion never penetrates a well-developed mind.

15. The evil-doer grieves here and hereafter; he grieves in both the worlds. He laments and is afflicted, recollecting his own impure deeds.

16. The doer of good rejoices here and hereafter; he rejoices in both the worlds. He rejoices and exults, recollecting his own pure deeds.

17. The evil-doer suffers here and hereafter; he suffers in both the worlds. The thought, "Evil have I done," torments him, and he suffers even more when gone to realms of woe.

18. The doer of good delights here and hereafter; he delights in both the worlds. The thought, "Good have I done," delights him, and he delights even more when gone to realms of bliss.

19. Much though he recites the sacred texts, but acts not accordingly, that heedless man is like a cowherd who only counts the cows of others-he does not partake of the blessings of the holy life.

20. Little though he recites the sacred texts, but puts the Teaching into practice, forsaking lust, hatred, and delusion, with true wisdom and emancipated mind, clinging to nothing of this or any other world-he indeed partakes of the blessings of a holy life.

21. Heedfulness is the path to the Deathless. Heedlessness is the path to death. The heedful die not. The heedless are as if dead already.

22. Clearly understanding this excellence of heedfulness, the wise exult therein and enjoy the resort of the Noble Ones.

23. The wise ones, ever meditative and steadfastly persevering, alone experience Nibbana, the incomparable freedom from bondage.

24. Ever grows the glory of him who is energetic, mindful and pure in conduct, discerning and self-controlled, righteous and heedful.

25. By effort and heedfulness, discipline and self-mastery, let the wise one make for himself an island which no flood can overwhelm.

26. The foolish and ignorant indulge in heedlessness, but the wise one keeps his heedfulness as his best treasure.

27. Do not give way to heedlessness. Do not indulge in sensual pleasures. Only the heedful and meditative attain great happiness.

28. Just as one upon the summit of a mountain beholds the groundlings, even so when the wise man casts away heedlessness by heedfulness and ascends the high tower of wisdom, this sorrowless sage beholds the sorrowing and foolish multitude.

29. Heedful among the heedless, wide-awake among the sleepy, the wise man advances like a swift horse leaving behind a weak jade.

30. By Heedfulness did Indra become the overlord of the gods. Heedfulness is ever praised, and heedlessness ever despised.

31. The monk who delights in heedfulness and looks with fear at heedlessness advances like fire, burning all fetters, small and large.

32. The monk who delights in heedfulness and looks with fear at heedlessness will not fall. He is close to Nibbana.

33. Just as a fletcher straightens an arrow shaft, even so the discerning man straightens his mind-so fickle and unsteady, so difficult to guard.

34. As a fish when pulled out of water and cast on land throbs and quivers, even so is this mind agitated. Hence should one abandon the realm of Mara.

35. Wonderful, indeed, it is to subdue the mind, so difficult to subdue, ever swift, and seizing whatever it desires. A tamed mind brings happiness.

36. Let the discerning man guard the mind, so difficult to detect and extremely subtle, seizing whatever it desires. A guarded mind brings happiness.

37. Dwelling in the cave (of the heart), the mind, without form, wanders far and alone. Those who subdue this mind are liberated from the bonds of Mara.

38. Wisdom never becomes perfect in one whose mind is not steadfast, who knows not the Good Teaching and whose faith wavers.

39. There is no fear for an awakened one, whose mind is not sodden (by lust) nor afflicted (by hate), and who has gone beyond both merit and demerit.

40. Realizing that this body is as fragile as a clay pot, and fortifying this mind like a well-fortified city, fight out Mara with the sword of wisdom. Then, guarding the conquest, remain unattached.

41. Ere long, alas! this body will lie upon the earth, unheeded and lifeless, like a useless log.

42. Whatever harm an enemy may do to an enemy, or a hater to a hater, an ill-directed mind inflicts on oneself a greater harm.

43. Neither mother, father, nor any other relative can do one greater good than one's own well-directed mind.

44. Who shall overcome this earth, this realm of Yama and this sphere of men and gods? Who shall bring to perfection the well-taught path of wisdom as an expert garland-maker would his floral design?

45. A striver-on-the path shall overcome this earth, this realm of Yama and this sphere of men and gods. The striver-on-the-path shall bring to perfection the well-taught path of wisdom, as an expert garland-maker would his floral design.

46. Realizing that this body is like froth, penetrating its mirage-like nature, and plucking out Mara's flower-tipped arrows of sensuality, go beyond sight of the King of Death!

47. As a mighty flood sweeps away the sleeping village, so death carries away the person of distracted mind who only plucks the flowers (of pleasure).

48. The Destroyer brings under his sway the person of distracted mind who, insatiate in sense desires, only plucks the flowers (of pleasure).

49. As a bee gathers honey from the flower without injuring its colour or fragrance, even so the sage goes on his alms-round in the village.

50. Let none find fault with others; let none see the omissions and commissions of others. But let one see one's own acts, done and undone.

51. Like a beautiful flower full of colour but without fragrance, even so, fruitless are the fair words of one who does not practice them.

52. Like a beautiful flower full of colour and also fragrant, even so, fruitful are the fair words of one who practices them.

53. As from a great heap of flowers many garlands can be made, even so should many good deeds be done by one born a mortal.

54. Not the sweet smell of flowers, not even the fragrance of sandal, tagara, or jasmine blows against the wind. But the fragrance of the virtuous blows against the wind. Truly the

virtuous man pervades all directions with the fragrance of his virtue.

55. Of all the fragrances-sandal, tagara, blue lotus and jasmine-the fragrance of virtue is the sweetest.

56. Faint is the fragrance of tagara and sandal, but excellent is the fragrance of the virtuous, wafting even amongst the gods.

57. Mara never finds the path of the truly virtuous, who abide in heedfulness and are freed by perfect knowledge.

58. Upon a heap of rubbish in the road-side ditch blooms a lotus, fragrant and pleasing.

59. Even so, on the rubbish heap of blinded mortals the disciple of the Supremely Enlightened One shines resplendent in wisdom.

60. Long is the night to the sleepless; long is the league to the weary. Long is worldly existence to fools who know not the Sublime Truth.

61. Should a seeker not find a companion who is better or equal, let him resolutely pursue a solitary course; there is no fellowship with the fool.

62. The fool worries, thinking, "I have sons, I have wealth." Indeed, when he himself is not his own, whence are sons, whence is wealth?

63. A fool who knows his foolishness is wise at least to that extent, but a fool who thinks himself wise is a fool indeed.

64. Though all his life a fool associates with a wise man, he no more comprehends the Truth than a spoon tastes the flavour of the soup.

65. Though only for a moment a discerning person associates with a wise man, quickly he comprehends the Truth, just as the tongue tastes the flavour of the soup.

66. Fools of little wit are enemies unto themselves as they move about doing evil deeds, the fruits of which are bitter.

67. Ill done is that action of doing which one repents later, and the fruit of which one, weeping, reaps with tears.

68. Well done is that action of doing which one repents not later, and the fruit of which one, reaps with delight and happiness.

69. So long as an evil deed has not ripened, the fool thinks it as sweet as honey. But when the evil deed ripens, the fool comes to grief.

70. Month after month a fool may eat his food with the tip of a blade of grass, but he still is not worth a sixteenth part of the those who have comprehended the Truth.

71. Truly, an evil deed committed does not immediately bear fruit, like milk that does not turn sour all at once. But smoldering, it follows the fool like fire covered by ashes.

72. To his own ruin the fool gains knowledge, for it cleaves his head and destroys his innate goodness.

73. The fool seeks undeserved reputation, precedence among monks, authority over monasteries, and honour among householders.

74. "Let both laymen and monks think that it was done by me. In every work, great and small, let them follow me"- such is the ambition of the fool; thus his desire and pride increase.

75. One is the quest for worldly gain, and quite another is the path to Nibbana. Clearly understanding this, let not the monk, the disciple of the Buddha, be carried away by worldly acclaim, but develop detachment instead.

76. Should one find a man who points out faults and who reproves, let him follow such a wise and sagacious person as one would a guide to hidden treasure. It is always better, and never worse, to cultivate such an association.

77. Let him admonish, instruct and shield one from wrong; he, indeed, is dear to the good and detestable to the evil.

78. Do not associate with evil companions; do not seek the fellowship of the vile. Associate with the good friends; seek the fellowship of noble men.

79. He who drinks deep the Dhamma lives happily with a tranquil mind. The wise man ever delights in the Dhamma made known by the Noble One (the Buddha).

80. Irrigators regulate the rivers; fletchers straighten the arrow shaft; carpenters shape the wood; the wise control themselves.

81. Just as a solid rock is not shaken by the storm, even so the wise are not affected by praise or blame.

82. On hearing the Teachings, the wise become perfectly purified, like a lake deep, clear and still.

83. The good renounce (attachment for) everything. The virtuous do not prattle with a yearning for pleasures. The wise show no elation or depression when touched by happiness or sorrow.

84. He is indeed virtuous, wise, and righteous who neither for his own sake nor for the sake of another (does any wrong), who does not crave for sons, wealth, or kingdom, and does not desire success by unjust means.

85. Few among men are those who cross to the farther shore. The rest, the bulk of men, only run up and down the hither bank.

86. But those who act according to the perfectly taught Dhamma will cross the realm of Death, so difficult to cross.

87-88. Abandoning the dark way, let the wise man cultivate the bright path. Having gone from home to homelessness, let him yearn for that delight in detachment, so difficult to enjoy. Giving up sensual pleasures, with no attachment, let the wise man cleanse himself of defilements of the mind.

89. Those whose minds have reached full excellence in the factors of enlightenment, who, having renounced acquisitiveness, rejoice in not clinging to things-rid of cankers, glowing with wisdom, they have attained Nibbana in this very life.

90. The fever of passion exists not for him who has completed the journey, who is sorrowless and wholly set free, and has broken all ties.

91. The mindful ones exert themselves. They are not attached to any home; like swans that abandon the lake, they leave home after home behind.

92. Those who do not accumulate and are wise regarding food, whose object is the Void, the Unconditioned Freedom-their track cannot be traced, like that of birds in the air.

93. He whose cankers are destroyed and who is not attached to food, whose object is the Void, the Unconditioned Freedom-his path cannot be traced, like that of birds in the air.

94. Even the gods hold dear the wise one, whose senses are subdued like horses well trained by a charioteer, whose pride is destroyed and who is free from the cankers.

95. There is no more worldly existence for the wise one who, like the earth, resents nothing, who is firm as a high pillar and as pure as a deep pool free from mud.

96. Calm is his thought, calm his speech, and calm his deed, who, truly knowing, is wholly freed, perfectly tranquil and wise.

97. The man who is without blind faith, who knows the Uncreated, who has severed all links, destroyed all causes (for karma, good and evil), and thrown out all desires-he, truly, is the most excellent of men. 11

98. Inspiring, indeed, is that place where Arahants dwell, be it a village, a forest, a vale, or a hill.

99. Inspiring are the forests in which worldlings find no pleasure. There the passionless will rejoice, for they seek no sensual pleasures.

100. Better than a thousand useless words is one useful word, hearing which one attains peace.

101. Better than a thousand useless verses is one useful verse, hearing which one attains peace.

102. Better than reciting a hundred meaningless verses is the reciting of one verse of Dhamma, hearing which one attains peace.

103. Though one may conquer a thousand times a thousand men in battle, yet he indeed is the noblest victor who conquers himself.

104-105. Self-conquest is far better then the conquest of others. Not even a god, an angel, Mara or Brahma can turn into defeat the victory of a person who is self-subdued and ever restrained in conduct.

106. Though month after month for a hundred years one should offer sacrifices by the thousands, yet if only for a moment one should worship those of perfected minds that honour is indeed better than a century of sacrifice.

107. Though for a hundred years one should tend the sacrificial fire in the forest, yet if only for a moment one should worship those of perfected minds, that worship is indeed better than a century of sacrifice.

108. Whatever gifts and oblations one seeking merit might offer in this world for a whole year, all that is not worth one fourth of the merit gained by revering the Upright Ones, which is truly excellent.

109. To one ever eager to revere and serve the elders, these four blessing accrue: long life and beauty, happiness and power.

110. Better it is to live one day virtuous and meditative than to live a hundred years immoral and uncontrolled.

111. Better it is to live one day wise and meditative than to live a hundred years foolish and uncontrolled.

112. Better it is to live one day strenuous and resolute than to live a hundred years sluggish and dissipated.

113. Better it is to live one day seeing the rise and fall of things than to live as hundred years without ever seeing the rise and fall of things.

114. Better it is to live one day seeing the Deathless than to live a hundred years without ever seeing the Deathless.

115. Better it is to live one day seeing the Supreme Truth than to live a hundred years without ever seeing the Supreme Truth.

116. Hasten to do good; restrain your mind from evil. He who is slow in doing good, his mind delights in evil.

117. Should a person commit evil, let him not do it again and again. Let him not find pleasure therein, for painful is the accumulation of evil.

118. Should a person do good, let him do it again and again. Let him find pleasure therein, for blissful is the accumulation of good.

119. It may be well with the evil-doer as long as the evil ripens not. But when it does ripen, then the evil-doer sees (the painful results of) his evil deeds.

120. It may be ill with the doer of good as long as the good ripens not. But when it does ripen, then the doer of good sees (the pleasant results of) his good deeds.

121. Think not lightly of evil, saying, "It will not come to me." Drop by drop is the water pot filled. Likewise, the fool, gathering it little by little, fills himself with evil.

122. Think not lightly of good, saying, "It will not come to me." Drop by drop is the water pot filled. Likewise, the wise man, gathering it little by little, fills himself with good.

123. Just as a trader with a small escort and great wealth would avoid a perilous route, or just as one desiring to live avoids poison, even so should one shun evil.

124. If on the hand there is no wound, one may carry even poison in it. Poison does not affect one who is free from wounds. For him who does no evil, there is no ill.

125. Like fine dust thrown against the wind, evil falls back upon that fool who offends an inoffensive, pure and guiltless man.

126. Some are born in the womb; the wicked are born in hell; the devout go to heaven; the stainless pass into Nibbana.

127. Neither in the sky nor in mid-ocean, nor by entering into mountain clefts, nowhere in the world is there a place where one may escape from the results of evil deeds.

128. Neither in the sky nor in mid-ocean, nor by entering into mountain clefts, nowhere in the world is there a place where one will not be overcome by death.

129. All tremble at violence; all fear death. Putting oneself in the place of another, one should not kill nor cause another to kill.

130. All tremble at violence; life is dear to all. Putting oneself in the place of another, one should not kill nor cause another to kill.

131. One who, while himself seeking happiness, oppresses with violence other beings who also desire happiness, will not attain happiness hereafter.

132. One who, while himself seeking happiness, does not oppress with violence other beings who also desire happiness, will find happiness hereafter.

133. Speak not harshly to anyone, for those thus spoken to might retort. Indeed, angry speech hurts, and retaliation may overtake you.

134. If, like a broken gong, you silence yourself, you have approached Nibbana, for vindictiveness is no longer in you.

135. Just as a cowherd drives the cattle to pasture with a staff, so do old age and death drive the life force of beings (from existence to existence).

136. When the fool commits evil deeds, he does not realize (their evil nature). The witless man is tormented by his own deeds, like one burnt by fire.

137. He who inflicts violence on those who are unarmed, and offends those who are inoffensive, will soon come upon one of these ten states:

138-140 Sharp pain, or disaster, bodily injury, serious illness, or derangement of mind, trouble from the government, or grave charges, loss of relatives, or loss of wealth, or houses destroyed by ravaging fire; upon dissolution of the body that ignorant man is born in hell.

141. Neither going about naked, nor matted locks, nor filth, nor fasting, nor lying on the ground, nor smearing oneself with ashes and dust, nor sitting on the heels (in penance) can purify a mortal who has not overcome doubt.

142. Even though he be well-attired, yet if he is posed, calm, controlled and established in the holy life, having set aside violence towards all beings-he, truly, is a holy man, a renunciate, a monk.

143. Only rarely is there a man in this world who, restrained by modesty, avoids reproach, as a thoroughbred horse avoids the whip.

144. Like a thoroughbred horse touched by the whip, be strenuous, be filled with spiritual yearning. By faith and moral purity, by effort and meditation, by investigation of the truth, by being rich in knowledge and virtue, and by being mindful, destroy this unlimited suffering.

145. Irrigators regulate the waters, fletchers straighten arrow shafts, carpenters shape wood, and the good control themselves.

146. When this world is ever ablaze, why this laughter, why this jubilation? Shrouded in darkness, will you not see the light?

147. Behold this body-a painted image, a mass of heaped up sores, infirm, full of hankering-of which nothing is lasting or stable!

148. Fully worn out is this body, a nest of disease, and fragile. This foul mass breaks up, for death is the end of life.

149. These dove-colored bones are like gourds that lie scattered about in autumn. Having seen them, how can one seek delight?

150. This city (body) is built of bones, plastered with flesh and blood; within are decay and death, pride and jealousy.

151. Even gorgeous royal chariots wear out, and indeed this body too wears out. But the Dhamma of the Good does not age; thus the Good make it known to the good.

152. The man of little learning grows old like a bull. He grows only in bulk, but, his wisdom does not grow.

153. Through many a birth in samsara have I wandered in vain, seeking in the builder of this house (of life). Repeated birth is indeed suffering!

154. O house-builder, you are seen! You will not build this house again. For your rafters are broken and your ridgepole shattered. My mind has reached the Unconditioned; I have attained the destruction of craving.

155. Those who in youth have not led the holy life, or have failed to acquire wealth, languish like old cranes in the pond without fish.

156. Those who in youth have not lead the holy life, or have failed to acquire wealth, lie sighing over the past, like worn out arrows (shot from) a bow.

157. If one holds oneself dear, one should diligently watch oneself. Let the wise man keep vigil during any of the three watches of the night.

158. One should first establish oneself in what is proper; then only should one instruct others. Thus the wise man will not be reproached.

159. One should do what one teaches others to do; if one would train others, one should be well controlled oneself. Difficult, indeed, is self-control.

160. One truly is the protector of oneself; who else could the protector be? With oneself fully controlled, one gains a mastery that is hard to gain.

161. The evil a witless man does by himself, born of himself and produced by himself, grinds him as a diamond grinds a hard gem.

162. Just as a single creeper strangles the tree on which it grows, even so, a man who is exceedingly depraved harms himself as only an enemy might wish.

163. Easy to do are things that are bad and harmful to oneself. But exceedingly difficult to do are things that are good and beneficial.

164. Whoever, on account of perverted views, scorns the Teaching of the Perfected Ones, the Noble and Righteous Ones-that fool, like the bamboo, produces fruits only for self destruction.

165. By oneself is evil done; by oneself is one defiled. By oneself is evil left undone; by oneself is one made pure. Purity and impurity depended on oneself; no one can purify another.

166. Let one not neglect one's own welfare for the sake of another, however great. Clearly understanding one's own welfare, let one be intent upon the good.

167. Follow not the vulgar way; live not in heedlessness; hold not false views; linger not long in worldly existence.

168. Arise! Do not be heedless! Lead a righteous life. The righteous live happily both in this world and the next.

169. Lead a righteous life; lead not a base life. The righteous live happily both in this world and the next.

170. One who looks upon the world as a bubble and a mirage, him the King of Death sees not.

171. Come! Behold this world, which is like a decorated royal chariot. Here fools flounder, but the wise have no attachment to it.

172. He who having been heedless is heedless no more, illuminates this world like the moon freed from clouds.

173. He, who by good deeds covers the evil he has done, illuminates this world like the moon freed from clouds.

174. Blind is the world; here only a few possess insight. Only a few, like birds escaping from the net, go to realms of bliss.

175. Swans fly on the path of the sun; men pass through the air by psychic powers; the wise are led away from the world after vanquishing Mara and his host.

176. For a liar who has violated the one law (of truthfulness) who holds in scorn the hereafter, there is no evil that he cannot do.

177. Truly, misers fare not to heavenly realms; nor, indeed, do fools praise generosity. But the wise man rejoices in giving, and by that alone does he become happy hereafter.

178. Better than sole sovereignty over the earth, better than going to heaven, better even than lordship over all the worlds is the supramundane Fruition of Stream Entrance.

179. By what track can you trace that trackless Buddha of limitless range, whose victory nothing can undo, whom none of the vanquished defilements can ever pursue?

180. By what track can you trace that trackless Buddha of limitless range, in whom exists no longer, the entangling and embroiling craving that perpetuates becoming?

181. Those wise ones who are devoted to meditation and who delight in the calm of renunciation-such mindful ones, Supreme Buddhas, even the gods hold dear.

182. Hard is it to be born a man; hard is the life of mortals. Hard is it to gain the opportunity of hearing the Sublime Truth, and hard to encounter is the arising of the Buddhas.

183. To avoid all evil, to cultivate good, and to cleanse one's mind-this is the teaching of the Buddhas.

184. Enduring patience is the highest austerity. "Nibbana is supreme," say the Buddhas. He is not a true monk who harms another, nor a true renunciate who oppresses others.

185. Not despising, not harming, restraint according to the code of monastic discipline, moderation in food, dwelling in solitude, devotion to meditation-this is the teaching of the Buddhas.

186-187. There is no satisfying sensual desires, even with the rain of gold coins. For sensual pleasures give little satisfaction and much pain. Having understood this, the wise man finds no delight even in heavenly pleasures. The disciple of the Supreme Buddha delights in the destruction of craving.

188. Driven only by fear, do men go for refuge to many places-to hills, woods, groves, trees and shrines.

189. Such, indeed, is no safe refuge; such is not the refuge supreme. Not by resorting to such a refuge is one released from all suffering.

190-191. He who has gone for refuge to the Buddha, the Teaching and his Order, penetrates with transcendental wisdom the Four Noble Truths-suffering, the cause of suffering, the cessation of suffering, and the Noble Eightfold Path leading to the cessation of suffering.

192. This indeed is the safe refuge, this the refuge supreme. Having gone to such a refuge, one is released from all suffering.

193. Hard to find is the thoroughbred man (the Buddha); he is not born everywhere. Where such a wise man is born, that clan thrives happily.

194. Blessed is the birth of the Buddhas; blessed is the enunciation of the sacred Teaching; blessed is the harmony in the Order, and blessed is the spiritual pursuit of the united truth-seeker.

195-196. He who reveres those worthy of reverence, the Buddhas and their disciples, who have transcended all obstacles and passed beyond the reach of sorrow and lamentation-he who reveres such peaceful and fearless ones, his merit none can compute by any measure.

197. Happy indeed we live, friendly amidst the hostile. Amidst hostile men we dwell free from hatred.

198. Happy indeed we live, friendly amidst the afflicted (by craving). Amidst afflicted men we dwell free from affliction.

199. Happy indeed we live, free from avarice amidst the avaricious. Amidst the avaricious men we dwell free from avarice.

200. Happy indeed we live, we who possess nothing. Feeders on joy we shall be, like the Radiant Gods.

201. Victory begets enmity; the defeated dwell in pain. Happily the peaceful live, discarding both victory and defeat.

202. There is no fire like lust and no crime like hatred. There is no ill like the aggregates (of existence) and no bliss higher than the peace (of Nibbana).

203. Hunger is the worst disease, conditioned things the worst suffering. Knowing this as it really is, the wise realize Nibbana, the highest bliss.

204. Health is the most precious gain and contentment the greatest wealth. A trustworthy person is the best kinsman, Nibbana the highest bliss.

205. Having savored the taste of solitude and peace (of Nibbana), pain-free and stainless he becomes, drinking deep the taste of the bliss of the Truth.

206. Good is it to see the Noble Ones; to live with them is ever blissful. One will always be happy by not encountering fools.

207. Indeed, he who moves in the company of fools grieves for longing. Association with fools is ever painful, like partnership with an enemy. But association with the wise is happy, like meeting one's own kinsmen.

208. Therefore, follow the Noble One, who is steadfast, wise, learned, dutiful and devout. One should follow only such a man, who is truly good and discerning, even as the moon follows the path of the stars.

209. Giving himself to things to be shunned and not exerting where exertion is needed, a seeker after pleasures, having given up his true welfare, envies those intent upon theirs.

210. Seek no intimacy with the beloved and also not with the unloved, for not to see the beloved and to see the unloved, both are painful.

211. Therefore hold nothing dear, for separation from the dear is painful. There are no bonds for those who have nothing beloved or unloved.

212. From endearment springs grief, from endearment springs fear. From him who is wholly free from endearment there is no grief, whence then fear?

213. From affection springs grief, from affection springs fear. From him who is wholly free from affection there is no grief, whence then fear?

214. From attachment springs grief, from attachment springs fear. From him who is wholly free from attachment there is no grief, whence then fear?

215. From lust springs grief, from lust springs fear. From him who is wholly free from craving there is no grief; whence then fear?

216. From craving springs grief, from craving springs fear. From him who is wholly free from craving there is no grief; whence then fear?

217. People hold dear him who embodies virtue and insight, who is principled, has realized the truth, and who himself does what he ought to be doing.

218. One who is intent upon the Ineffable (Nibbana), dwells with mind inspired (by supramundane wisdom), and is no more bound by sense pleasures-such a man is called "One Bound Upstream."

219. When, after a long absence, a man safely returns from afar, his relatives, friends and well-wishers welcome him home on arrival.

220. As kinsmen welcome a dear one on arrival, even so his own good deeds will welcome the doer of good who has gone from this world to the next.

221. One should give up anger, renounce pride, and overcome all fetters. Suffering never befalls him who clings not to mind and body and is detached.

222. He who checks rising anger as a charioteer checks a rolling chariot, him I call a true charioteer. Others only hold the reins.

223. Overcome the angry by non-anger; overcome the wicked by goodness; overcome the miser by generosity; overcome the liar by truth.

224. Speak the truth; yield not to anger; when asked, give even if you only have a little. By these three means can one reach the presence of the gods.

225. Those sages who are inoffensive and ever restrained in body, go to the Deathless State, where, having gone, they grieve no more.

226. Those who are ever vigilant, who discipline themselves day and night, and are ever intent upon Nibbana-their defilements fade away.

227. O Atula! Indeed, this is an ancient practice, not one only of today: they blame those who remain silent, they blame those who speak much, they blame those who speak in moderation. There is none in the world who is not blamed.

228. There never was, there never will be, nor is there now, a person who is wholly blamed or wholly praised.

229. But the man whom the wise praise, after observing him day after day, is one of flawless character, wise, and endowed with knowledge and virtue.

230. Who can blame such a one, as worthy as a coin of refined gold? Even the gods praise him; by Brahma, too, is he praised.

231. Let a man guard himself against irritability in bodily action; let him be controlled in deed. Abandoning bodily misconduct, let him practice good conduct in deed.

232. Let a man guard himself against irritability in speech; let him be controlled in speech. Abandoning verbal misconduct, let him practice good conduct in speech.

233. Let a man guard himself against irritability in thought; let him be controlled in mind. Abandoning mental misconduct, let him practice good conduct in thought.

234. The wise are controlled in bodily action, controlled in speech and controlled in thought. They are truly well-controlled.

235. Like a withered leaf are you now; death's messengers await you. You stand on the eve of your departure, yet you have made no provision for your journey!

236. Make an island for yourself! Strive hard and become wise! Rid of impurities and cleansed of stain, you shall enter the celestial abode of the Noble Ones.

237. Your life has come to an end now; You are setting forth into the presence of Yama, the king of death. No resting place is there for you on the way, yet you have made no provision for the journey!

238. Make an island unto yourself! Strive hard and become wise! Rid of impurities and cleansed of stain, you shall not come again to birth and decay.

239. One by one, little by little, moment by moment, a wise man should remove his own impurities, as a smith removes his dross from silver.

240. Just as rust arising from iron eats away the base from which it arises, even so, their own deeds lead transgressors to states of woe.

241. Non-repetition is the bane of scriptures; neglect is the bane of a home; slovenliness is the bane of personal appearance, and heedlessness is the bane of a guard.

242. Unchastity is the taint in a woman; niggardliness is the taint in a giver. Taints, indeed, are all evil things, both in this world and the next.

243. A worse taint than these is ignorance, the worst of all taints. Destroy this one taint and become taintless, O monks!

244. Easy is life for the shameless one who is impudent as a crow, is backbiting and forward, arrogant and corrupt.

245. Difficult is life for the modest one who always seeks purity, is detached and unassuming, clean in life, and discerning.

246-247. One who destroys life, utters lies, takes what is not given, goes to another man's wife, and is addicted to intoxicating drinks-such a man digs up his own root even in this world.

248. Know this, O good man: evil things are difficult to control. Let not greed and wickedness drag you to protracted misery.

249. People give according to their faith or regard. If one becomes discontented with the food and drink given by others, one does not attain meditative absorption, either by day or by night.

250. But he in who this (discontent) is fully destroyed, uprooted and extinct, he attains absorption, both by day and by night.

251. There is no fire like lust; there is no grip like hatred; there is no net like delusion; there is no river like craving.

252. Easily seen is the fault of others, but one's own fault is difficult to see. Like chaff one winnows another's faults, but hides one's own, even as a crafty fowler hides behind sham branches.

253. He who seeks another's faults, who is ever censorious-his cankers grow. He is far from destruction of the cankers.

254. There is no track in the sky, and no recluse outside (the Buddha's dispensation). Mankind delights in worldliness, but the Buddhas are free from worldliness.

255. There is not track in the sky, and no recluse outside (the Buddha's dispensation). There are no conditioned things that are eternal, and no instability in the Buddhas.

256. Not by passing arbitrary judgments does a man become just; a wise man is he who investigates both right and wrong.

257. He who does not judge others arbitrarily, but passes judgment impartially according to the truth, that sagacious man is a guardian of law and is called just.

258. One is not wise because one speaks much. He who is peaceable, friendly and fearless is called wise.

259. A man is not versed in Dhamma because he speaks much. He who, after hearing a little Dhamma, realizes its truth directly and is not heedless of it, is truly versed in the Dhamma.

260. A monk is not Elder because his head is gray. He is but ripe in age, and he is called one grown old in vain.

261. One in whom there is truthfulness, virtue, inoffensiveness, restraint and self-mastery, who is free from defilements and is wise-he is truly called an Elder.

262. Not by mere eloquence nor by beauty of form does a man become accomplished, if he is jealous, selfish and deceitful.

263. But he in whom these are wholly destroyed, uprooted and extinct, and who has cast out hatred-that wise man is truly accomplished.

264. Not by shaven head does a man who is indisciplined and untruthful become a monk. How can he who is full of desire and greed be a monk?

265. He who wholly subdues evil both small and great is called a monk, because he has overcome all evil.

266. He is not a monk just because he lives on others' alms. Not by adopting outward form does one become a true monk.

267. Whoever here (in the Dispensation) lives a holy life, transcending both merit and demerit, and walks with understanding in this world-he is truly called a monk.

268. Not by observing silence does one become a sage, if he be foolish and ignorant. But that man is wise who, as if holding a balance-scale accepts only the good.

269. The sage (thus) rejecting the evil, is truly a sage. Since he comprehends both (present and future) worlds, he is called a sage.

270. He is not noble who injures living beings. He is called noble because he is harmless towards all living beings.

271-272. Not by rules and observances, not even by much learning, nor by gain of absorption, nor by a life of seclusion, nor by thinking, "I enjoy the bliss of renunciation, which is not experienced by the worldling" should you, O monks, rest content, until the utter destruction of cankers (Arahantship) is reached.

273. Of all the paths the Eightfold Path is the best; of all the truths the Four Noble Truths are the best; of all things passionlessness is the best: of men the Seeing One (the Buddha) is the best.

274. This is the only path; there is none other for the purification of insight. Tread this path, and you will bewilder Mara.

275. Walking upon this path you will make an end of suffering. Having discovered how to pull out the thorn of lust, I make known the path.

276. You yourselves must strive; the Buddhas only point the way. Those meditative ones who tread the path are released from the bonds of Mara.

277. "All conditioned things are impermanent"-when one sees this with wisdom, one turns away from suffering. This is the path to purification.

278. "All conditioned things are unsatisfactory"-when one sees this with wisdom, one turns away from suffering. This is the path to purification.

279. "All things are not-self"-when one sees this with wisdom, one turns away from suffering. This is the path to purification.

280. The idler who does not exert himself when he should, who though young and strong is full of sloth, with a mind full of vain thoughts-such an indolent man does not find the path to wisdom.

281. Let a man be watchful of speech, well controlled in mind, and not commit evil in bodily action. Let him purify these three courses of action, and win the path made known by the Great Sage.

282. Wisdom springs from meditation; without meditation wisdom wanes. Having known these two paths of progress and decline, let a man so conduct himself that his wisdom may increase.

283. Cut down the forest (lust), but not the tree; from the forest springs fear. Having cut down the forest and the underbrush (desire), be passionless, O monks!

284. For so long as the underbrush of desire, even the most subtle, of a man towards a woman is not cut down, his mind is in bondage, like the sucking calf to its mother.

285. Cut off your affection in the manner of a man plucks with his hand an autumn lotus. Cultivate only the path to peace, Nibbana, as made known by the Exalted One.

286. "Here shall I live during the rains, here in winter and summer"-thus thinks the fool. He does not realize the danger (that death might intervene).

287. As a great flood carries away a sleeping village, so death seizes and carries away the man with a clinging mind, doting on his children and cattle.

288. For him who is assailed by death there is no protection by kinsmen. None there are to save him-no sons, nor father, nor relatives.

289. Realizing this fact, let the wise man, restrained by morality, hasten to clear the path leading to Nibbana.

290. If by renouncing a lesser happiness one may realize a greater happiness, let the wise man renounce the lesser, having regard for the greater.

291. Entangled by the bonds of hate, he who seeks his own happiness by inflicting pain on others, is never delivered from hatred.

292. The cankers only increase for those who are arrogant and heedless, who leave undone what should be done and do what should not be done.

293. The cankers cease for those mindful and clearly comprehending ones who always earnestly practice mindfulness of the body, who do not resort to what should not be done, and steadfastly pursue what should be done.

294. Having slain mother (craving), father (self-conceit), two warrior-kings (eternalism and nihilism), and destroyed a country (sense organs and sense objects) together with its treasurer (attachment and lust), ungrieving goes the holy man.

295. Having slain mother, father, two brahman kings (two extreme views), and a tiger as the fifth (the five mental hindrances), ungrieving goes the holy man.

296. Those disciples of Gotama ever awaken happily who day and night constantly practice the Recollection of the Qualities of the Buddha.

297. Those disciples of Gotama ever awaken happily who day and night constantly practice the Recollection of the Qualities of the Dhamma.

298. Those disciples of Gotama ever awaken happily who day and night constantly practice the Recollection of the Qualities of the Sangha.

299. Those disciples of Gotama ever awaken happily who day and night constantly practice Mindfulness of the Body.

300. Those disciples of Gotama ever awaken happily whose minds by day and night delight in the practice of non-violence.

301. Those disciples of Gotama ever awaken happily whose minds by day and night delight in the practice of meditation.

302. Difficult is life as a monk; difficult is it to delight therein. Also difficult and sorrowful is the household life. Suffering comes from association with unequals; suffering comes from wandering in samsara. Therefore, be not an aimless wanderer, be not a pursuer of suffering.

303. He who is full of faith and virtue, and possesses good repute and wealth-he is respected everywhere, in whatever land he travels.

304. The good shine from afar, like the Himalaya mountains. But the wicked are unseen, like arrows shot in the night.

305. He who sits alone, sleeps alone, and walks alone, who is strenuous and subdues himself alone, will find delight in the solitude of the forest.

306. The liar goes to the state of woe; also he who, having done (wrong), says, "I did not do it." Men of base actions both, on departing they share the same destiny in the other world.

307. There are many evil characters and uncontrolled men wearing the saffron robe. These wicked men will be born in states of woe because of their evil deeds.

308. It would be better to swallow a red-hot iron ball, blazing like fire, than as an immoral and uncontrolled monk to eat the alms of the people.

309. Four misfortunes befall the reckless man who consorts with another's wife: acquisition of demerit, disturbed sleep, ill-repute, and (rebirth in) states of woe.

310. Such a man acquires demerit and an unhappy birth in the future. Brief is the pleasure of the frightened man and woman, and the king imposes heavy punishment. Hence, let no man consort with another's wife.

311. Just as kusa grass wrongly handled cuts the hand, even so, a recluse's life wrongly lived drags one to states of woe.

312. Any loose act, any corrupt observance, any life of questionable celibacy-none of these bear much fruit.

313. If anything is to be done, let one do it with sustained vigour. A lax monastic life stirs up the dust of passions all the more.

314. An evil deed is better left undone, for such a deed torments one afterwards. But a good deed is better done, doing which one repents not later.

315. Just as a border city is closely guarded both within and without, even so, guard yourself. Do not let slip this opportunity (for spiritual growth). For those who let slip this opportunity grieve indeed when consigned to hell.

316. Those who are ashamed of what they should not be ashamed of, and are not ashamed of what they should be ashamed of-upholding false views, they go to states of woe.

317. Those who see something to fear where there is nothing to fear, and see nothing to fear where there is something to fear-upholding false views, they go to states of woe.

318. Those who imagine evil where there is none, and do not see evil where it is-upholding false views, they go to states of woe.

319. Those who discern the wrong as wrong and the right as right-upholding right views, they go to realms of bliss.

320. As an elephant in the battlefield withstands arrows shot from bows all around, even so shall I endure abuse. There are many, indeed, who lack virtue.

321. A tamed elephant is led into a crowd, and the king mounts a tamed elephant. Best among men is the subdued one who endures abuse.

322. Excellent are well-trained mules, thoroughbred Sindhu horses and noble tusker elephants. But better still is the man who has subdued himself.

323. Not by these mounts, however, would one go to the Untrodden Land (Nibbana), as one who is self-tamed goes by his own tamed and well-controlled mind.

324. Musty during rut, the tusker named Dhanapalaka is uncontrollable. Held in captivity, the tusker does not touch a morsel, but only longingly calls to mind the elephant forest.

325. When a man is sluggish and gluttonous, sleeping and rolling around in bed like a fat domestic pig, that sluggard undergoes rebirth again and again.

326. Formerly this mind wandered about as it liked, where it wished and according to its pleasure, but now I shall thoroughly master it with wisdom as a mahout controls with his ankus an elephant in rut.

327. Delight in heedfulness! Guard well your thoughts! Draw yourself out of this bog of evil, even as an elephant draws himself out of the mud.

328. If for company you find a wise and prudent friend who leads a good life, you should, overcoming all impediments, keep his company joyously and mindfully.

329. If for company you cannot find a wise and prudent friend who leads a good life, then, like a king who leaves behind a conquered kingdom, or like a lone elephant in the elephant forest, you should go your way alone.

330. Better it is to live alone; there is no fellowship with a fool. Live alone and do no evil; be carefree like an elephant in the elephant forest.

331. Good are friends when need arises; good is contentment with just what one has; good is merit when life is at an end, and good is the abandoning of all suffering (through Arahantship).

332. In this world, good it is to serve one's mother, good it is to serve one's father, good it is to serve the monks, and good it is to serve the holy men.

333. Good is virtue until life's end, good is faith that is steadfast, good is the acquisition of wisdom, and good is the avoidance of evil.

334. The craving of one given to heedless living grows like a creeper. Like the monkey seeking fruits in the forest, he leaps from life to life (tasting the fruit of his kamma).

335. Whoever is overcome by this wretched and sticky craving, his sorrows grow like grass after the rains.

336. But whoever overcomes this wretched craving, so difficult to overcome, from him sorrows fall away like water from a lotus leaf.

337. This I say to you: Good luck to all assembled here! Dig up the root of craving, like one in search of the fragrant root of the birana grass. Let not Mara crush you again and again, as a flood crushes a reed.

338. Just as a tree, though cut down, sprouts up again if its roots remain uncut and firm, even so, until the craving that lies dormant is rooted out, suffering springs up again and again.

339. The misguided man in whom the thirty-six currents of craving strongly rush toward pleasurable objects, is swept away by the flood of his passionate thoughts.

340. Everywhere these currents flow, and the creeper (of craving) sprouts and grows. Seeing that the creeper has sprung up, cut off its root with wisdom.

341. Flowing in (from all objects) and watered by craving, feelings of pleasure arise in beings. Bent on pleasures and seeking enjoyment, these men fall prey to birth and decay.

342. Beset by craving, people run about like an entrapped hare. Held fast by mental fetters, they come to suffering again and again for a long time.

343. Beset by craving, people run about like an entrapped hare. Therefore, one who yearns to be passion-free should destroy his own craving.

344. There is one who, turning away from desire (for household life) takes to the life of the forest (i.e., of a monk). But after being freed from the household, he runs back to it. Behold that man! Though freed, he runs back to that very bondage!

345-346. That is not a strong fetter, the wise say, which is made of iron, wood or hemp. But the infatuation and longing for jewels and ornaments, children and wives-that, they say, is a far stronger fetter, which pulls one downward and, though seemingly loose, is hard to remove. This, too, the wise cut off. Giving up sensual pleasure, and without any longing, they renounce the world.

347. Those who are lust-infatuated fall back into the swirling current (of samsara) like a spider on its self-spun web. This, too, the wise cut off. Without any longing, they abandon all suffering and renounce the world.

348. Let go of the past, let go of the future, let go of the present, and cross over to the farther shore of existence. With mind wholly liberated, you shall come no more to birth and death.

349. For a person tormented by evil thoughts, who is passion-dominated and given to the pursuit of pleasure, his craving steadily grows. He makes the fetter strong, indeed.

350. He who delights in subduing evil thoughts, who meditates on the impurities and is ever mindful-it is he who will make an end of craving and rend asunder Mara's fetter.

351. He who has reached the goal, is fearless, free from craving, passionless, and has plucked out the thorns of existence-for him this is the last body.

352. He who is free from craving and attachment, is perfect in uncovering the true meaning of the Teaching, and knows the arrangement of the sacred texts in correct sequence-he, indeed, is the bearer of his final body. He is truly called the profoundly wise one, the great man.

353. A victor am I over all, all have I known. Yet unattached am I to all that is conquered and known. Abandoning all, I am freed through the destruction of craving. Having thus directly comprehended all by myself, whom shall I call my teacher?

354. The gift of Dhamma excels all gifts; the taste of the Dhamma excels all tastes; the delight in Dhamma excels all delights. The Craving-Freed vanquishes all suffering.

355. Riches ruin only the foolish, not those in quest of the Beyond. By craving for riches the witless man ruins himself as well as others.

356. Weeds are the bane of fields, lust is the bane of mankind. Therefore, what is offered to those free of lust yields abundant fruit.

357. Weeds are the bane of fields, hatred is the bane of mankind. Therefore, what is offered to those free of hatred yields abundant fruit.

358. Weeds are the bane of fields, delusion is the bane of mankind. Therefore, what is offered to those free of delusion yields abundant fruit.

359. Weeds are the bane of fields, desire is the bane of mankind. Therefore, what is offered to those free of desire yields abundant fruit.

360. Good is restraint over the eye; good is restraint over the ear; good is restraint over the nose; good is restraint over the tongue.

361. Good is restraint in the body; good is restraint in speech; good is restraint in thought. Restraint everywhere is good. The monk restrained in every way is freed from all suffering.

362. He who has control over his hands, feet and tongue; who is fully controlled, delights in inward development, is absorbed in meditation, keeps to himself and is contented-him do people call a monk.

363. That monk who has control over his tongue, is moderate in speech, unassuming and who explains the Teaching in both letter and spirit-whatever he says is pleasing.

364. The monk who abides in the Dhamma, delights in the Dhamma, meditates on the Dhamma, and bears the Dhamma well in mind-he does not fall away from the sublime Dhamma.

365. One should not despise what one has received, nor envy the gains of others. The monk who envies the gains of others does not attain to meditative absorption.

366. A monk who does not despise what he has received, even though it be little, who is pure in livelihood and unremitting in effort-him even the gods praise.

367. He who has no attachment whatsoever for the mind and body, who does not grieve for what he has not-he is truly called a monk.

368. The monk who abides in universal love and is deeply devoted to the Teaching of the Buddha attains the peace of Nibbana, the bliss of the cessation of all conditioned things.

369. Empty this boat, O monk! Emptied, it will sail lightly. Rid of lust and hatred, you shall reach Nibbana.

370. Cut off the five, abandon the five, and cultivate the five. The monk who has overcome the five bonds is called one who has crossed the flood.

371. Meditate, O monk! Do not be heedless. Let not your mind whirl on sensual pleasures. Heedless, do not swallow a red-hot iron ball, lest you cry when burning, "O this is painful!"

372. There is no meditative concentration for him who lacks insight, and no insight for him who lacks meditative

concentration. He in whom are found both meditative concentration and insight, indeed, is close to Nibbana.

373. The monk who has retired to a solitary abode and calmed his mind, who comprehends the Dhamma with insight, in him there arises a delight that transcends all human delights.

374. Whenever he sees with insight the rise and fall of the aggregates, he is full of joy and happiness. To the discerning one this reflects the Deathless.

375. Control of the senses, contentment, restraint according to the code of monastic discipline-these form the basis of holy life here for the wise monk.

376. Let him associate with friends who are noble, energetic, and pure in life, let him be cordial and refined in conduct. Thus, full of joy, he will make an end of suffering.

377. Just as the jasmine creeper sheds its withered flowers, even so, O monks, should you totally shed lust and hatred!

378. The monk who is calm in body, calm in speech, calm in thought, well-composed and who has spewn out worldliness-he, truly, is called serene.

379. By oneself one must censure oneself and scrutinize oneself. The self-guarded and mindful monk will always live in happiness.

380. One is one's own protector, one is one's own refuge. Therefore, one should control oneself, even as a trader controls a noble steed.

381. Full of joy, full of faith in the Teaching of the Buddha, the monk attains the Peaceful State, the bliss of cessation of conditioned things.

382. That monk who while young devotes himself to the Teaching of the Buddha illumines this world like the moon freed from clouds.

383. Exert yourself, O holy man! Cut off the stream (of craving), and discard sense desires. Knowing the destruction of all the conditioned things, become, O holy man, the knower of the Uncreated (Nibbana)!

384. When a holy man has reached the summit of two paths (meditative concentration and insight), he knows the truth and all his fetters fall away.

385. He for whom there is neither this shore nor the other shore, nor yet both, he who is free of cares and is unfettered-him do I call a holy man.

386. He who is meditative, stainless and settled, whose work is done and who is free from cankers, having reached the highest goal-him do I call a holy man.

387. The sun shines by day, the moon shines by night. The warrior shines in armor, the holy man shines in meditation. But the Buddha shines resplendent all day and all night.

388. Because he has discarded evil, he is called a holy man. Because he is serene in conduct, he is called a recluse. And because he has renounced his impurities, he is called a renunciate.

389. One should not strike a holy man, nor should a holy man, when struck, give way to anger. Shame on him who strikes a holy man, and more shame on him who gives way to anger.

390. Nothing is better for a holy man than when he holds his mind back from what is endearing. To the extent the intent to harm wears away, to that extent does suffering subside.

391. He who does no evil in deed, word and thought, who is restrained in these three ways-him do I call a holy man.

392. Just as a brahman priest reveres his sacrificial fire, even so should one devoutly revere the person from whom one has learned the Dhamma taught by the Buddha.

393. Not by matted hair, nor by lineage, nor by birth does one become a holy man. But he in whom truth and righteousness exist-he is pure, he is a holy man.

394. What is the use of your matted hair, O witless man? What of your garment of antelope's hide? Within you is the tangle (of passion); only outwardly do you cleanse yourself.

395. The person who wears a robe made of rags, who is lean, with veins showing all over the body, and who meditates alone in the forest-him do I call a holy man.

396. I do not call him a holy man because of his lineage or high-born mother. If he is full of impeding attachments, he is just a supercilious man. But who is free from impediments and clinging-him do I call a holy man.

397. He who, having cut off all fetters, trembles no more, who has overcome all attachments and is emancipated-him do I call a holy man.

398. He who has cut off the thong (of hatred), the band (of craving), and the rope (of false views), together with the appurtenances (latent evil tendencies), he who has removed the crossbar (of ignorance) and is enlightened-him do I call a holy man.

399. He who without resentment endures abuse, beating and punishment; whose power, real might, is patience-him do I call a holy man.

400. He who is free from anger, is devout, virtuous, without craving, self-subdued and bears his final body-him do I call a holy man.

401. Like water on a lotus leaf, or a mustard seed on the point of a needle, he who does not cling to sensual pleasures-him do I call a holy man.

402. He who in this very life realizes for himself the end of suffering, who has laid aside the burden and become emancipated-him do I call a holy man.

403. He who has profound knowledge, who is wise, skilled in discerning the right or wrong path, and has reached the highest goal-him do I call a holy man.

404. He who holds aloof from householders and ascetics alike, and wanders about with no fixed abode and but few wants-him do I call a holy man.

405. He who has renounced violence towards all living beings, weak or strong, who neither kills nor causes others to kill-him do I call a holy man.

406. He who is friendly amidst the hostile, peaceful amidst the violent, and unattached amidst the attached-him do I call a holy man.

407. He whose lust and hatred, pride and hypocrisy have fallen off like a mustard seed from the point of a needle-him do I call a holy man.

408. He who utters gentle, instructive and truthful words, who imprecates none-him do I call a holy man.

409. He who in this world takes nothing that is not given to him, be it long or short, small or big, good or bad-him do I call a holy man.

410. He who wants nothing of either this world or the next, who is desire-free and emancipated-him do I call a holy man.

411. He who has no attachment, who through perfect knowledge is free from doubts and has plunged into the Deathless-him do I call a holy man.

412. He who in this world has transcended the ties of both merit and demerit, who is sorrowless, stainless and pure-him do I call a holy man.

413. He, who, like the moon, is spotless and pure, serene and clear, who has destroyed the delight in existence-him do I call a holy man.

414. He who, having traversed this miry, perilous and delusive round of existence, has crossed over and reached the other shore; who is meditative, calm, free from doubt, and, clinging to nothing, has attained to Nibbana-him do I call a holy man.

415. He who, having abandoned sensual pleasures, has renounced the household life and become a homeless one; has destroyed both sensual desire and continued existence-him do I call a holy man.

416. He who, having abandoned craving, has renounced the household life and become a homeless one, has destroyed both craving and continued existence-him do I call a holy man.

417. He who, casting off human bonds and transcending heavenly ties, is wholly delivered of all bondages-him do I call a holy man.

418. He who, having cast off likes and dislikes, has become tranquil, is rid of the substrata of existence and like a hero has conquered all the worlds-him do I call a holy man.

419. He who in every way knows the death and rebirth of all beings, and is totally detached, blessed and enlightened-him do I call a holy man.

420. He whose track no gods, no angels, no humans trace, the arahant who has destroyed all cankers-him do I call a holy man.

421. He who clings to nothing of the past, present and future, who has no attachment and holds on to nothing-him do I call a holy man.

422. He, the Noble, the Excellent, the Heroic, the Great Sage, the Conqueror, the Passionless, the Pure, the Enlightened one-him do I call a holy man.

423. He who knows his former births, who sees heaven and hell, who has reached the end of births and attained to the perfection of insight, the sage who has reached the summit of spiritual excellence-him do I call a holy man.

ENLIGHTENED NUNS

In this section we will be exploring poems composed by the arahant bhikkhunis or enlightened Buddhist nuns of old, looking at these poems as springs of inspiration for contemporary Buddhists. Most of the poems we will consider come from the Therigatha, a small section of the vast Pali canon. The Therigatha has been published twice in English translation by the Pali Text Society, London: first in 1909 (reprinted in 1980) by C. A. R. Rhys Davids in verse under the title Psalms of the Early Buddhists: The Sisters; and second in 1971 by K. R. Norman in prose under the title The Elders' Verses, II. We have used quotations from both translations here, referring to Psalms of the Early Buddhists by page number and to The Elders' Verses by verse number. Mrs. Rhys Davids' translations have sometimes been slightly modified. Our discussion will also draw upon the verses of bhikkhunis from the Samyutta Nikaya (Kindred Sayings), included by Mrs. Rhys Davids at the end of Psalms of the Sisters.

From the poems of the enlightened nuns of the Buddha's time contemporary followers of the Noble Eightfold Path can receive a great deal of instruction, help and encouragement. These verses can assist us in developing morality, concentration and wisdom, the three sections of the path. With their aid we will be able to work more effectively towards eliminating our mental defilements and towards finding lasting peace and happiness. In some respects, the inspiration from these poems may be stronger for women than for men, since these are in fact women's voices that are speaking. And when the theme of the poem is the mother-child bond, this is bound to be the case. However, at a deeper level the sex of the speakers is irrelevant, for the ultimate truths which they enunciate explain the universal principles of reality which are equally valid for men and for women.

The verses of the nuns, if systematically examined, can help serious Buddhist meditators to understand many central aspects of the Dhamma. The background to the verses, including biographical information on the nuns who uttered them, is provided by the ancient commentary on the Therigatha by the venerable Acariya Dhammapala. Mrs. Rhys Davids has included some of these background stories in Psalms of the Early Buddhists, and in the first part of this essay we will look at these stories and consider the themes they suggest that are relevant to contemporary students of Buddhist meditation. Then we will go on to discuss a selection of the poems themselves, which deal with many specific teachings of the Buddha.

We of the twentieth century who are seeking to attain liberation will find ourselves deeply grateful to these fully awakened Buddhist nuns of old for their profound assistance in illuminating the Dhamma for us in their own distinctly personal ways.

THE BACKGROUND STORIES

The ancient commentaries give us information about each nun's background and also explain the poems themselves. Two major themes of relevance to contemporary students of the Dhamma run through these stories: (1) the immeasurably long time that we have all been lost in samsara, the round of birth and death; and (2) the working of the impersonal law of kammic cause and effect which brought these women into contact with the Buddha's teachings in what was to be their final lifetime.

The Long Duration of Samsara

In the original Pali commentaries, the tales of the nuns began many, many re-births and eons prior to their final existence at the time of Buddha Gotama. We read how over ages and ages all these women had been living out the results of their old kamma and how they created powerful new kamma based on wisdom, which finally culminated in the attainment of Arahatship, full awakening. Each woman-or, more accurately, each succession of aggregates-had to undergo infinite eons of suffering in its gross and subtle forms before she was prepared to gain complete insight. But finally she gave up all clinging and was freed from the need ever again to be reborn and suffer, on any plane.

Vipassana meditators trying to develop this same understanding of the ultimate nature of conditioned existence can find inspiration if they would apply these tales to their own lives. When we realize how long we ourselves have been wandering in ignorance, constantly generating more and more unwholesome kamma, we will be able to remain patient when our early efforts to train the mind tend to falter or fail. Some of the bhikkhunis who had sufficient paramis-virtues cultivated in previous lives-even to gain Arahatship, still had to put in many years of arduous and sometimes seemingly fruitless effort before they could attain the goal.

For example, Siha entered the Sangha as a young woman but could not learn to contain her mind's attraction to external objects for seven years. Another nun worked for twenty-five years without finding any substantial peace because of her strong attachment to sense desire. But both these bhikkhunis, when all the appropriate conditions were finally fulfilled, found their patience and continued efforts fully rewarded. So too will we, if we diligently and strictly keep to the Noble Eightfold Path until we become Ariyas, noble ones. Once we have done this, we are assured that we will completely eliminate the causes of all suffering.

By making this effort to live in accordance with the Dhamma and to understand the true nature of existence, we begin to develop strong wholesome mental volitions, kamma that will have effects in future births as well as in this one. The continued efforts in this direction become easier and more natural because, as we wear away ignorance and the other defilements through insight meditation, our minds come to be more strongly conditioned by wisdom (panna). Recollecting this infinite span of time behind us, and the vast mass of wholesome volitional activities accumulated therein, will help us keep our efforts at purification balanced and strong.

These rebirth stories, illustrating the continuous suffering which every sentient being has undergone during the rounds of samsara, can also encourage us to work hard in the Dhamma. Understanding this weighty aspect of the First Noble Truth stimulates us to put forth the great effort required to overcome suffering by penetrating and uprooting its causes, which the Buddha explains are basically craving and ignorance.

Bhikkhuni Sumedha, in her poem, repeats one of the Buddha's powerful injunctions to eliminate the source of the ceaseless stream of suffering that has rushed on in our previous lives, and will otherwise continue on in the same way throughout the infinite future. Sumedha is pleading with her parents and fiance to allow her to enter the Sangha rather than force her to marry: Journeying-on is long for fools and for those who lament again and again at that which is without beginning and end, at the death of a father, the slaughter of a brother, and their own slaughter. Remember the tears, the milk, the blood, the journeying-on as being without beginning and end; remember the heap of bones of beings who are journeying-on.

Remember the four oceans compared with the tears, milk and blood; remember the heap of bones (of one man) for one eon, (as) equal (in size) to Mount Vepula. (vv. 495-497)

"Journeying-on" is samsara. In the lines beginning "Remember the four oceans compared," Sumedha is reminding her family of a discourse which they must have heard from the Buddha. Each of us, the Buddha tells us, has shed vast oceans of tears over the loss of loved ones and in fear of our own doom as the succession of aggregates has arisen and vanished throughout samsara's weary ages. During all these lifetimes, as the verse declares, we have drunk seas and seas of mother's milk, and the blood that was shed when violent death ended our lives also amounts to an immeasurable volume. How could even one gory death be anything but terrible suffering? The Buddha perceived all this with his infinite wisdom and so described it to his followers.

The vastness of samsara that we endured before meeting the Dhamma in this life can easily be extrapolated from the stories of these nuns. We must also sustain the patience in our endeavour to wear down ignorance and to develop the awareness of omnipresent suffering which is life in samsara, as the First Noble Truth makes known.

Kammic Cause and Effect

The second commentarial theme that can be helpful to us in developing our own understanding of the ultimate nature of reality is the working of the law of kammic cause and effect. None of these nuns was emancipated because one day she decided, "Now I am going to cut off all craving." Nor did the grace of a guru or the power of God or the Buddha himself enlighten them. Rather, it was a very long process in the evolution of the "life continuum" that gradually permitted the conditions for liberation to develop and eventually culminate in Arahatship. Freeing the mind of ignorance, like all activities, is an impersonal cause and effect process. Natural laws of this sort are cultivated and utilized by mental volition to bring about purification. By repeatedly seeing all the phenomena of life as they are by means of concentrated Vipassana meditation, we gradually wear away the defilements that becloud the mind and cause rebirth with its attendant misery.

For example, Sela took robes when she was a young woman and "worked her way to insight and because of the promise in her and the maturity of her knowledge, crushing the sankharas (conditioned phenomena), she soon won Arahatship" (p. 43). For eons, Sela had done many good deeds, such as making offerings to and looking after previous Buddhas and their monks.

As a result of these meritorious actions over many lifetimes, she was reborn in the heavenly deva planes or in comfortable situations on earth. Eventually, at the time of Buddha Gotama, each of the bhikkhunis, including Sela, came into the Sangha in her own way. Because the time was right for their paramis to bear fruit, all the factors conducive to enlightenment could develop, their defilements could be effaced, and the goal could be achieved.

Sukha left the world under one of the earlier Buddhas, but she died without becoming an Ariya. Under subsequent Buddhas "she kept the precepts and was learned and proficient in the doctrine." Finally, "in this Buddha era she found faith in the Master at her own home, and became a lay disciple. Later, when she heard Bhikkhuni Dhammadinna preach, she was thrilled with emotion and renounced the world under her" (pp. 40-41).1 All her efforts in past lives then bore their appropriate fruit as Sukha attained Arahatship and became in turn a great preacher of the Dhamma.

Only a small number of nuns are renowned for their skill in teaching, and it is likely that the need to develop the extra paramis to teach the Dhamma made it necessary for Sukha to study under earlier Buddhas for so long without gaining the paths and fruits.

Similar stories tell of how other bhikkhunis performed good works and put forth effort in previous lives, building various kinds of paramis which allowed them to completely give up all attachment to the world at the time of our Buddha. If we consider the process by which they gradually matured towards liberation, we can see how every mental volition and every deed of body and speech at some time or other bears fruit.

It is due to our own paramis, our own good kamma of the past, that we have the rare and great opportunity to come into contact with the teachings of a Buddha in this lifetime. It is because of wisdom already cultivated that we now have the opportunity to develop greater wisdom (pannaparami) through insight meditation. Wisdom has the power to obliterate the results of past kamma since it comprehends reality correctly.

In addition, if we continue to generate such wholesome volitions now, more good kamma is built up which will continue to bear beneficial fruit and bring us closer to the goal.

However, wisdom cannot be cultivated in the absence of morality. The Buddha taught that in order to move towards liberation, it is necessary to keep a minimum of five precepts strictly at all times: abstention from killing, stealing, sexual misconduct, lying and consuming intoxicants. If the precepts are broken, the bad kamma thus created will bring very painful results. Without purity of body and speech, purity of mind cannot be developed as the mind will be too agitated by sense desires, regrets and aversion to settle on its meditation subject properly.

Some of the earlier rebirth stories of arahant bhikkhunis tell of lives in which they did not keep the precepts. Several of them suffered the results of their unwholesome deeds in animal births or in low forms of human existence. Addhakasi, for example, had a mixed background. She had become a bhikkhuni established in morality under Kassapa Buddha, the Buddha immediately preceding Gotama.

But once, due to anger, she referred to a fully liberated senior nun as a prostitute. As a result of that wrong speech, she was reborn in one of the lower realms, for to say or do anything wrong to an Ariya creates worse kamma than to say or do the same thing against a non-Ariya. When the fruit of that bad deed was mostly used up, as a residual effect she herself became a prostitute in her final life. By this time her previous good kamma was the stronger and she ordained as a nun. Keeping the bhikkhuni life pure, Addhakasi attained the goal.

Causes and effects work themselves out and keep the life process going through samsara. So long as the mind is attached to anything at all, we will engage in volitional actions, make new kamma, and will have to experience their results. Cultivating good kamma will save one from much suffering and prepare the mind for the most powerful wholesome kamma of all, that born of wisdom, which can eliminate all kammic creation.

THE TEACHINGS OF THE POEMS

The actual poems composed by the nuns exhibit a wide range in tone and subject matter. They were almost all spoken after the author had realized that rebirth and all its associated suffering had been brought to an end by the perfection of insight and total elimination of defilements. So virtually all the poems contain some form of "lion's roar," an exclamation that the author has become awakened.

Trivial Incidents Spark Enlightenment

In some cases the poems describe the circumstances which brought the woman into the Sangha or which precipitated her awakening. Both of these can inspire contemporary followers of the Buddha. Sometimes the most mundane event stimulates a ripe mind to see the truth perfectly. Bhikkhuni Dhamma returned from her almsround one day exhausted from heat and exertion. She stumbled, and as she sprawled on the ground a clear perception arose in her of the utter suffering inherent in the body, bringing about total relinquishment. She describes the incident in the following lines: Having wandered for alms, leaning on a stick, weak, with trembling limbs I fell to the ground in that very spot, having seen peril in the body. Then my mind was completely released. (v.17)

If someone could gain awakening based on such an event, surely there are an infinite number of potentially enlightening experiences available to all of us for contemplation. Systematic attention (yoniso manasikara) given to any subject will show up its impermanence (anicca), unsatisfactoriness (dukkha), and essenceless nature (anatta) and so encourage us to stop craving. However, unless we carefully apply our minds in Vipassana meditation under the guidance of a competent teacher, it is unlikely that we will be able to utilize our daily encounters with these basic characteristics as means towards liberation. This is because the mind's old conditioning is based on ignorance-the very inability to see things as they really are. Only concentrated mindfulness of phenomena in meditation can enable us to comprehend correctly our everyday experiences, because such methodical culture of insight through Vipassana meditation loosens the old mental tendencies by giving us direct experience of the impermanence of our mind and body.

Entering the Sangha after a Child's Death

Quite a number of women entered the Sangha after their small children had died. Grief is put to good use if it is made the motivation to develop the "path leading to the cessation of suffering." Ubbiri greatly mourned the death of her infant daughter until the Buddha pointed out to her that right in the same charnel ground where she had left this baby's body, she had similarly parted with thousands of children to whom she had given birth in previous lives. Because she had acquired strong merit in the past, this brief personalized discourse was enough to turn Ubbiri from a lamenting mother into an arahant on the spot. As she clearly saw the vastness of samsara, she was prepared to leave it behind. Her profound gratitude to the Buddha is described in these simple lines:

> He has thrust away for me my grief for my daughter... I am without hunger, quenched. (vv. 51, 53)

With the quenching of ignorance and craving, nothing remains but a pure mind, inherently peaceful. Ubbiri had a pliable, well-prepared mind, and thus she understood, through the Buddha's instructions, that the source of all her suffering had been craving. After countless millions of lifetimes spent rolling in samsara, Ubbiri realized how her deep motherly attachment to her children had always caused her much anguish; for sons and daughters, like everything else, are subject to the law of impermanence. We cannot make our loved ones live beyond the span set by their own kamma. This was an insight so powerful for her that no object at all seemed worthy of interest any longer because of the potential pain permeating them all. Thus all tendency to cling was broken, never to reappear.

The life story of Patacara before she came to the Dhamma, described in considerable detail in the commentary to the Therigatha, is even more dramatic. She lost her entire family, her husband, two small children, parents and brothers in various accidents within a few days. She went insane from the sorrow, but the Buddha's compassion combined with Patacara's paramis from the past enabled her to regain her right mind. When she came into his presence, he taught her to understand how often before she had hopelessly exhausted herself grieving for the dead. She became a stream-enterer (sotapanna), one at the first stage of irreversible progress on the path to liberation, and she was ordained.

Later, as she was one day pouring water to wash her feet and watching it trickle away-as life does sooner or later for all beings-her mind became utterly free from clinging. Patacara, like Dhamma, had thoroughly developed seeds of understanding, so a very minor mundane incident at just the right moment cleared her mind of every trace of ignorance.

Many other women entered the Sangha in circumstances similar to those of Ubbiri or Patacara. A woman distraught over the death of a child must have been very common in India in those days when limited medical knowledge could not counter a very high infant mortality rate. Theri Patacara spoke to a group of five hundred such grief-stricken mothers, expressing what she had so powerfully learned from similar experience herself:

The way of which men come we cannot know;

Nor can we see the path by which they go.

Why mourn then for him who came to you,

Lamenting through the tears?...

Weep not, for such is the life of man.

Unasked he came and unbidden he went.

Ask yourself again whence came your child

To live on earth this little time?

By one way come and by another gone,

As human to die, and pass to other births-

So hither and so hence-why should you weep?(p. 78)

In this way Patacara illustrates for these mothers the natural connection, the invisible, impersonal causal nexus between death and life, life and death. They too took robes and eventually became Arahats. Their joint "lion's roar" culminates in the lines:

Today my heart is healed, my yearning stayed,

Perfected deliverance wrought in me.

I go for refuge to the Buddha, the Sangha, and the Dhamma. (p. 77)

Because of their physiology and their conditioning by family and society, women are more prone to attachment to their offspring than are men, and so will suffer all the more from their loss. However, if women train their minds to understand how clinging causes enormous suffering, how birth and death are natural processes happening as effects of specific causes, and how infinite the history of such misery is, they can utilize their feminine sufferings in the quest for awakening. In the Kindred Sayings (Vol. IV, pp. 62-163), the Buddha himself pointed out the five kinds of suffering unique to women. Three are physiological-menstruation, pregnancy, and childbirth. The other two are social, and perhaps not as widely relevant today as they were in ancient Indian society: having to leave her own family to live with her husband and in-laws, and having "to wait upon a man." All five must be the results of past unwholesome deeds, yet each one can be made a basis for insight. Women can train their minds to turn to advantage these apparent disadvantages. They can then make full use of their stronger experiences of the universality and omnipresence of suffering to condition themselves to let go of everything in the conditioned realm.

For some individuals, intense suffering is needed to make the mind relinquish its misconceptions and desires. Patacara is one example of this; Kisa Gotami is a second. The latter was so unwilling to face the truth of her child's death that she carried the dead baby around with her hoping to find one who could give her medicine to cure him. The Buddha guided her into a realization of the omnipresence of death by sending her in search of some mustard seed. This is a common ingredient in Indian kitchens, but the Buddha specified that these seeds must come from a household where no one had ever died.

Kisa Gotami went looking for this "medicine" for her baby, but because of the prevalent joint family system in which three or more generations lived together under one roof, every house she went to had seen death. Gradually, as she wandered through the village, she realized that all who are born must die. Her great paramis then enabled her to understand impermanence so thoroughly that soon afterwards the Buddha confirmed her attainment of stream-entry. She then spoke these lines:

No village law is this, no city law,

No law for this clan, or for that alone;

For the whole world-and for the gods too-

This is the law: All is impermanent. *(p. 108)*

Kisa Gotami thus transcended the limits of a woman's personal grief to understand one of the basic characteristics of all existence.

Kisa Gotami later attained Arahatship. Some of the verses she spoke on that occasion give useful lessons to any striver on the Noble Eightfold Path: Resorting to noble friends, even a fool would be wise. Good men are to be resorted to; thus the wisdom of those who resort to them increases. Resorting to good men one would be released from all pains.

One should know suffering, the cause of suffering and its cessation, and the Eightfold Path; (these are) the Four Noble Truths. (vv. 213-215)

The company of the wise, especially the guidance of a teacher, is an invaluable help in getting oneself established on the path. But the company of people not involved in the Dhamma will tend to be distracting. Those who are not trying to practice the Buddha's teachings will usually lead us in the worldly direction to which their own minds incline. Thus, when we can, it is best to choose our friends from among meditators.

The Four Noble Truths

As Kisa Gotami urges in the final lines quoted above, meditators need to train their minds constantly to see the Four Noble Truths in all their ramifications. This is wisdom, panna, the remedy for the ignorance and delusion which are at the root of all suffering as shown in the formula of dependent origination. To develop wisdom one has to ponder these four truths over and over again:

(1) the Noble Truth of Suffering (dukkha) which includes all forms of suffering from severe agony to the pervasive unsatisfactoriness and instability inherent in individual existence in all planes of becoming;

(2) the Noble Truth of the Cause of Suffering-craving (tanha), which drives the mind outwards after sense objects in a state of perpetual unrest;

(3) the Noble Truth of the Cessation of Suffering-Nibbana, which is attained when the causes of suffering, ignorance and craving, have been utterly uprooted; and

(4) the Noble Truth of the Way leading to the Cessation of Suffering-the Noble Eightfold Path discovered and taught by the Buddha, consisting in the assiduous practice of morality (sila), concentration (samadhi) and wisdom (panna).

The Four Noble Truths are concisely expressed in a verse spoken by Maha Pajapati, the Buddha's maternal aunt who brought him up when his own mother, Queen Mahamaya, died a week after his birth. It was at the insistence of Maha Pajapati that the Buddha founded the Bhikkhuni Sangha. In her poem she first praises the Buddha for the unique help he has given to so many beings by training them in the way to liberation; then she briefly sums up the Four Noble Truths which she has so thoroughly experienced as ultimate truth. It would be beneficial for modern meditators to consider these lines carefully:

Now have I understood how ill does come,
Craving, the Cause, is dried up in me.
Have I not walked, have I not touched the End
Of ill-the Ariyan, the Eightfold Noble Path. (p. 89)

Buddhist meditators have to train themselves to know these truths as deeply as they can by seeing them in every aspect of existence. We follow the mundane level of the Noble

Eightfold Path in order to reach the supramundane (lokuttara) path with the attainment of stream-entry. Then the constituents of the path-morality, concentration and wisdom-are cultivated to the highest degree and the end of suffering, Nibbana, is realized.

Reaching the Goal after a Long Struggle

When we read the stories of these great bhikkhunis, we see that many of them attained the highest fruits either instantaneously or soon after coming into contact with the Buddha or his Dhamma. This could have happened because they had built up paramis in many previous lives, creating pure kamma of body, speech and mind, while simultaneously wearing out the effects of past kamma.

Yet not all the people whose paramis permitted them to actually hear the Buddha preach were able to become Arahats so quickly in their final lives. When we confront our rebellious minds as we try to follow his path, we can take heart from the tales of nuns who had to put forth years and years of intense persistent effort before they eliminated all their defilements.

A youthful Citta ordained at her home town of Rajagaha and spent her whole adult life as a nun striving for enlightenment. She finally attained her goal only as a weak old woman, as she laboriously climbed up the landmark of Vultures' Peak. When she had done so, she said:

> *Having thrown down my outer robe, and having turned my bowl upside down, I propped myself against a rock, having torn asunder the mass of darkness (of ignorance). (v. 27)*

If we diligently, strictly, and vigorously practice the Noble Eightfold Path, developing insight into the true nature of existence, the opacity of delusion must eventually become completely transparent, cleared by wisdom. It may require many years or many lifetimes of work, but then patience is one of the qualities we must cultivate from the time we first set foot on the path. Another bhikkhuni who took years to reach enlightenment was Mittakali. She took robes after hearing the Satipatthana Sutta. In her "lion's roar" she describes the errors that cost her seven years to gain Nibbana. Her poem can be instructive to other meditators both within and outside the Sangha:

> *Having gone forth in faith from the house to the houseless state, I wandered here and there, greedy for gain and honour.*
>
> *Having missed the highest goal, I pursued the lowest goal. Having gone under the mastery of the defilements, I did not know the goal of the ascetic's state. (vv. 9293)*

The Buddha pointed out on many occasions that it is dangerous for monks and nuns to pursue gains or favors from the laity, as such activities nullify any attempts they may make to purify their minds. The layman gives gifts to bhikkhus and bhikkhunis to earn merit. If the mind of the recipient is pure, free from greed and other defilements, the merit accruing to the lay disciple is far greater than if the recipient's mind is filled with craving. One of the epithets given to Arahats, whose purity is permanently perfect, is "worthy of the highest offerings." All those, ordained or not, who allow craving to overtake them and waste the precious opportunity they have to practice the Dhamma, will delay their own liberation and increase their suffering.

In the simile of the poisonous snake in the Middle Length Sayings (Vol I, pp. 171-72), the Buddha points out that his teaching has only one aim, freedom from suffering. An incorrect approach that seeks to misuse the Dhamma will lead to increased suffering, just as grasping a snake by the body or tail will result in one's being bitten. The same venomous snake, if grabbed with the help of a forked stick by the neck just behind its head, will safely yield up its poison for medicinal use. The Buddha declares that similarly only those who wisely examine the purpose of his teachings will be able to gain insight and actually experience their purpose-the elimination of the causes of suffering.

When Mittakali perceived that old age and death were rapidly approaching, she finally came to realize the urgency of the task after wasting years in the pursuit of gain and honour.

Since we can never be sure how much longer we will live, it is risky to put off meditation. We have come into contact with the Dhamma under conditions conducive to pursuing the Buddha's goal. Such conditions as youth and human birth will come to an end-either gradually or abruptly-so we can never be certain that the conditions to practice the Dhamma will remain ideal. Mittakali took years to comprehend that with advancing age, rigidity of mind and bodily ailments were making the job of purification ever more difficult. But once she did realize this, she was able to achieve the goal. Studying this verse of hers may help us to avoid wasting precious time: I felt a sense of urgency as I was seated in my little cell; (thinking) "I have entered upon the wrong road; I have come under the mastery of craving.

> *"My life is short. Old age and sickness are destroying it. There is no time for me to be careless before this body is broken."*
>
> *Looking at the arising and passing away of the elements of existence as they really are, I stood up with my mind completely released. The Buddha's Teaching has been done.(vv. 94-95)*

By observing the rise and fall at every instant of body, feelings, perceptions, mental formations, and consciousness, Mittakali's mind was freed from misconceptions of any lasting "I" or self. After those seven long years of being trapped in the net of desires, she saw through her foolish and dangerous interest in mundane matters. She was then able to see the elements or aggregates as they actually are: utterly transient (anicca), hence incapable of providing any satisfaction (so dukkha), working automatically without any lasting core (anatta). All her worldly involvements dropped away as she attained Arahatship and thenceforth passed beyond all sorrow and suffering.

Perhaps the most moving story of a nun who had to undergo a long struggle from the time she first ordained until she became fully enlightened is that of Punna. Under six earlier Buddhas, in the vast eons prior to the Buddha Gotama's dispensation, Punna was a bhikkhuni "perfect in virtue, and learning the three Pitakas [the Buddhist scriptures] she became very learned in the Norm and a teacher of it. But because of her tendency to pride [each time], she was unable to root out the defilements." Even at the time of Buddha Gotama, she had to work out some bad kamma and so was born as a slave. Hearing one of the Buddha's discourses, she became a stream-enterer. After she helped her master clear his wrong view, in gratitude he freed her and she ordained. After so many lifetimes of striving, the paramis she had built up as a nun under previous Buddhas ripened. Pride or conceit, always one of the last defilements to go, finally dissolved and she attained Arahatship.

By pondering the accounts of women who attained full awakening after much application and effort, we can be encouraged to continue our own exertions no matter how slow our progress may appear at a given time. In the Gradual Sayings (Vol. IV, pp. 83-84), the Buddha gives an analogy of the wearing down of the carpenter's axe handle to illustrate how the mental impurities are to be gradually worn away. Even though the woodcutter cannot say, "This much of the handle was rubbed off today, this much last week," it is clear to him that slowly, over time, the handle is being destroyed. Similarly, a meditator who has a good guide and who constantly attempts to understand the Four Noble Truths and to live in accordance with the Noble Eightfold Path, will gradually eliminate his defilements, even though the steps in the process are imperceptible. Even the Buddha declined to predict the amount of time that will elapse before the final goal is reached. This is conditioned by many interacting factors, such as the good and bad kamma built up in the past and the amount of effort put forth now and in the future. Whether it takes us millions of more lifetimes or a week, we will be sustained in our efforts by the faith that perfection of morality, concentration and wisdom will bring utter detachment and freedom from all suffering.

Liberation means renouncing attachment to oneself and to the world. We cannot rush the process of detachment; insight into the suffering brought about by clinging will do it, slowly.

While trying to eliminate mental impurities, we have to accept their existence. We would not be here at all were it not for the ignorance and other defiling tendencies that brought us into this birth. We need to learn to live equanimously with the dirt of the mind while it is slowly being cleared away. Purification, like all other mental activities, is a cause and effect process. Clarity comes slowly with the repeated application of the wisdom of impermanence. If we are patient and cheerfully bear with moments of apparent backsliding or stupidity, if we continue to work energetically with determination, not swerving off the path, the results will begin here and now. And in due time they have to ripen fully.

Contemplation on the Sangha

The Sangha, the order of monks and nuns, preserves and perpetuates the Buddha's pure teachings, and its members have dedicated their lives to practicing them. Thus contemplation on the Sangha is recommended by the Buddha to help cultivate wholesome mental states. We could begin such contemplation based on the poem of a bhikkhuni named Rohini.

Her father had asked her why she thought recluses and monks were great beings. He claimed, as might many people today-particularly in the West with its strong "work ethic"-that ascetics are just lazy; they are "parasites" who do nothing worthwhile and live off the labour of others. But Rohini proclaimed her faith in the work and lives of pure recluses. She thereby inspired her father's confidence, and at her bidding he then took refuge in the Buddha, the Dhamma, and the Sangha. Her poem can also inspire us:

They are dutiful, not lazy, doers of the best actions; they abandon desire and hatred...

They shake off the three roots of evil doing pure actions; all their evil is eliminated...

Their body-activity is pure; and their speech-activity is likewise; their mind-activity is pure...

They are spotless like mother-of-pearl, purified inside and out; full of good mental states...

Having great learning, expert in the doctrine, noble, living in accordance with the doctrine, they teach the goal and the doctrine... with intent minds, (they are) possessed of mindfulness...

Travelling far, possessed of mindfulness, speaking in moderation, not conceited, they comprehend the end of suffering...

If they go from any village, they do not look back (longingly) at anything; they go without longing indeed...

They do not deposit their property in a store-room, nor in a pot, nor in a basket, (rather) seeking that which is cooked...

They do not take gold, coined or uncoined, or silver; they live by means of whatever turns up...

Those who have gone forth are of various families and from various countries; (nevertheless) they are friendly to one another; therefore ascetics are dear to me. (vv. 275-285)

The Buddhist texts speak of two kinds of Sangha, both referred to in this poem, the Ariya Sangha and the Bhikkhu Sangha. In the opening lines Rohini describes the Ariyas, "noble ones," and those striving to attain that state. The three lower kinds of Ariyas may be lay disciples or ordained monks and nuns. But because of their utter purity, the highest type, the filly liberated Arahats, can continue to live only within the Bhikkhu Sangha. It is Arahats who have completely rid their minds of greed, hatred and ignorance, the three roots of evil which Rohini mentions. Other Ariyas are striving to abandon whatever of these three still remains in their minds. All Ariyas to some extent "comprehend the end of suffering," the Third Noble Truth, for it is this experience of Nibbana which sets them apart as "noble."

Beginning with the next line, Rohini specifically talks about the behavior of monks and nuns. They wander on almsrounds through the streets with their eyes trained just a few steps ahead of them. "They do not look back" as they have no idle interest in the events that are going on around them.

They do not handle money and are content with the minimum by way of the requisites-whatever their lay followers may offer them. Students of the Dhamma who are not in the monastic order would also do well to cultivate the monk's lack of interest in his surroundings. A good monk does not let his gaze wander about uncontrolled, especially when he is on almsround, because when going into the village every morning he encounters a plethora of sense objects that might entice him if he does not restrain his senses and maintain mindfulness. Attentively, the good bhikkhu goes silently from door to door and leaves when there is enough food in his bowl, without letting craving disturb his balance of mind. Such a monk is not interested in the details of the lives of those around him. His focus is always on the ultimate nature of things their impermanence, painfulness and essencelessness. As lay meditators we too need to train ourselves to be like these bhikkhus, to remain equanimous and detached amidst all the clamor and distractions of life by reminding ourselves that none of these things is worth running after.

Rohini also states that the noble monks are not greedy about money or other possessions. They do not save up their requisites out of fear for the future. Instead, they trust their good kamma to fulfill their daily needs. While, as laymen, we must work for our living, we should heed this behavior and similarly adopt a detached attitude towards wealth. We work in order to sustain our bodies and those of the people who are dependent on us. But if we can learn to do this without intense longing for the "security" that money seems to provide, we will see how the law of kamma works.

The last verse states that within the Sangha, the family, class or national background of its members does not impede their cordial relations with each other. This kind of open good will is surely useful for laymen to put into practice in their daily lives too. Since it is by ordaining that individuals can completely dedicate their lives to the Dhamma, bhikkhus and bhikkhunis offer us laymen many examples of how we should try to apply the teachings within the limitations of "the dust of household life." Rohini's poem has pointed out some of these.

The Danger of Worldly Desire

A large number of poems by the nuns emphasize the danger of worldly desire. The bhikkhuni named Sumedha shaved off her hair herself in order to force her parents to cancel her proposed marriage and permit his to enter the Sangha. But before she left home, Sumedha convinced her whole family and its retinue of the validity of the Buddha's message. To her fiance, King Anikaratta, she explained the futility of sense desires and the insatiability of the senses:

Even if the rain-god rained all seven kinds

Of gems, until earth and heaven were full,

Still senses would crave and men die unsatiated. (p. 176)

No matter how large a quantity of worldly goods we may have, if the mind has not gained insight, craving will recur. If ignorance has not been uprooted, desire will seek more and different objects, always hoping for lasting satisfaction. Durable happiness is impossible in the mundane sphere because all sense objects change and decay every moment, as does the mind itself.

This perpetual state of underlying dissatisfaction-craving looking for gratification-is one of the many forms of present suffering. In addition, desire itself generates the kammic energy which propels life towards rebirth in order for it to continue its efforts at finding fulfillment. If desire is present in the mind at the moment of death, rebirth has to ensue.

After speaking the above verse, Sumedha gave a lengthy discourse to the whole assembly in her palace on the great value of a human birth in the infinity of samsara. Life in this world is precious because it provides a very rare opportunity for learning the way to put an end to rebirth and suffering, for putting into practice the teachings of the Buddha.

Sumedha also spoke on the danger inherent in sensual joy and sense desire and she uttered verses about the Noble Eightfold Path as well. She enthusiastically exhorted her audience:

When the undying (Nibbana) exists, what do you want with sensual pleasures which are burning fevers? For all delights in sensual pleasures are on fire, aglow, seething. (v. 504)

When craving momentarily gains its aim, mind's enjoyment of the sense object brings it to a feverish state of excitement and activity. Sumedha urges her family to look beyond such unsettling, binding pleasures and to heed the words of the Awakened One which show the way beyond all desire to utter peace. She exhorts them to keep in mind their long-term benefit and not get caught up in the fragile momentary happiness that comes with the occasional satisfaction of sense desire. She reminds them in words we too should recall: "Desires of sense burn those who do not let go" (p. 176). Clinging to pleasure always brings pain. Such agitated emotions, although perhaps pleasant in a gross way, are gone in a moment.

They arise and cease due to conditions we cannot completely control. We always tend to want the pleasant to last in spite of the fact that its nature is to change, vanish, and give way to the unpleasant. Sumedha's poem expounding this wisdom is the last one in the original Therigatha and it summarizes what the Buddha taught about the dangers of craving.

The bhikkhuni named Subha also dwells at length on the dangers of mundane wishes, using some terrifying metaphors to show the tremendous dangers inherent in attachment to the world. In the following poem taken from the Samyutta Nikaya a meditator can discover much by reflecting on Subha's intense imagery:

May I not meet (again) with sensual pleasures, in which no refuge is found. Sensual pleasures are enemies, murderers, like a mass of fire, pain-(ful).

Greed is an obstacle, full of fear, full of annoyance, full of thorns, and it is very disagreeable. It is a great cause of stupefaction...

Sensual pleasures are maddening, deceiving, agitating the mind; a net spread out by Mara for the defilement of creatures.

> *Sensual pleasures have endless perils, they have much pain, they are great poisons, they give little enjoyment, they cause conflict, drying up the virtuous.(vv. 351f., 357f.)*

These lines show us the peril and suffering we must face when we allow ourselves to become entangled in mundane desires. Only personal comprehension of these dangers motivates a meditator to become truly mindful, aware of his physical and mental activities with ever-present detachment. Otherwise his "mindfulness" may be forced, suppressing reactions without helping to untie mental knots. Studying the suffering we have to encounter if we are carried away by our desires, naturally loosens their hold on the mind. We will realize along with Subha that worldly lusts are enemies and that they herald all the misery of successive births.

One of our tasks in seeking liberation is to train our minds to see desire as it arises at the sense doors. We must also see desire as it persists and as it passes away. Having done this over and over again, we will understand that all desire or attachment is bound to result in unhappiness. In this way we will gradually train our minds to let go of all craving and aversions towards sense objects.

To try to practice this mindfulness without any specific training is likely to fail because the worldling, the average person, perceives no suffering in craving. A worldling can only see the expected happiness. He invariably thinks, "If only this would happen just right, all would be well." But as we purify our bodily and vocal activities through morality, still our minds through concentration, and take up insight meditation under a good teacher, we will come to see more and more clearly how all desire is suffering and brings still more suffering in the future.

We will then also realize how often attaining a desired object turns out to be an anti-climax which leaves-not the anticipated happiness-but only emptiness. With a calm mind we can clearly perceive the tension, distress, and uneasiness caused by the continual dissatisfaction, which in turn is due to craving impelling the mind to various sense objects.

Thus the mind is always running-now towards what it foolishly regards as a "desirable" thing, now away from what it considers "undesirable." In Vipassana meditation, the one-pointed mind is trained to experience directly the transitory nature of body and of mind itself, and also of external sense objects. With this direct knowledge or experiential insight, the "happiness" which is so avidly sought by the worldling is seen as really just another form of suffering, and the perpetual tension caused by the ignorance and craving latent in any unliberated mind becomes evident. As sensual pleasure is understood to be the seething fire described by our bhikkhunis, the mind naturally lets go of all these different manifestations of craving. Such a mind has thoroughly learned the lesson that the nuns gleaned from their Master and passed on to us: suffering is inherent in desire.

The Danger in Attachment to One's Beauty

In ancient times as well as at present, women in all stations of life have used various means to enhance their beauty and to hide the signs of advancing age. This, however, is just a futile attempt to pretend that the body is not growing old, to keep it from showing outwardly that it is actually falling apart. But if, instead of creams and lotions, wisdom is applied to the aging process, it can deepen our understanding of impermanence on all levels.

Ambapali was a wealthy and beautiful courtesan during the time of the Buddha. Before she heard the Buddha preach, her main concern had been to cultivate and maintain her renowned beauty. With the Buddha's guidance, she was able to face the inevitability of aging and the loss of her beauty and to comprehend the suffering of old age. Her verses can also stimulate our own understanding:

> *My eyes were shining, very brilliant like jewels, very black and long. Overwhelmed by old age, they do not look beautiful. Not otherwise is the utterance of the speaker of truth...*
>
> *Formerly my hands looked beautiful, possessing delicate signet rings, decorated with gold. Because of old age*

they are like onions and radishes. Not otherwise is the utterance of the speaker of the truth...
Formerly my body looked beautiful, like a well-polished sheet of gold. (Now) it is covered with very fine wrinkles. Not otherwise is the utterance of the speaker of the truth...
Such was this body. (Now) it is decrepit, the abode of many pains, an old house with its plaster fallen off. Not otherwise is the utterance of the speaker of the truth. (vv. 257, 264, 266, 270)

Ambapali sees how all the body's charms give way to ugliness and pain as the aging process takes its toll, as the Buddha teaches it must. All physical beauty, no matter how perfect it might seem at one youthful moment, is utterly impermanent. Even at its peak, the brilliance of the eyes is already, if invisibly, starting to grow dim; the firmness of limbs is withering; the smoothness of skin is wrinkling. Impermanence and decay, Ambapali reminds us, is the nature of all bodies and of everything else in the universe as well. Khema, the queen of King Bimbisara, was another woman who had been enthralled with her own beauty prior to meeting the Buddha. But Khema had made a vow before one of the earlier Buddhas to become great in wisdom under the Buddha Gotama. During the dispensations of several of the intervening Buddhas, she had parks made which she donated to each Buddha and his Sangha.

But in her final lifetime Khema strongly resisted going to see the Buddha Gotama. Perhaps her "Mara forces" were making a last effort to keep her in samsara. They were, however, doomed to fail since by the force of her merits this was to be her final existence. King Bimbisara almost had to trick her into going to the Buddha because Queen Khema was so attached to her looks and was afraid that this would provoke the Buddha's disapproval. If we ever find ourselves resisting the Dhamma, we can use Khema's example to remind ourselves of the temporary nature of this mental state. Then we will not take it as a major personal fault. Mind's old habits are not pure, so at times it is bound to struggle against the process of purification.

But the Buddha knew how to tame Khema's vanity and conceit. He created the vivid image of a woman even more attractive than she was. When she came into his presence, Khema saw this other lady fanning the Buddha. Then, before the queen's very eyes, the Buddha made the beautiful image grow older and older until she was just a decaying bag of bones. Seeing this, first Khema realized that her own beauty was not unmatched. This broke her pride. Second and more important, she understood that she herself would likewise have to grow old and decrepit.

The Buddha next spoke a verse and Khema became a stream-enterer. Then in rapid succession she went through all the stages of enlightenment to attain Arahatship on the spot. Thereupon the Buddha told King Bimbisara that she would either have to ordain or to pass away, and the king, unable to bear the thought of losing her so soon, gave her permission to ordain.

So, already an arahant, she was ordained-one of the very rare cases of a human being who had achieved Arahatship before entering the Sangha. Khema had clearly built up truly unique paramis by giving great gifts to earlier Buddhas and by learning their teachings thoroughly.2 Here again we see the great importance of creating in the present strong good kamma based on wisdom, even if we do not attain any of the paths or fruits in this lifetime. The more good deeds accompanied by wisdom that we do now, the easier will it be when the time actually comes for us to reach the goal. Meditation is, of course, the most valuable of such deeds.

In the Therigatha, Khema's poem takes the form of a conversation with Mara, the being who controls and symbolizes the forces of evil. Mara praised her beauty, and her reply shows how totally her view of herself and of life had changed now that she fully understood the true nature of things:

Through this body vile, foul seat of disease and corruption,

Loathing I feel, and oppression. Cravings of lust are uprooted.

Lusts of the body and mind cut like daggers and javelins.

Speak not to me of delighting in any sensuous pleasure!

All such vanities cannot delight me any more.(p. 83)

Then she identifies Mara with those who believe that mere ritual observances will lead to mental purification. Khema states that such people, who worship fire or the constellations, etc., are ignorant of reality and cannot eliminate their defiling tendencies through such practices. This is why the belief that rites and rituals can bring about liberation has to be eliminated to attain even the stage of stream-entry.

Khema concludes her verses with an exclamation of deep gratitude to the Buddha, the supreme among men. Her last line is a resounding "lion's roar":

(I am) utterly free from all sorrow,

A doer of the Buddha's teachings. (pp. 3-4)

Khema had "done," i.e., put into practice, the message of all the Buddhas, and this had taken her beyond the realms of suffering.

Further Conversations with Mara

Some of the other discourse-type verses in the Therigatha also take the form of a discussion with Mara. Typically, Mara asks the arahant nun why she is not interested in the "good things of life." Mara urged Sela, for example, to enjoy sensual pleasures while youth allowed her to do so. The theri's reply on the dangers of such delights offers similes as powerful as those used by Bhikkhuni Sumedha:

Sensual pleasures are like sword and stakes; the elements of existence are a chopping block for them; what you call 'delight in sensual pleasures' is now 'non-delight' for me. (v. 58)

Surely many of us have also heard our own internal Mara urge us to "go have a good time and never mind the long-term kammic consequences." But if we can remind ourselves often enough and early enough of the painful after-effects of such "joys"-especially of those that involve breaking moral precepts-we may see through the pleasures of the senses and so gradually lose our attachment to them.

In one of the discourses from the Samyutta Nikaya, Cala tells Mara that, unlike most beings, she finds no delight in birth in spite of the so-called sensual pleasures that life makes possible. With clear simplicity she shows that ultimately all that birth produces is suffering:

Once born we die. Once born we see life's ills-

The bonds, the torments, and the life cut off. (p. 186)

We too should cultivate this understanding in order to develop detachment from the poison-soaked sensual pleasures offered by mundane life.

The Doctrine of Anatta

One of the unique aspects of the Buddha's teaching is its doctrine of anatta, the impersonal, essenceless, egoless or soul-less nature of all phenomena. This universal characteristic is difficult to comprehend as it is contrary to our most deeply held assumption that "I" exist, that "I" act and "I" feel. Sakula, in the following lines of her poem in the Therigatha, briefly expresses her understanding of the impersonal quality of all compounded things:

Seeing the constituent elements as other, arisen causally, liable to dissolution, I eliminated all taints. I have become cool, quenched. (v. 101)

Sakula has attained Nibbana because she saw with total clarity that everything normally taken to be "myself" is, in fact, devoid of any such self. She knew that all these phenomena arise and dissolve every moment strictly dependent on causes. This comprehension has rooted out all tendency to cling to the sankharas or "constituent elements" and so all the defiling mental tendencies have ceased.

When Mara asks Sister Sela, "Who made this body, where did it come from and where will it go?", she gives him in reply (in one of the poems added from the Samyutta Nikaya) a discourse on egolessness:

Neither self-made the puppet is, nor yet
By another is this evil fashioned.
By reason of a cause it came to be;
By rupture of a cause it dies away.
Like a given seed sown in the field,
Which, when it gets the taste of earth,
And moisture too-by these two does grow,
So the five aggregates, the elements,
And the six spheres of sense-all of these-
By reason of a cause they came to be;
By rupture of a cause they die away. (pp.189-190)

After the seed analogy, the last four lines discuss the "self" as it actually is-a compound of conditioned, changing phenomena. The five aggregates make up nama (mentality) and rupa (materiality), each of which is turn made up of groups of ephemeral factors. Nama, the mental side of existence, consists of the four immaterial aggregates-feeling (vedana), perception (sanna), mental formations (sankhara), and consciousness (vinnana)-which arise together at every moment of experience. Rupa, which may be external matter or the matter of one's own body, consists of the four essential material qualities-solidity, cohesion, temperature, and vibration-along with the derivative types of matter coexisting with them in the very minute material groupings called kalapas, arising and passing away millions of times per second. Each aggregate arises due to certain causes and when these causes end, the aggregate also ceases. Causes, or conditions, are connected with effects in the law of dependent arising (paticcasamuppada), which is at the centre of the Buddha's own awakening. The refrain from Sela's poem (lines 3-4 and 10-11) is, in fact, a reformulation of the most general exposition of that law often stated thus in the suttas:

When there is this, that comes to be;
With the arising of this, that arises.
When this is absent, that does not come to be;
With the cessation of this, that ceases.

The specific link in the cycle of dependent arising most relevant to Sela's verse is: "With consciousness as condition, mentality-materiality arises." That is, at the moment of conception, nama-rupa (in this case excluding consciousness) arises due to rebirth-linking consciousness. Later on, during the course of an existence, nama, the mental aggregates, comes into being due to ignorance, past kamma, objects at the sense doors, and many other conditions. Rupa, the matter which makes up the body, arises during life because of food, climate, present state of mind, and past kamma.

Sela also refers to the elements, dhatu, a word which the Buddha uses for several groups of phenomena. Let us look here at the eighteen elements. The five sense faculties (eye, ear, nose, tongue, body), their objects (sights, sounds, smells, tastes, touches), and the five types of consciousness dependent on their coming together make up fifteen of the elements. Mind as a faculty, mental objects (ideas), and the mind-consciousness that arises when those two come together are the sixth in each set, completing the eighteen.

The Buddha analyzed the totality of conditioned phenomena into ultimate constituents in a number of ways for the benefit of listeners of varying proclivities. To some, the eighteen elements are clear, to others, the five aggregates. Either way, what we need to understand as Sela did is that none of these things is "me" or "mine" or "my self." All these phenomena-the aggregates, the elements, the spheres-arise because of certain conditions, and when those conditions end, naturally they also have to end. When the relevant causes have expended their force, all these aspects of what we erroneously take to be "me" and "mine" cease. So we see with Sela that nowhere is there any real, independent, or lasting "I" with the power to create and sustain itself. There is only the concept "I am" which is conditioned by ignorance, i.e., our inability to see mind-and-body as it really is. The idea "I" is itself essenceless, it arises due to causes; and it is also inherently impermanent, bound to completely disappear when the ignorance and other supporting conditions behind it are uprooted. This is the attainment of Arahatship.

The removal of ignorance takes place step by step in Vipassana meditation. Every aspect of the mind-body complex comes to be clearly known at its ultimate level as conditioned, essenceless, transitory, oppressive. One comes to fully understand that only when the appropriate conditions come about will a so-called "being" be born. Only then will a five-aggregate life-continuum commence a new life with its bases, elements and sense organs.

If we explore Bhikkhuni Sela's seed analogy, we will see in relation to ourselves how a strict succession of causes and effects, kammic and other, governs all of life. We will discover that there is no underlying or ongoing "I" doing or experiencing anything, and will begin to loosen our attachment to this non-existent "self." Then we start to eliminate the dreadful suffering that comes attendant on this delusion.

Suffering follows from the mistaken belief in an "I," technically called sakkayaditthi, wrong view of a lasting self. On the basis of this idea the mind generates all its thoughts of craving: "I must have this," "I don't like that," "This is mine." It is basically due to this misconception of a controlling self that we have been wandering and suffering throughout eons in samsara. If we are to eliminate all the dukkha of existence, as Theri Sela did, we must develop insight through Vipassana meditation to the point at which understanding of the ultimate truth about mind and body dissolves the mistaken belief in an "I." We can use this bhikkhuni's words to stimulate our own personal meditative experience of the essenceless nature of the five aggregates.

Men and Women in the Dhamma

The difference between the male and female in connection with the Dhamma is a minor theme running through the Therigatha. It takes two forms: poems whose subject matter is the irrelevance of one's gender for gaining insight, and instances in which a nun specifically inspires or instructs a man with a discourse. The stories of Sumedha and Rohini already discussed fit into the latter type. An example of the first type is Soma's challenge to Mara's query about women's ability to attain Arahatship. Soma showed Mara that the capacity to gain the requisite insight for liberation need not be hindered by "woman's nature." Soma's encounter with Mara in the Therigatha proper is explained in her verses from the Samyutta Nikaya, where she rhetorically asks him:

What should the woman's nature do to them

Whose hearts are firmly set, who ever move

With growing knowledge onward in the Path?(pp. 45; 182-183)

If one is really developing morality, concentration and wisdom, it does not matter whether one was born male or female. The insight to "truly comprehend the Norm" is completely irrespective of superficial distinctions of sex, race, caste, etc. Soma adds that if one even thinks, "Am I a woman in these matter, or an I a man, or what not am I then?" one is under Mara's sway. To be much concerned with such subjects is to remain on the level of conventional truth, clinging to the non-existent self. Repeatedly worrying about which sex is better or about the "inequities" women suffer generates unwholesome kamma. Thoughts like this are rooted in attachment to "I" and "mine" and are associated with ill will or desire.

Moreover, spending time on such matters distracts us from the urgent task of self-purification. Meditators who wish to escape Mara's net need to cast off such thoughts as soon as they are noticed. We should not indulge in or expand upon them. Soma and all the other nuns follow the Buddha's advice closely when they urge us to stick exclusively to the work that will allow us to liberate ourselves from all suffering. All side issues will lose their importance and so pass away with further growth of wisdom. When we know fully that all beings are just impersonal, unstable mind-body processes, generating kamma and feeling its results, our minds will remain with the ultimate truths and have no interest in any conventional concerns. The story of the bhikkhuni known as "Vaddha's Mother" is one in which a nun specifically guides a man in the Dhamma. This woman joined the Sangha when her son Vaddha was small; thus he had been brought up by relatives. Later, he too ordained and one day went to visit his mother in the bhikkhunis' quarters. On that occasion, she exhorted and inspired him to seek and attain the highest goal:

> *Vaddha, may you not have craving for the world at any time. Child, do not be again and again a sharer in pain.*
>
> *Happy, indeed, Vaddha, dwell the sages, free from lust, with doubts cut off, become cool, having attained self-taming, (being) without taints.*
>
> *O Vaddha, devote yourself to the way practiced by seers for the attainment of insight, for the putting an end to pain. (vv. 204-205)*

From these lines Vaddha deduced that his mother had reached the goal, a fact she confirmed. She again urged him to develop "the path leading to the cessation of suffering" himself. Vaddha, being deeply inspired by his mother's words, also attained the goal and then spoke the following lines praising her:

> *Truly my mother, because of being sympathetic, applied an excellent goad to me, (namely) verses connected with the highest goal.*
>
> *Having heard her utterance, the instruction of my mother, I reached a state of religious excitement in the doctrine, for the attainment of rest-from-exertion. (vv. 210-211)*

Here we find a woman's example of perfect sainthood, combined with her timely Dhamma instruction, inspiring a man whose paramis were ripe to put forth the utmost effort and attain complete liberation.

The Five Aggregates and Nibbana

The Culavedalla Sutta (Middle Length Sayings, Vol. I) is another sutta in which a bhikkhuni instructs a man. This important text takes the form of a discourse on some fine points of the Dhamma given by the theri Dhammadinna in reply to questions put to her by her former husband, the lay disciple Visakha. They had been married for some time when he attained the third stage of holiness, that of the non-returner (anagami), by eradicating all traces of ill will and sense desire. Dhammadinna then learned from him that women too could purity their minds and she obtained his permission to take robes as a nun. By the time of this discussion, she must have already attained Arahatship, the fourth and final stage of holiness.

Visakha first asks Dhammadinna what the Buddha actually refers to when, using conventional language, he says "own self." As a non-returner, Visakha knew the answer to this basic question, but he put it by way of introduction to his progressive series of queries. Dhammadinna's reply is something for us to ponder. She says that the "five aggregates of grasping" (pancupadanakkhandha) comprise "own self." She defines the aggregates or groups of grasping as:

the group of grasping after material shape,

the group of grasping after feeling,

the group of grasping after perception,

the group of grasping after habitual tendencies,

the group of grasping after consciousness.

The aggregates are viewed and clung to as myself or mine: this is sakkayaditthi, the view that there is a lasting self. Actually, there is no lasting controller or core corresponding to the concept "me" or "I." It is merely the grasping after these five groups, which are all that actually makes up "myself," that perpetuates our illusion that there is something substantial. If we can see this, we will be attacking sakkayaditthi and will come to know that in reality there is no essence, just these five aggregates, all of whose components are continually changing.

The next question Visakha asks Dhammadinna concerns the reasons for the arising of the aggregates. Quoting the Buddha, she replies that the cause for the aggregates is "craving (that is) connected with again-becoming, accompanied by delight and attachment, finding delight in this and that, namely, the craving for sense pleasures, the craving for becoming, the craving for annihilation." All craving contributes to the arising of the aggregates over and over again. Being attracted to the things of this world or of the heavenly planes ("craving for sense pleasures") will lead to rebirth there with renewed suffering, gross or subtle. Wanting to keep on going ("craving for becoming") strengthens clinging and ignorance to force us to continue in samsara. The belief that there is no form of life after death (rooted in "craving for annihilation") undermines the doctrine of kamma and its result, the understanding of which is essential to moral living.

After a long series of questions and answers which cover the Four Noble Truths, the attainment of cessation, feeling, etc., Visakha asks a final question: "And what, lady, is the counterpart [i.e., equal] of Nibbana?" Here Dhammadinna has to stop him: This question goes too far, friend Visakha, it is beyond the compass of an answer. Friend Visakha, the Brahmafaring is for immergence in Nibbana, for going beyond to Nibbana, for culminating in Nibbana.

Nothing can possibly be compared with Nibbana as everything else, be it mental or physical, arises and ceases due to conditions. Nibbana alone is unconditioned and unchanging. Going beyond the realm of transitory, unsatisfactory phenomena to the utter peace of Nibbana is the aim of the teaching of the Buddha and so of serious Buddhists. It is useful to keep this goal in mind even during the early stages of meditation, when it may seem remote and vague.

The aspiration to attain Nibbana is cumulative. If it is frequently considered, repeated and combined with the practice of Vipassana, this aspiration will become a supporting condition for the attainment itself. Frequent recollection of the goal will also keep us from being sidetracked by the pleasurable experiences one may encounter on the path.

After this question and answer session, Dhammadinna suggests that Visakha should ask the Buddha about all this so that he is certain and learns the answers well. Visakha takes up the idea and later repeats to the Buddha his entire conversation with the theri. The Lord replies in her praise: Clever, Visakha, is the nun Dhammadinna, of great wisdom... If you had asked me, Visakha, about this matter, I too would have answered exactly as the nun Dhammadinna answered.

Kamma and its Fruit

Finally, let us look at a poem in which a bhikkhuni describes in detail a few of her previous lives and shows her questioner how she comprehended the law of kammic cause and effect working out behind her present-life experiences.

Isidasi had built up many good paramis long ago during the times of former Buddhas. But some seven lifetimes back, when she was a young man, she had committed adultery. After passing away from that existence Isidasi had to suffer the results of this immoral action:

Therefrom deceasing, long I ripened in Avici hell

And then found rebirth in the body of an ape.

Scarce seven days I lived before the great

Dog-ape, the monkey's chief, castrated me.

Such was the fruit of my lasciviousness.

Therefrom deceasing in the woods of Sindh,

Born the offspring of a one-eyed goat

And lame, twelve years a gelding, gnawn by worms.

Unfit, I carried children on my back.

Such was the fruit of my lasciviousness. (p. 157)

The next time she was born a calf and was again castrated, and as a bullock pulled a plow and a cart. Then, as the worst of that evil kamma's results had already ripened, Isidasi returned to the human realm. But it was still an uncertain kind of birth as she was the hermaphroditic child of a slave. That life too did not last long.

Next, she was the daughter of a man oppressed by debts. One of her father's creditors took her in lieu of payment. She became the wife of that merchant's son, but she "brought discord and enmity within that house."

In her final lifetime, no matter how hard she tried, no home she was sent to as a bride would keep her more than a brief while. Several times her virtuous father had her married to appropriate suitors. She tried to be the perfect wife, but each time she was thrown out. This inability to remain with a husband created an opportunity for her to break through the cycle of results. After her third marriage disintegrated, she decided to enter the Sangha. All her mental defilements were eliminated by meditation, insight into the Four Noble Truths matured, and Isidasi became an arahant.

She also developed the ability to see her past lives and thus saw how this whole causal chain of unwholesome deeds committed long ago brought their results in her successive existences:

Fruit of my kamma was it thus that they

In this last life have slighted me even though

I waited on them as their humble slave.

The last line of her poem puts the past, rebirth and all its sufferings, completely behind with a "lion's roar": "Enough! Of all that now have I made an end." (p. 163)

In Isidasi's tale we have several instructive illustrations of the inexorable workings of the law of kamma. The suffering she had to undergo because of sexual misconduct lasted through seven difficult lives.

But the seeds of wisdom had also been sown and when the force of the bad kamma was used up, the powerful paramis she had created earlier bore their fruit. Hence Isidasi was able to become a bhikkhuni, purify her mind perfectly, and so eliminate all possible causes of future suffering. The beginning, the middle, and the ending of every life are always due to causes and conditions.

We have now come full circle with these stories of the theris and have returned to the theme of impersonal causes and effects working themselves out, without any lasting being committing deeds or experiencing results.

The infinite sequence of lifetimes steeped in ignorance and suffering is repeated over and over until accumulated paramis and present wisdom, aided by other factors, become sufficiently strong to enable one to see through the craving which has perpetually propelled the succession of aggregates. Through this process these bhikkhunis clearly perceived that their attachments and aversions were the source of all their suffering. Because of this insight, they were able to dissolve the knots of old delusion-based conditioning.

With their completed understanding of suffering, the First Noble Truth, and the abandoning of craving, the Second Noble Truth, their practice of the Noble Eightfold Path, the Fourth Noble Truth, was perfected. They attained the cessation of suffering, the Third Noble Truth, in that very lifetime, and were never reborn again.

The poems of these enlightened nuns, telling how they came to meet the Buddha, how they had built up wisdom and other meritorious kamma over many previous lives, how they understood the Buddha's teachings, and how they attained Arahatship, offer us inspiration and guidance. They can help us present-day Buddhists to practice Vipassana meditation and to gain insight into suffering and its causes. Then we too will be able to give up all craving by developing wisdom. We can use the messages of the theris to assist us in putting an end to our own suffering.

Grateful for their assistance, may we all follow in the footsteps of these great nuns, true daughters of the Buddha. May our minds be perfect in wisdom, perfectly pure, and utterly free from all possibility of future suffering.

6

Buddha's Teachings to Nirvana

ADMISSION OF MAHAPRAJAPATI

Mahaprajapati was musing. She knew the vanity of this world. She wanted to flee the palace, to flee Kapilavastu, and lead a life of holiness. "How happy is the Master! How happy are the disciples!" she thought. "Why can I not do as they do? Why can I not live as they live? But they oppose women. We are not admitted to the community, and I must remain in this mournful city, to me deserted; I must remain in this mournful palace, empty in my sight!"

She grieved. She laid aside her costly robes; she gave her jewels to her handmaidens, and she was humble before all creatures.

One day, she said to herself:

"The Master is kind; he will take pity on me. I shall go to him, and perhaps he will be willing to receive me into the community."

The Master was in a wood, near Kapilavastu. Mahaprajapati went to him, and in a timid voice, she said: "Master, only you and your disciples can be really happy. Yet I, too, like you and those who accompany you, wish to walk in the path of salvation. May the favour be granted me to enter the community, O Blessed One."

The Master remained silent. She continued:

"How can I be happy in a world I despise? I know its meretricious joys. I long to walk in the path of salvation.

May the favour be granted me to enter the community, O Blessed One. And I know many women who are willing to follow me. May the favour be granted us to enter the community, O Blessed One."

The Master still remained silent. She continued:

"My palace is cheerless and dreary. The city is wrapped in darkness. The embroidered veils weigh heavily upon my brow; the diadems, the bracelets and the necklaces hurt me. I must walk in the path of salvation. Many earnest women, many women of great piety, are ready to follow me. May the favour be granted women to enter the community, O Blessed One."

For the third time, the Master remained silent. Mahaprajapati, her eyes full of tears, returned to her gloomy palace. But she would not accept defeat. She resolved to seek the Master once again and plead with him.

He was then in the great wood, near Vaisali. Mahaprajapati cut off her hair, and putting on a reddish-coloured robe made of a coarse material, she set out for Vaisali.

She made the trip on foot; she never once complained of weariness. Covered with dust, she finally arrived at the hall where the Buddha was meditating. But she did not dare to enter; she stood outside the door, with tears in her eyes. Ananda happened to pass by. He saw her and asked:

"O queen, why have you come here, dressed in this manner? Why are you standing before the Master's door?"

"I dare not enter his presence. Three times, already, he has denied my plea, and that which he has thrice refused, I have come to ask him again: that the favour be granted me, that the favour be granted women, to enter the community."

"I shall intercede for you, O queen," said Ananda.

He entered the hall. He saw the Master, and he said to him:

"Blessed One, Mahaprajapati, our revered queen, is standing before your door. She dares not appear before you; she is afraid you will again turn a deaf ear to her

plea. Yet it is not the plea of a foolish woman, Blessed One. Would it mean so much to you to grant it? The queen was a mother to you, once; she was always kind to you; surely she deserves to be heard. Why should you not receive women into the community? There are women of great piety, women with the saintly courage to keep in the path of holiness."

"Ananda," said the Master, "do not ask me to permit women to enter the community."

Ananda left. The queen was waiting for him.

"What did the Master say," she asked, anxiously.

"He denies your plea. But do not lose hope."

The following day, Ananda again went to the Blessed One.

"Mahaprajapati has not left the wood," said he. "She is thinking of the happy days of her youth. Maya was then alive; Maya, the most beautiful of all women; Maya, to whom a son would be born. Maya's sister was a noble woman: she knew nothing of envy she loved this child, even before it came into the world. And when it was born, to bring joy to all creatures, Queen Maya died. Mahaprajapati was kind to the motherless boy: he seemed so frail. She protected him from harm; she gave him devoted nurses; she shielded him from the influence of evil servants; she lavished her care and her tenderness upon him. He grew older, and still she would not leave him. She anticipated his least wishes; she worshipped him. And he attained the happiest fortune; he is the giant tree that shelters the wise; and now, when she would seek a humble place in his shadow, she is refused the peace and rest to which she aspires. O Master, be not unjust; receive Mahaprajapati into the community."

The Master pondered; then he gravely spoke these words:

"Listen, Ananda. Go to Mahaprajapati and tell her that I am willing to receive her into the community, but that she must conform to certain very strict rules. These are the observances I shall require of the women in the community: a nun, even if she has been a nun for a

hundred years, must rise in the presence of a monk and show him every mark of deep respect, even though he has been a monk for only a day; the nuns must go to the monks for a public confession of their transgressions and for instruction in the sacred word; nuns guilty of a grave offense must submit to a fitting punishment, for fifteen days, in front of the whole community of monks and nuns; before nuns are admitted to the community, their constancy and their virtue must be tried for a period of two years; the nuns will not be allowed to exhort the monks, but the monks will be allowed to exhort the nuns. These are the observances which, in addition to the observances already known to the monks, will be required of all the nuns."

Mahaprajapati joyfully promised to observe these rules. She entered the community, and within a few months, many women had followed her example.

But, one day, the Master said to Ananda:

"If women had not been admitted to the community, Ananda, chastity would have been preserved a long time, and the true faith would have lived, vigorous and serene, for a thousand years.. But now that women are admitted to the community, Ananda, chastity will be in danger, and the true faith, in all its vigour, will live only five hundred years."

BUDDHA EXPOSES THE IMPOSTERS

From Vaisali, the Master went to Cravasti, to Jeta's park. One day, King Prasenajit came to see him. "My Lord," said the king, "six hermits have recently arrived in Cravasti. They

do not believe in your law. They maintain that your knowledge is not equal to theirs, and they have tried to astonish me by performing numerous prodigies. I believe their statements to be untrue, but it would be well, my Lord, if you were to confound their audacity. The world's salvation depends upon your glory. So appear before these cheats and impostors and silence them."

"King," replied the Buddha, "order a great hall to be built near the city. Have it finished in seven days. I shall proceed there. Arrange to have the evil hermits present, and you will then see who performs the greatest prodigies, they or I."

Prasenajit ordered the hall to be built.

While awaiting the day of the trial, the lying hermits sought to delude the Master's faithful followers, and those who refused to listen to their evil words incurred their bitter enmity. Now, the Master had no truer friend in Cravasti than Prince Kala, a brother of Prasenajit. Kala had shown his utter contempt for the hermits, and they decided to take their revenge.

Kala was a very handsome man. One day, as he was walking through the royal gardens, he met one of Prasenajit's wives, and she playfully threw him a garland of flowers. The hermits heard of the incident, and they told the king that his brother had tried to seduce one of his wives. The king flew into a great rage, and without giving Kala a chance to justify himself, he had his hands and feet cut off.

Poor Kala suffered pitifully. His friends stood around his couch, weeping. One of the evil hermits happened to pass by.

"Come, show your power," they said to him. "You know that Kala is innocent. Make him well again!"

"He believes in the son of the Sakyas," replied the hermit. "It behooves the Sakyas' son to make him well again."

Then Kala began to sing:

"How can the Master of the worlds fail to see my misery? Let us worship the Lord who no longer knows desire; let us adore the Blessed One who takes pity on all creatures."

Ananda suddenly appeared before him.

"Kala," said he, "the Master has taught me the words that will heal your wounds." He recited a few verses, and the prince immediately recovered the use of his limbs.

"Henceforth," he exclaimed, "I shall serve the Master! However humble the tasks which he may assign to me, I shall perform them with joy, to please him."

And he followed Ananda to Jeta's park. The Master received him graciously and admitted him to the community.

The day arrived on which the Master was to compete with the hermits. Early in the morning, King Prasenajit went to the hall he had built for this occasion. The six hermits were already there. They exchanged glances and smiled.

"King," said one of them, "we are the first to arrive at the place of meeting."

"Do you suppose the one we are expecting will really come?" said another.

"Hermits," said the king, "do not scoff at him. You know how he sent one of his disciples to cure my brother whom I had unjustly punished. He will come. He may even be here, in our midst, without our knowing it."

As the king finished speaking, a luminous cloud filled the hall. It became lighter and lighter; it melted into the daylight, and the Buddha appeared, arrayed in golden splendour. Behind him stood Ananda and Kala. Ananda held a red flower in his hand, Kala a yellow flower, and never, in all the gardens of Cravasti, had any one seen two such flowers as these.

Prasenajit showed his profound admiration. The evil hermits ceased their laughter.

The Blessed One spoke:

"The glowworm shines for all to see, as long as the sun stays hidden, but when the blazing star appears, the poor worm quenches his feeble light. The impostors spoke loudly as long as the Buddha was silent, but now that the Buddha speaks, they weep with fear and are silent."

The hermits were alarmed. They saw the king viewing them with a scornful eye, and they hung their heads in shame.

Suddenly, the roof of the hall disappeared, and on the dome of the sky, stretching from the east to the west, the Master traced a course over which he proceeded to travel. At the sight of this prodigy, his most insolent rival fled in terror. The hermit imagined he was being pursued by a howling pack of hounds, and he never stopped running until he came to the edge of a pool. There, he tied a stone to his neck and threw himself into the water. A fisherman found his body the following day.

In the meanwhile, the Master had created a being in his own image, and, with him, he was now walking in the celestial path. And his great voice was heard, saying:

"O my disciples, I am about to ascend to the abode of the Gods and the Goddesses. Maya, my mother, has summoned me; I must instruct her in the law. I shall remain with her three months. But, each day, I shall descend to earth, and Sariputra, alone, will know where to find me; he will rule the community according to my instructions. And while I am absent from the sky, I shall leave with my mother, to instruct her, this being whom I have created in mine own image."

SUPRABHA

At the end of three months, the Master descended to earth and took the road to Cravasti. As he was approaching Jeta's park, he met a young girl. She was the servant of a wealthy inhabitant of the city who happened to be working in the fields that day. She was taking him a bowl of rice for his meal. At the sight of the Buddha, she felt strangely happy.

"It is the Master, the Blessed One," she thought. "My eyes behold him; my hands could almost touch him, he is so near. Oh, what a holy joy it would be to give him alms! But I have nothing of my own."

She sighed. Her glance fell on the bowl of rice.

"This rice... My master's meal... No master can reduce to slavery one who is already a slave. Mine could strike me, but what of that! He could put me in chains, but I would bear them lightly. I shall give the rice to the Blessed One."

She presented the bowl to the Buddha. He accepted it and continued on his way to Jeta's park. The young girl, her eyes shining with happiness, went to look for her master.

"Where is my rice?" he asked, as soon as he saw her.

"I gave it to the Buddha as an alms. Punish me if you will, I shall not weep; I am too happy for what I have done."

He did not punish her. He bowed' his head and said:

"No, I shall not punish you. I am asleep and your eyes are open. Go; you are no longer a slave."

The young girl made a deep obeisance.

"With your permission then," said she, "I shall go to Jeta's park, and I shall ask the Blessed One to instruct me in the law."

"Go," said the man.

She went to Jeta's park; she sat at the Buddha's feet, and she became one of the most saintly women in the community.

Among those who sought instruction from the Blessed One at the same time as this young slave was Suprabha, the daughter of a prominent citizen of Cravasti. Suprabha was very beautiful. To see her was to fall in love with her, and she was courted by all the distinguished young men of the city. This caused her father no little concern. "To which one shall I give her in marriage?" he would repeatedly ask himself; "those whom I refuse will become my bitter enemies."

And for hours at a time, he would remain deep in thought.

One day, Suprabha said to him:

"You seem to be troubled, dear father. What is the reason?"

"Daughter," he replied, "you alone are the cause of my anxiety. There are so many in Cravasti who wish to marry you!"

"You are afraid to make a choice from among my suitors," said Suprabha. "Poor men! If they but knew my thoughts! Do not be anxious, father! Tell them to assemble, and, according to the ancient custom, I shall go among them, and I myself shall choose a husband from their number."

"I shall do as you wish, daughter."

Suprabha's father went to King Prasenajit and received permission to have a herald proclaim throughout the city:

"That seven days from this day, there will be held an assembly of all the young men who wish to marry Suprabha. The young girl herself will select a husband from among their number."

On the seventh day, a host of suitors gathered in the magnificent garden belonging to Suprabha's father. She appeared, riding in a chariot. She was holding a yellow banner on which was painted the picture of the Blessed One. She was singing his praises. They all looked at her in amazement, and they wondered, "What will she say to us?" She finally addressed the young men.

"I can not love any of you," said she, "but do not think that I spurn you. Love is not my aim in life; I want to take refuge with the Buddha. I shall go to the park where he dwells, and he will instruct me in the law."

Mournfully, the young men withdrew, and Suprabha went to Jeta's park. She heard the Blessed One speak; she was admitted to the community, and she became a most devoted nun.

One day, as she was leaving the sacred gardens, she was recognized by one of her former suitors who happened to be passing with several friends.

"We must carry off this woman," said he. "I loved her once; I still love her. She shall be mine."

His friends agreed to help him. Before Suprabha was aware of it, she was surrounded, and they suddenly rushed upon her. But as they were about to seize her, she directed her thought toward the Buddha, and, immediately, she rose in the air. A crowd gathered; Suprabha soared above them for a while, then, flying with the grace and majesty of a swan, she returned to her sacred dwelling.

And their cries followed her:

"O saintly one, you make manifest the power of the faithful; O saint, you render manifest the power of the Buddha. It would be unjust to condemn you to the earthly pleasures of love, O saintly one, O saint."

VIRUPA

King Prasenajit had a daughter named Virupa. She had reached a marriageable age. Unfortunately, she was extremely ugly; no prince or warrior would have her for a wife, and even the merchants looked at her askance.

But presently a wealthy stranger came to live in Cravasti. His name was Ganga. The king thought, "Ganga has never seen my daughter. Perhaps he will not refuse to marry her." And he summoned him to the palace.

Ganga was highly flattered by Prasenajit's offer. He was of humble birth, and although, as a merchant, he had amassed a great fortune, he had never dreamed of marrying a princess. He therefore accepted the proposal.

"Then come to the palace this very evening," said the king, "and take my daughter home with you."

He obeyed. The night was dark, and the wedding took place without Ganga having seen his betrothed. Then Virupa accompanied her husband to his home.

Ganga saw his wife the next day. Her ugliness frightened him. He wanted to turn her out of the house, but he did not dare; he feared the king's vengeance. He kept her at home, but she was virtually a prisoner; she was not allowed to go out, for any reason whatsoever.

She was very unhappy. In vain she gave her husband constant proof of her affection; he only showed his aversion and his contempt for her. He never looked at her. He hardly spoke to her. And Virupa felt lonely and forlorn.

One day, Ganga was invited to a feast given by some of his friends. "Whoever comes without wife," he was warned, "will be fined five hundred pieces of gold."

Ganga decided to attend; it would relieve the monotony of his existence. But he did not want to show Virupa to his friends; he was afraid of being ridiculed. "I shall pay the five hundred pieces of gold," he thought, "and they will not make fun of me." That day, Virupa was sadder than usual. She knew where her husband had gone, and she wept. She said to herself:

"What good is a life as dreary as mine? I never have any pleasure. My master loathes me. And I can not blame him; I am ugly; every one has told me so. I have brought joy to no one. Oh, I loathe myself. Death would be better than this life I lead; death would be sweet. I shall kill myself."

She took a rope and hung herself.

At that same moment, in Jeta's park, the Master was wondering, "Who is suffering today in Cravasti? Whom can I save from misery? To what unfortunate being can I lend a helping hand?"

By his power of divination, he learned of Virupa's distress. He flew to Ganga's house; he entered. Virupa was still alive. The Master loosened the rope she had fastened about her neck. She breathed deeply and looked around. She recognized the Master. She fell at his feet and made him a pious offering. Then he said:

"Look at yourself in a mirror, Virupa."

She obeyed. She uttered a cry of joy and astonishment. She was as beautiful as a daughter of the Gods. Again she wanted to worship the Buddha, but he had disappeared. In the meanwhile, Ganga had not been spared the banter of his friends.

"Why did you come without your wife?" they asked him. "Are you afraid to let us see her? She must be very beautiful. You jealous husband!"

Ganga was at a loss for an answer. The feast bored him. One of his friends handed him a cup of intoxicating wine.

"Drink, Ganga," said he. "We laugh, and you are almost in tears. Come, laugh with us. Drink; this wine will teach you to laugh."

Ganga took the cup. He drank. He became livelier. He drank again. Presently, he was drunk. And he kept on drinking until, finally, he fell into a heavy sleep.

"Let us hurry over to his house, while he is asleep," said his friends. "We shall see his wife, and we shall find out why he keeps her out of sight."

They entered Ganga's home. Virupa had the mirror in her hand; she was looking at herself. Her eyes were bright with happiness. All the guests admired her, and they went away, quietly, saying, "We now understand Ganga's jealousy."

Ganga was still sleeping. They awoke him and said:

"Great is your felicity, friend. What did you do that was so pleasing to the Gods, to deserve a wife of such rare beauty?"

"This is too much!" cried Ganga. "What have I ever done to you that you should insult me so cruelly?"

And he abruptly left them. He was raging with anger and mortification. He flung open the door of his house; he strode through the halls, muttering imprecations; but, suddenly, the curses died upon his lips. He turned pale with astonishment. Before him was standing a woman of incomparable beauty. She was smiling. He slowly came to his senses; then he, too, smiled, and he asked:

"O you who appear before me like some radiant Goddess new-risen from her bed of flowers, O well-beloved, who made you so beautiful?"

Virupa told him the story. From that day, she and her husband knew true happiness, and they both sought every opportunity to evince their faith in the Buddha and show him their gratitude.

SINCA'S DECEIT

In the meanwhile, the evil hermits, whose imposture the Buddha had exposed, were being treated with contempt by the populace, and each day their desire for vengeance grew more intense. They had established themselves near Jeta's park, and night and day they spied upon the Buddha and his disciples. But all in vain; they saw nothing that gave them the slightest excuse for slandering the community.

At last, one of the hermits said to his companions:

"We have long been observing the conduct of these monks. Their virtue can not be denied. Still, we must turn the

minds of the people against them, and I think I have found a way. I know a young girl of great charm. Her name is Sinca. She is very clever at practising deceit. She will not refuse to help us, and soon the glory of this Sakya will vanish."

The hermits sent word to Sinca. She came. "Why did you send for me?" she asked.

"Do you know the monk from Kapilavastu, the one who is worshipped as the Buddha?"

"No, but I know of his great fame. I have been told of the many prodigies he has performed."

"This man is our bitterest enemy, Sinca. He treats us shamefully and would destroy our power. Now, you believe in us; come, take our part. She who will have conquered the conqueror may well be proud; she will be famous among women, and the world will ring with her praises."

Sinca was carried away by the hermit's words. She assured him that the Buddha would soon be disgraced and his name hated throughout the earth.

Each day, now, she went to Jeta's park, at a time when those who had been listening to the Master preach were beginning to leave. She was dressed in flaming red, and she carried flowers in her arms. And if, by chance, some one asked her, "Where are you going?" she would reply, "What business is it of yours?" When she came to the park, she waited until she was quite alone; then, instead of entering the Buddha's domain, she set out for the dwelling of the evil hermits. There, she spent the night, but at dawn she returned to the gates of the park, and when she was sure to be seen by the early risers on their way to their devotions, she would leave and return home. And to those who asked, "Where do you come from, so early in the morning?" she would reply, "What business is it of yours?"

At the end of one month, she gave a different answer. In the evening she would say, "I am going to Jeta's park, where the Blessed One is waiting for me," and in the morning, "I have just come from Jeta's park, where I spent the night with the

Blessed One." And there were some poor, credulous people who believed her and who suspected the Master of unchastity.

The sixth month, she took a piece of cloth and wrapped it around her body. "She is pregnant," they thought, and the fools maintained that the Master's virtue was only a pretense.

When the ninth month arrived, she tied a wooden ball to the thick girdle about her waist, and when she walked, she assumed a languorous gait. Finally, one night, she entered the hall where the Master was expounding the law. Boldly, she faced him, and her strident voice interrupted his speech.

"Sweet is your voice and honeyed your words as you instruct the people in the law. While I, who am pregnant because of you, I, who am soon to become a mother, have not even a place for my confinement! You would deny me the very oil and butter I need. If it would make you blush, now, to look after me, you could at least entrust me to one of your disciples, or to King Prasenajit, or to the merchant Anathapindika. But no! I am nothing to you any more, and little you care about the child that will be born! You would know all the joys of love, but the responsibilities you would ignore!" "Is that a lie or are you telling the truth, Sinca?" asked the Master, calmly. "Only you and I know."

"You know very well I am not lying," cried Sinca.

The Master retained his composure. But Indra, who had been watching from the sky, decided it was time to expose Sinca's impudence. He had four Gods take the form of mice. They crawled under her robe and gnawed at the string that was holding the wooden ball. The ball fell to the ground.

"There, your child is born," exclaimed the Master with a laugh.

The disciples turned upon. Sinca in their rage. They reviled her; they spat in her face; they beat her. She fled. She was weeping with pain and shame and anger. Suddenly, red flames sprang up around her and enveloped her in a mantle of fire, and she, who had dared to slander the Buddha, came to a cruel and terrible end.

TAMING A WILD BUFFALO

The Master left Jeta's park. He stopped in the cities and in the villages to preach the law, and full many there were to adopt the true faith.

One day, an old man and his wife invited the Master to take his meal with them.

"My Lord," said the old man, "we have long been eager to hear your word. We are happy, now that we know the sacred truths, and among your friends you will find none more devout than we."

"I am not surprised," replied the Buddha, "for you and I were near relations in our former existences."

"Master," said the woman, "my husband and I have lived together since our early youth; we have now attained a ripe old age. Life has been kind to us. Never has the slightest quarrel come between us. We still love each other as in the days gone by, and the evening of our lives is as sweet as was the dawn. May it be granted us, my Lord, to love each other in our next existence as we have loved one another in this life."

"It will be granted," said the Master; "the Gods have protected you!"

He continued on his way. He saw an old woman drawing water from a well by the side of the road. He approached her.

"I am thirsty," said he. "Will you give me a drink?"

The old woman stared at him. She was deeply moved. She began to weep. She wanted to embrace the Master, but she was afraid. The tears coursed down her cheeks.

"Embrace me," said the Master.

The old woman ran to his arms, and she murmured:

"Now I can die happy. I have seen the Blessed One, and it was given me to embrace him."

He went on. He came to a vast forest where a herd of buffaloes lived with their keepers. One of these buffaloes was a very powerful animal. He had an ugly temper. He barely tolerated the presence of his keepers, and at the approach of a stranger he would become aggressive. When the stranger came near, he would attack him with his horns, and he would often wound him seriously. Sometimes he killed him.

The keepers saw the Blessed One walking along, quietly, and they shouted:

> *"Take care, traveller. Do not come near us. There is a vicious buffalo here."*

But he paid no attention to the warning. He made straight for the spot where the buffalo was grazing.

All at once, the buffalo raised his head and sniffed noisily; then, lowering his horns, he rushed at the Master. The keepers trembled. "Our voices were not loud enough," they cried; "he did not hear us." But, suddenly, the animal stopped short; he knelt before the Master and began licking his feet. There was a look of pleading in his eyes. The Master gently stroked the buffalo. He spoke to him in a quiet voice.

"Say to yourself that all earthly things are transitory, that peace is found only in nirvana. Do not weep. Believe in me, believe in my goodness, in my compassion, and your condition will change. You will not be reborn among the animals, and, in time, you will attain the sky and dwell among the Gods."

From that day, the buffalo was extremely docile. And the keepers, who had expressed their admiration for the Master and who had given him what alms they could afford, were instructed in the law, and they became known for their piety, even among the most pious.

DISSENSION AMONG THE MONKS

The Master arrived at the city of Kausambi, and there, at first, he was very happy. The inhabitants eagerly listened to his words, and many of them became monks. King Udayana was among the believers, and he allowed his son Rashtrapala to enter the community.

Yet it was in Kausambi that the Master met with one of his great sorrows. A monk, one day, was reprimanded for committing some minor offense. He would not own himself in the wrong; so he was punished. He refused to submit to the punishment, and, as he was a pleasant man, of great wit and learning, there were many to take his part. In vain the others besought him to return to the straight path.

"Do not assume that conceited air," they said to him; "do not consider yourself incapable of making mistakes. Heed our wise advice. Address the other monks as they should be addressed who profess a faith that is also yours; they will address you as he should be addressed who professes a faith that is also theirs. The community will grow, the community will flourish, only if the monks will take counsel from one another."

"It is not for you to tell me what is right or wrong," he replied. "Stop reproving me."

"Do not say that. Your words offend against the law. You are defying discipline; you are sowing discord in the community. Come, mend your ways. Live at peace with the community. Avoid these quarrels, and be faithful to the law."

It was useless. They then decided to expel the rebel, but, once again, he refused to obey. He would remain in the community: since he was innocent, there was no need to submit to an unjust punishment.

The Master finally intervened. He tried to pacify the monks; he pleaded with them to forget their grievances and to unite, as before, in the performance of their sacred duties, but no one paid any attention. And, one day, a monk even had the audacity to say to him:

> *"Keep still, O Master; do not bother us with your speeches. You have arrived at a knowledge of the law; meditate upon it. You will find your meditations quite delightful. As for us, we shall know where to go; our quarrels will not keep us from finding the way. Meditate, and be quiet."*

The Master was not angry. He tried to speak, but it was impossible, He saw then that he could never convince the monks of Kausambi; they seemed to be possessed with some sudden folly. The Master decided to forsake them, but first he said to them:

> *"Happy is he who has a faithful friend; happy is he who has a discerning friend. What obstacles could two wise and virtuous friends not overcome? But he who has no faithful friend resembles a king without a country: he must roam in solitude, like the elephant in the wild forest. Yet it is better to travel alone than in the company of a fool. The wise man should follow a lonely path; he should avoid evil and should preserve his serenity, like the elephant in the wild forest."*

He left. No one tried to stop him. He went to a village where he knew he would find his disciple Bhrigu. Bhrigu was overjoyed to see him, and the Master was not a little comforted. Then, Anuruddha, Nanda and Kimbala joined him. They gave him every proof of their respect and friendship, and they lived at peace with one another. And the Master thought, "So there are some, among my disciples, who love me and who do not quarrel."

One day, as he sat down in the shade of a tree and began thinking of the troublous times in Kausambi, a herd of elephants stopped to rest not far from him. The biggest elephant went down to the river and drew water which he brought back to the others. They drank; then, instead of thanking him for doing them this service, they abused him, they beat him with their trunks, and, finally, they drove him away.

And the Master saw that his own experience was not unlike that of the elephant: they were both victims of gross ingratitude. The elephant noticed the sadness in his face; he drew near and looked at him tenderly; then left, to go in search of food and drink for him.

The Master finally returned to Cravasti and rested in Jeta's park.

But it still grieved him to think of the cruel monks of Kausambi. One morning, however, he saw them enter the park. They were in great distress: alms had been denied them, for every one was indignant at their treatment of the Master. They had come to beg his forgiveness. The guilty monk confessed himself to have been in the wrong, and his punishment was light. His adversaries, as well as his friends, admitted the error of their ways, and all promised strictly to obey the rules. And the Master was happy: there was no longer any dissension in the community.

KUVALAYA THE DANCER

One day, he returned to the country of Rajagriha.

In a field, not far from the city, he came upon a Brahman named Bharadvaja. It was the harvest season, and the Brahman and his servants were joyously celebrating. They were laughing and singing as the Master went by. He held out his alms-bowl, and those who recognized him, greeted him and made him many friendly offerings. This displeased Bharadvaja. He went up to the Master, and he said to him in a loud voice:

> *"Monk, tarry not in our midst; you set an evil example. We work, we that are here, and with watchful eyes, we observe the changes of seasons. When it is time to plow, my servants plow; when it is time to sow, they sow; and I plow and sow with them. Then the day comes when we harvest the fruit of our labour. We provide our own food, and when it is stored away, we have good reason to rest and play. While you, you roam the streets and walk the roads, and the only trouble you deign to take is to hold out a bowl to those you meet. It would be better far for you to work; it would be better far to plow and sow."*

The Master smiled and answered:

> *"Friend, like you I plow and sow, and when my work is done, I eat."*

"You plow? You sow?" said Bharadvaja. "How can I believe that? Where are your cattle? Where is your grain? Where is your plow?"

The Master said:

> *"Purity of understanding, that is the glorious seed I sow. Works of holiness are the rain that falls upon the fertile earth where the seed sprouts and ripens. And mine is a mighty plow: it has wisdom for its plowshare,*

the law for its handles, and an active faith is the powerful bullock yoked to its pole. Desire is uprooted like weeds in the fields I plow, and I gather in the richest of harvests, nirvana."

He continued on his way. But the Brahman Bharadvaja followed him; he would now hear the sacred word.

They entered the city. On the public square, a large crowd was watching a troop of dancers. The daughter of the leader-was attracting particular attention. Such grace and beauty had seldom been seen, and, whenever she appeared, those who were not master of their passions burned with the desire to possess her. Her name was Kuvalaya.

She had just finished dancing. Ardent eyes were still fastened upon her. She was aware of her power, and full of pride and audacity, she shouted 'to the crowd:

"Admire me, my lords! In all Rajagriha is there one who can surpass Kuvalaya in beauty, are there any who can even equal her?"

"Yes, woman," replied the Brahman Bharadvaja. "What is your beauty when compared with the beauty of the Master?"

"I would see this Master whose beauty you praise," said Kuvalaya; "lead me to him."

"Here he is," said the Blessed One.

And he came forward.

The dancer stared at him.

"You are beautiful," she said at last. "I shall dance for you."

Kuvalaya danced. The dance began slowly. She had wrapped all her veils about her, even covering her face, and the beauty once so boldly flaunted was now only a dim promise. She was like the moon, hiding behind soft clouds from the gaze of night. A cloud flew away; a faint ray escaped through the rift. The dance became more rapid; one by one the veils fell away, and the queen of the stars appeared in all her glory. Faster and faster she whirled; suddenly, a blinding light flashed in her eyes, and she stopped. She was naked. The crowd gasped and surged forward.

"Unhappy woman!" said the Buddha.

He looked at her intently. Whereupon Kuvalaya's cheeks became sunken, her forehead wrinkled and her eyes grew dull. Only a few ugly teeth were left in her mouth; only a few thin strands of grey hair still hung from her head, and she was stooped as with age. The Blessed One had punished her as he had once punished Mara's daughters when they had tried to tempt him; he had changed the beautiful dancer into a shrivelled old woman.

She sighed:

"Master, I know the great wrong I have done. An ephemeral beauty had made me vain. You taught me a bitter lesson, but I feel that some day I shall be happy to have received it. Let me learn the sacred truths; then may I be released for ever from this body that, even when it was the delight of men, was nothing but a loathsome corpse."

The Master granted Kuvalaya's request, and she became one of the most devout of the Buddha's faithful followers.

GOD ALAVAKA DEFEATED BY THE BUDDHA

In the city of Atavi there ruled a king who was very fond of hunting. One day, he saw an enormous deer and started in pursuit. The deer was fleet of foot, and in the heat of the chase, the king lost sight of the other hunters. Finally, the prey escaped, and weary and discouraged, the king sat down under a tree. He fell asleep.

It happened that a wicked God named Alavaka lived in the tree. He liked to feed on human flesh, and he killed and devoured all who came near him. He saw the king; he rejoiced, and the poor hunter was about to be dealt a severe blow when a noise fortunately awoke him. He realized that his life was threatened; he made an attempt to rise, but the God took him by the throat and held him down. Then the king tried to plead with him.

"Spare me, my lord!" said he. "By your terrifying appearance, I know you to be one of the Gods that eat human flesh. Oh, deign to be kind to me. You will have no cause to regret your mercy. I shall reward you with magnificent gifts."

"What care I for gifts!" replied Alavaka. "It is your flesh I want; it will appease my hunger."

"My lord," replied the king, "if you let me return to Atavi, I shall send you a man every day to satisfy your hunger."

"When you get back to your home, you will forget this promise."

"No," said the king, "I never forget a promise. Besides, if I should once fail to make this daily offering, you have only to come to my palace and tell me of your grievance, and, immediately, without resisting, I shall follow you, and you may devour me."

The God allowed himself to be persuaded, and the king returned to the city of Atavi. But he kept thinking of his cruel promise; there was no way he could evade it, and henceforth he would have to he a hard and ruthless master.

He sent for his minister and told him what had happened. The minister considered for a moment, then said to the king:

> *"My lord, in the prison of Atavi there are criminals who have been condemned to death. We can send them to the God. When he sees that you are keeping faith with him, perhaps he will relieve you of your promise."*

The king approved of the suggestion. Guards were sent to the prison, and to those whose days were numbered they said:

> *"Not far from the city there is a tree inhabited by a God who is very fond of rice. Whoever leaves a plate of rice for him at the foot of the tree will be granted a full pardon."*

Whereupon, each day, one of these men, carrying a plate of rice, joyously set out for the tree, never to return.

Presently, there were no men condemned to death left in prison. The minister ordered the judges to be extremely severe and to acquit no one accused of murder except on irrefutable proof of his innocence, but it was in vain; some new way had to be found for appeasing the hunger of the God. Then they began to sacrifice the thieves.

In spite of all their efforts to apprehend the guilty, the prison was again empty, and the king and his minister were compelled to look for victims among the worthy inhabitants of the city. Old people were carried off and forcibly led to the tree, and if the guards were not fleet-footed, the God would sometimes devour them and the victims as well.

A vague uneasiness possessed the city of Atavi. The old people were seen to disappear; no one knew what became of them. And, each day, the king's remorse grew more poignant. But he lacked the courage to sacrifice his life to the welfare of his people. He thought:

"Will no one come to my assistance? There lives in Cravasti, and sometimes in Rajagriha, I have been told, a man of great power, a Buddha, whose prodigies are loudly praised. They say he is fond of travelling. Why, then, does he not come into my kingdom?"

By his power of divination, the Buddha knew of the king's desire. He flew through the air and came to Alavaka's tree. There, he sat down. The God saw him. He started walking toward him, but, suddenly, he became powerless. His knees trembled. Fury seized him.

"Who are you?" he asked, fiercely.

"A being far more powerful than yourself," replied the Buddha.

Alavaka was in a terrible rage. He would have liked to torture this man who was sitting on the ground in front of him, this man whom he could not reach; he would have liked to torture him to death. The Buddha never lost his composure.

Alavaka finally managed to control himself. He thought that cunning would perhaps succeed where strength had failed, and in a pleasant voice he said:

"I see you are a wise man, my Lord; it is always a pleasure for me to interrogate men of wisdom. I ask

them four questions. If they can answer, they are free to go wherever they please; if they can not answer, they remain my prisoners, and I devour them when I feel so disposed."

"Ask me the four questions," said the Buddha.

"I must warn you," said Alavaka, "that no one has ever answered them. You will find scattered around the bones of those I interrogated in the past."

"Ask me the four questions," repeated the Buddha.

"Well then," said Alavaka, "how can man avoid the river of passions? How can he cross the sea of existences and find safe harbour? How can he escape the tempests of evil? How can he be left untouched by the storm of desires?"

In a quiet voice, the Buddha replied:

"Man avoids the river of passions if he believes in the Buddha, in the law and in the community; he crosses the sea of existences and finds safe harbour if he understands works of holiness; he will escape the tempests of evil if he performs works of holiness; he will be left untouched by the storm of desires if he knows the sacred path that leads to deliverance."

When Alavaka heard the Master's answers, he fell at his feet and worshipped him, and he promised to change his savage ways. Then, together, they went to Atavi, to the palace of the king.

"King," said the God, "I release you from your pledge."

The king was happier than he had ever been before. When he knew who had saved him, he cried:

"I believe in you, my Lord, who have saved me and saved my people; I believe in you, and I shall dedicate my life to proclaiming your glory, the glory of the law and the glory of the community."

DEVADATTA EXPELLED FROM THE COMMUNITY

The monk Devadatta was possessed of an arrogant nature. He was impatient of any restraint. He aspired to supplant the

Buddha, but the monks, he knew, would not join him in an open revolt. For that he needed the support of some king or prince.

"King Bimbasara is an old man," he said to himself, one day; "Prince Ajatashatru, who is young and brave, is eager to succeed him to the throne. I could advise the prince to his advantage, and, in return, he could help me to become the head of the community."

He went to see Ajatashatru. He addressed him in flattering terms; he praised his strength, his courage, his beauty.

"Oh, if you were king," said he, "what glory would come to Rajagriha! You would conquer the neighboring states; all the sovereigns of the world would pay you homage: you would be the omnipotent master, and you would be worshipped like a God."

With such words as these, Devadatta won Ajatashatru's confidence. He received many precious gifts, and he became still more arrogant.

Maudgalyayana noticed Devadatta's frequent visits to the prince. He decided to warn the Blessed One.

"My Lord," he began, "Devadatta is very friendly with Prince Ajatashatru."

The Blessed One interrupted him.

"Let Devadatta do as he pleases; we shall soon know the truth. I am aware that Ajatashatru pays him homage; it does not advance him a single step in the path of virtue. Let Devadatta glory in his arrogance! It will be his ruin. As the banana-tree and the bamboo-tree bear fruit only to die, so will the honours Devadatta is receiving simply hasten his downfall."

Devadatta soon reached the height of vanity. He could not abide the Buddha's grandeur, and, one day, he made bold to say to him:

> *"Master, you are now well along in years; it is a great hardship for you to rule the monks; you should retire. Meditate in peace upon the sublime law you have discovered, and the community let me take charge of."*

The Master smiled quizzically.

"Be not concerned about me, Devadatta; you are too kind. I shall know when it is time to retire. For the present, I shall stay in charge of the community.

Besides, when the time does come, I shall not give it even to Sariputra or Maudgalyayana, those two great minds that are like blazing torches, and you want it, Devadatta, you who have such a mediocre intelligence, you who shed even less light than a night-lamp!" Devadatta bowed respectfully before the Master, but he could not hide the fire of anger in his eyes.

The Master then sent for learned Sariputra.

"Sariputra," said he, "go through the city of Rajagriha and cry in a loud voice: 'Beware of Devadatta! He has strayed from the path of righteousness. The Buddha is not responsible for his words or for his actions; the law no longer inspires him, the community no longer interests him. Henceforth, Devadatta speaks only for himself.'"

It grieved Sariputra to have such a painful mission to perform; however, he understood the Master's reasons, and he went through the city crying Devadatta's shame. The inhabitants stopped to listen, and some thought, "The monks envy Devadatta his friendship for Prince Ajatashatru." But the others said, "Devadatta must have committed a serious offense, for the Blessed One thus publicly to denounce him."

AJATASHATRU'S TREACHERY

Devadatta was musing: "Siddhartha thought to humiliate me by making light of my intelligence. I shall show him he is mistaken. My glory will overshadow his: the night-lamp will become the sun. But King Bimbasara is his faithful friend; he protects him. As long as the king is living, I can do nothing. Prince Ajatashatru, on the other hand, honours me and holds me in high esteem; he reposes implicit confidence in me. If he were to reign, I would get everything I desire."

He went to Ajatashatru's palace.

"Oh, prince," said he, "we are living in an unfortunate age! They that are best fitted to govern are likely to die without ever having reigned. Human life is so brief a thing! Your father's longevity causes me no little concern for you." He kept on talking, and he was presently giving the prince most evil advice. The prince was weak; he listened. Before long, he had decided to kill his father." Night and day, now, Ajatashatru wandered through the palace, watching for an opportunity to slip into his father's apartments and make away with him. But he could not escape the vigilance of the guards. His restlessness puzzled them, and they said to King Bimbasara:

"O king, your son Ajatashatru has been behaving strangely of late. Could he be planning an evil deed?"

"Be silent," replied the king. "My son is a man of noble character. It would not occur to him to do anything base."

"You ought to send for him, O king, and question him."

"Be silent, guards. Do not accuse my son lightly."

The guards continued to keep a close watch, and at the end of a few days, they again spoke to the king. To convince them that they were mistaken, the king summoned Ajatashatru. The prince appeared before his father. He was trembling.

"My lord," said he, "why did you send for me?"

"Son," said Bimbasara, "my guards say that you have been behaving strangely of late. They tell me you wander through the palace, acting mysteriously, and that you shun the gaze of those you meet. Son, are they not lying?"

"They are not lying, father," said Ajatashatru

Remorse suddenly overwhelmed him. He fell at the king's feet, and out of the depths of his shame, he cried:

"Father, I wanted to kill you."

Bimbasara shuddered. In a voice full of anguish, he asked:

"Why did you want to kill me?"

"In order to reign."

"Then reign," cried the king. "Royalty is not worth a son's enmity."

Ajatashatru was proclaimed king the next day.

The first thing he did was to have great honours paid to his father. But Devadatta still feared the old king's authority; he decided to use his influence against him. "As long as your father is allowed his freedom," he said to Ajatashatru, "you are in danger of losing your power. He still retains many followers; you must take measures to intimidate them."

Devadatta again was able to impose his will on Ajatashatru, and poor Bimbasara was thrown into prison. Ajatashatru presently decided to starve him to death, and he allowed no one to take him any food.

But Queen Vaidehi was sometimes permitted to visit Bimbasara in his prison, and she would take rice to him which he ate ravenously. Ajatashatru, however, soon put a stop to this; he ordered the guards to search her each time she went to see the prisoner. She then tried to hide the food in her hair, and when this, too, was discovered, she had to use great ingenuity to save the king from dying of hunger. But she was repeatedly found out, and Ajatashatru, finally, denied her access to the prison.

In the meanwhile, he was persecuting the Buddha's faithful followers. They were forbidden to look after the temple where Bimbasara, formerly, had placed a lock of the Master's hair and the parings of his finger-nails. No longer were flowers or perfume left there as pious offerings, and the temple was not even cleaned or swept.

In Ajatashatru's palace there dwelt a woman named Srimati. She was very devout. It grieved her to be unable to perform works of holiness, and she wondered how, in these sad times, she could prove to the Master that she had kept her faith. Passing in front of the temple, she complained bitterly to see it so deserted, and when she noticed how unclean it was, she wept.

"The Master shall know that there is still one woman in this house who would honour him," thought Srimati, and at the risk of her life, she swept out the temple and decorated it with a bright garland.

Ajatashatru saw the garland. He was greatly incensed and wanted to know who had dared to disobey him. Srimati did not try to hide; of her own accord, she appeared before the king. "Why did you defy my orders?" asked Ajatashatru. "If I defied your orders," she replied, "I respected those of your father, King Bimbasara."

Ajatashatru did not wait to hear further. Pale with fury, he rushed at Srimati and stabbed her with his dagger. She fell, mortally wounded; but her eyes were shining with joy, and in a happy voice, she sang:

"My eyes have seen the protector of the worlds; my eyes have seen the light of the worlds, and for him, in the night, I have lighted the lamps. For him who dissipates the darkness, I have dissipated the darkness. His brilliance is greater than the brilliance of the sun; his rays are purer than the rays of the sun, and my rapt gaze is dazzled by the splendour. For him who dissipates the darkness, I have dissipated the darkness."

And, dead, she seemed to glow with the light of sanctity.

THE DEATH OF DEVADATTA

Devadatta was eager to succeed the Buddha as head of the community. One day, he said to King Ajatashatru: "My lord, the Buddha holds you in contempt. He hates you. You must put him to death, for your glory is at stake. Send some men to the Bamboo Grove with orders to kill him; I shall lead the way." Ajatashatru was easily persuaded. The assassins came to the Bamboo Grove, but when they saw the Master, they fell at his feet and worshipped him. This added fuel to Devadatta's rage. He went to the royal stables where a savage elephant was kept, and he bribed the guards to release him when the Master passed by, so that the animal could gore him with his tusks or trample him underfoot. But at the sight of the Master, the elephant became quite gentle, and going up to him, with his trunk he brushed the dust from the sacred robes. And the Master smiled and said:

"This is the second time, thanks to Devadatta, that an elephant has paid homage to me."

Then Devadatta himself tried to do harm to the Master. He saw him meditating in the shade of a tree; and he had the audacity to throw a sharp stone at him. It struck him in the foot; the wound began to bleed. The Master said:

> *"You have committed a serious offense, Devadatta; the punishment will be terrible. Vain are your criminal attempts upon the life of the Blessed One; he will not meet with an untimely death. The Blessed One will pass away of his own accord, and at the hour he chooses."*

Devadatta fled. He decided he would no longer obey the rules of the community, and, wherever he could, he would seek followers of his own.

In the meanwhile, Bimbasara was starving. But he did not die. A mysterious force sustained him. His son finally decided to have him put to death, and he gave orders to burn the soles of his feet, to slash his limbs and to pour boiling oil and salt on the open wounds. The executioner obeyed, and even he wept to see an old man tortured.

A son was born to Ajatashatru on the day he issued the order for his father's death. When he saw the child, a great joy came to him; he relented, and he hurriedly sent guards to the prison to stop the execution. But they arrived too late; King Bimbasara had died amid frightful suffering.

Then Ajatashatru began to repent. One day, he heard Queen Vaidehi saying to the infant prince, as she carried him in her arms:

"May your father be as kind to you as his father was to him. Once, when he was a child, he had a sore on his finger; it hurt him, and he cried; no ointment would heal it; so Bimbasara put the finger to his lips and drew out the pus, and Ajatashatru was able to laugh again and play. Oh, love your father, little child; do not punish him with your cruelty for having been cruel to Bimbasara."

Ajatashatru shed bitter tears. He was overwhelmed with remorse. At night, in his dreams, he saw his father, bleeding from his wounds, and he heard him moan. He was seized with a burning fever, and the physician Jivaka was summoned to attend him. "I can do nothing for you," said Jivaka. "Your body is not sick. Go to the Perfect Master, the Blessed One, the Buddha; he alone knows the words of consolation that will restore you to health."

Ajatashatru took Jivaka's advice. He went to the Blessed One; he confessed his misdeeds and his crimes, and he found peace.

"Your father," the Buddha said to him, "has been reborn among the most powerful Gods; he knows of your repentance, and he forgives you. Heed me, King Ajatashatru; know the law, and cease to suffer."

Ajatashatru issued a proclamation, banishing Devadatta from the kingdom, and ordering the inhabitants to close their doors to him if he were to seek refuge in their homes.

Devadatta was then near Cravasti where he hoped to be received by King Prasenajit, but he was scornfully denied an audience and was told to leave the kingdom. Thwarted in his attempts to enlist followers, he finally set out for Kapilavastu.

He entered the city as night was falling. The streets were dark, almost deserted; no one recognized him as he passed, for how could this lean, wretched monk, slinking in the shadow of the walls, be identified with the proud Devadatta? He went straight to the palace where princess Gopa dwelt in solitude.

He was admitted to her presence.

"Monk," said Gopa, "why do you wish to see me? Do you bring me a message of happiness? Do you come with orders from a husband I deeply reverence?"

"Your husband! Little he cares about you! Think of the time he wickedly deserted you!"

"He deserted me for the world's salvation." "Do you still love him?"

"My love would defile the purity of his life."

"Then hate him with all your heart."

"With all my heart I respect him."

"Woman, he spurned you; take your revenge."

"Be quiet, monk. Your words are evil."

"Do you not recognize me? I am Devadatta, who loves you."

"Devadatta, Devadatta, I knew you were false and evil; I knew you would be a faithless monk, but I never suspected the depths of your villainy."

"Gopa, Gopa, I love you! Your husband scorned you, he was cruel. Take your revenge. Love me!"

Gopa blushed. From her gentle eyes fell tears of shame.

"It is you who scorn me! Your love would be an insult if it were sincere, but you lie when you say you love me. You seldom noticed me in the days when I was young, in the days when I was beautiful! And now that you see me, an old woman, worn out by my austere duties, you tell me of your love, of your guilty love! You are the most contemptible of men, Devadatta! Go away! Go away!"

In his rage he sprang at her. She put out her hand to protect herself, and he fell to the ground. As he rolled over, blood gushed from his mouth.

He fled. The Sakyas heard that he was in Kapilavastu; they made him leave the city under an escort of guards, and he was taken to the Buddha who was to decide his fate. He pretended to be repentant, but he had dipped his nails in a deadly poison, and as he lay prostrate before the Maser, he tried to scratch his ankle. The Master pushed him away with his toe; then the ground opened; fierce flames burst forth, and they swallowed up the infamous Devadatta.

PRASENAJIT AND AJATASHATRU

Although the Buddha had chastened Ajatashatru's spirit, there were times when the king still gave way to anger. One day, because of a quarrel between a man from Rajagriha and one from Cravasti, he declared war on King Prasenajit. He collected a vast army. There were foot-soldiers and horsemen; there were some mounted on chariots, others enclosed in towers carried by elephants, and swords and lances flashed in the sun as they marched into battle.

King Prasenajit also assembled his troops. He too had chariots and horses and elephants, and he advanced to meet Ajatashatru.

It was a terrible battle. It lasted four days. The first day Prasenajit lost his elephants; the second day he lost his horses; on the third, his chariots were destroyed; and on the fourth, his foot-soldiers were killed or made prisoners; and Prasenajit himself, defeated and panic-stricken, fled in the only chariot that had been saved in the disaster and escaped to Cravasti.

There, in a small, unlighted hall, he flung himself down on a low couch. He was silent, a prey to his melancholy thoughts. He never stirred; he appeared to be dead, except for the tears that coursed down his cheeks.

A man entered; it was the merchant Anathapindika.

"My lord," said he, "long may you live, and may the tide of victory turn!"

"My soldiers are dead," the king lamented, "all my soldiers are dead! My soldiers! My soldiers!"

"Grieve not, O king. Raise another army."

"I lost my fortune when I lost my army."

"King," said Anathapindika, "I shall give you the gold you need, and you will be victorious."

Prasenajit sprang to his feet.

"You have saved me, Anathapindika!" he exclaimed. "I am grateful."

With Anathapindika's gold, Prasenajit raised a formidable host. He marched against Ajatashatru.

When the two armies met, the din terrified the Gods themselves. Prasenajit used a battle array he had been taught by men from a distant land. He attacked swiftly; Ajatashatru had no defense. He, in turn, was defeated, and he was captured.

"Kill me," he cried to Prasenajit.

"I shall spare your life," said Prasenajit. "I shall take you to the Blessed Master, and he will decide your fate."

The Master had recently arrived at Jeta's park. Prasenajit said to him:

> *"Behold, O Blessed One! King Ajatashatru is my prisoner. He hates me, though I bear him no ill will. He attacked me, for some trivial reason, and defeated me at first, but now he is at my mercy. I do not wish to kill him, O Blessed One. For the sake of his father, Bimbasara, who was my friend, I would like to set him free."*

"Then set him free," said the Master. "Victory begets hatred; defeat begets suffering. They that are wise will forgo both victory and defeat. Insult is born of insult, anger of anger. They that are wise will forgo both victory and defeat. Every murderer is struck down by a murderer; every conqueror is struck down by a conqueror. They that are wise will forgo both victory and defeat."

In the presence of the Master, Ajatashatru promised to be a faithful friend to Prasenajit.

"And," he added, "let us be more than friends. I have a son, as you know, and you have a daughter, Kshema, who is still unmarried. Will you give your daughter to my son?"

"So be it," said Prasenajit. "And may this happy marriage be the earnest of our happy friendship."

The Master approved. The two kings ever after lived at peace with each other, and Ajatashatru became known for his gentleness.

THE BUDDHA TEACHES THE DOCTRINE

The Master was growing old. When he was in Rajagriha, he called the monks together, and he spoke to them at great length: "Monks, do not forget the precepts I have given you. Observe them carefully. You will assemble twice a month, and you will confess your transgressions to one another.

If you feel that you have done evil, and you keep it to yourself, you will be guilty of a lie. Admit your transgressions: the confession will bring you rest and peace. The four gravest sins a monk can commit are, as you know: to have intercourse with a woman; to steal anything whatsoever; to kill a human being or instigate a murder; and to pretend to possess a superhuman power that he knows he does not possess.

A monk who has committed one of these four sins must be expelled from the community. Monks, do not bandy words with women, and do not corrupt them. Do not bear false witness against your brothers.

Do not try to sow discord in the community. Do not strive to evade a reprimand. Never lie, and insult no one. Observe carefully, O monks, all the precepts I have given you."

He said further:

"Seriousness is the province of immortality; frivolity, the province of death. They that are serious do not die; they that are frivolous are always dead. Therefore would the wise be serious. The wise attain the supreme blessing, nirvana. He sees his glory increase who is energetic and can remember, who thinks honestly and acts deliberately, who is continent, who lives within the law, and who is serious. It is frivolity the fools and the weak-minded pursue; the wise treasure seriousness as a miser his gold. The monk who would be serious, who sees the danger of frivolity, shakes the evil law like the wind does the leaves; he tears asunder the bonds that bind him to the world; he is close to nirvana. Standing on the terrace of wisdom, released from all suffering, the serious man who has conquered frivolity looks out over the unhappy multitude, as, from the summit of a mountain, one might gaze upon the crowd in the plains below."

BUDDHA AND THE SHEPHERD

Before he died, the Blessed One decided to go on a long journey. He wanted to visit certain of his disciples and exhort them to observe his teachings with scrupulous care. With only Ananda for a companion, he left the city of Rajagriha.

One day, while he was resting in the corner of a field, he said to Ananda:

"There will come a time when men will wonder why I once entered a woman's womb. They will question the perfect purity of my birth, and they will doubt whether I ever had supreme power. These benighted men will never understand that, for him who devotes his life to works of holiness, the body is free from the impurity of birth. He who would seek supreme knowledge must enter a woman's womb; he must, out of pity for mankind, be born into the world of men. For if he were a God, how could he set in motion the wheel of the law? Imagine the Buddha as a God, Ananda; men would soon lose heart. They would say, 'The Buddha, who is a God, has happiness, holiness, perfection; but we, how can we hope to attain them?' And they would be in deep despair. Oh, let them keep still, these benighted creatures! Let them not try to steal the law, for they would use it ill. Rather, let them consider the Buddha's nature incomprehensible, these men who will never be able to gauge my eminence!"

A shepherd was crossing the field. He had the serenity of a man who is quietly performing a labour of joy.

"Who are you, shepherd?" the Master asked him.

"My name is Dhaniya," replied the shepherd.

"Where are you going?" asked the Master.

"I am going home to my wife and children."

"You seem to know pure happiness, shepherd?"

"I have boiled my rice, I have milked my cows," said the shepherd Dhaniya; "I live with my family on the banks of the river; my house is well roofed, my fire is lighted; so fall if you will, O rain of the sky.

"I am rid of anger, I am rid of stubbornness," said the Master; "I bide for a night on the banks of the river; my house has no roof, the fire of passions is quenched in my being; so fall if you will, O rain of the sky."

"The gadflies never torment my herd," said the shepherd Dhaniya; "my cows roam in the grassy meadows; they can abide the coming rain; so fall if you will, O rain of the sky." "I built a sturdy raft, I set sail for nirvana," said the Master; "I crossed the torrent of passions and I reached the saintly shores; I need the raft no longer; so fall if you will, O rain of the sky."

"My wife is obedient, she is chaste and good," said the shepherd Dhaniya; "she has lived with me these many years; she is pleasant and kindly, no one speaks ill of her; so fall if you will, O rain of the sky."

"My mind is obedient, it is loosed from all bonds," said the Master; "I have trained it these many years; it is quite docile, no evil is left in me; so fall if you will, O rain of the sky."

"I myself pay my servants their wages," said the shepherd Dhaniya; "my children receive wholesome food at my board; no one has ever tried to speak ill of them; so fall if you will, O rain of the sky."

"I am the servant of no one," said the Master; "with what I earn I travel the whole world; there is for me no need of a servant; so fall if you will, O rain of the sky."

"I have cows, I have calves, I have heifers," said the shepherd Dhaniya, "and I have a dog that is lord of my herd; so fall if you will, O rain of the sky.

"I have neither cows nor calves nor heifers," said the Master, "and I have no dog to be on guard; so fall if you will, O rain of the sky." "The stakes are driven deep in the ground, nothing can move them," said the shepherd Dhaniya; the ropes are new and made of strong grasses; the cows will never break them now; so fall if you will, O rain of the sky."

"Like the dog that has broken his chain," said the Master, "like the elephant that has broken his shackles, never again will I enter a womb; so fall if you will, O rain of the sky."

The shepherd Dhaniya bowed before the Master and said:

"I know now who you are, O Blessed One; come with me to my home."

As they were about to enter the house, the rain fell in torrents and formed little streams that trickled over the ground. When Dhaniya heard the rain, he spoke these words:

> *"Verily, we have acquired great riches since we have seen the Buddha. O Master, you are our refuge, you who have looked at us with the eyes of wisdom. Be our protector, O Saint! We are obedient, my wife and I; if we lead a life of holiness, we shall conquer birth and death, and we shall have done with suffering."*

Then a voice was heard, and Mara, the Evil One, stood before them. No one had seen him come.

"He who has sons is happy to see his sons," said Mara, the Evil One; "he who has cows is happy to see his cows; happy is the man of substance, and he who has no substance has no happiness."

"He who has sons is worried to see his sons," said the Master; "he who has cows is worried to see his cows; worried is the man of substance, and he who has no substance has no worries."

But Mara had fled. Dhaniya and his wife were listening to the Master speak.

BUDDHA INSTRUCTS THE MONKS OF VAISALI

The Master came to the banks of the Ganges, to the place where the city of Pataliputra was being built. He bowed before the walls that were beginning to rise out of the ground, and he exclaimed:

> *"This city will one day have greatness and renown; many heroes will be born here, here will reign a famous king. A thriving city you will be, O Pataliputra, and down through the ages men will praise your name."*

He crossed the river. He set out for Vaisali, but in the village of Bailva he became gravely ill. He suffered intense pain. Ananda wept, for he thought he was dying. But the Master remembered the many disciples he had still to visit; he did not wish to enter nirvana until he had given them final instructions. By the strength of his will, he overcame the sickness, and life did not leave him. He recovered.

When he was well again, he went outside the house that had given him shelter, and he took a seat that had been prepared for him near the door. Ananda came and sat down beside him.

"My Lord," said he, "I see that you have recovered your health. When I found you so ill, my strength failed me; I was faint. There were times I could not realize that the Master was sick. And yet I was reassured, for I remembered that you had not disclosed your intentions regarding the community, and I knew you would not enter nirvana without first revealing them."

The Blessed One spoke these words:

"What more does the community want of me, Ananda? I have stated the doctrine, and I have taught it; there is not a single point I have not expounded! Let him who thinks, 'I want to rule over the community,' disclose his intentions regarding the community. The Blessed One, Ananda, never thought, 'I want to rule over the community.' Why then should he disclose his intentions? I am an old man, Ananda; my hair is white, and I have grown feeble.

I am eighty years old; I have come to the end of the road. Be, now, each one of you, your own torch; look to no one to bring you light. He who is his own torch, after I have left the world, will show that he has understood the meaning of my words; he will be my true disciple, Ananda; he will know the right way to live."

He set out again, and presently he arrived at Vaisali. He went through the city, begging his food from door to door. Suddenly, he saw Mara standing before him.

"The hour has come," said the Evil One; "enter nirvana, O Blessed One."

"No," replied the Buddha. "I know when I must enter nirvana; I know better than you, Evil One. A few months more, and it will be time. Three months more, and the Blessed One will enter nirvana."

At these words the earth shook, and thunder rolled across the sky: the Blessed One had destroyed the will by which he still held to life; he had set the time for his entry into nirvana. The earth shook, and thunder rolled across the sky. In the evening he assembled the monks of Vaisali, and he addressed them.

"O monks, preserve carefully, the knowledge I have acquired and that I have taught you, and walk in the right path, in order that the life of holiness may long endure, for the joy and salvation of the world, for the joy and salvation of the Gods, for the joy and salvation of mankind. A few months more, and my time will have come; three months more, and I shall enter nirvana. I go and you remain. But never cease to struggle, O monks. He who falters not in the path of truth avoids birth, avoids death, for ever and ever avoids suffering."

The following day, he again wandered through the city, in quest of alms; then, with a few disciples, he set out on the road to Kusinagara, where he had decided to enter nirvana.

THE MEAL AT CUNDA'S

The Master and his disciples stopped at Pava, in the garden of Cunda, the blacksmith. Cunda came and paid homage to the Master, and said to him:

"My Lord, do me the honour of taking your meal at my home, tomorrow."

The Master accepted. The next day, Cunda had pork and other delicacies prepared for his guests. They arrived and took their seats. When the Master saw the pork, he pointed to it and said:

"No one but me could eat that, Cunda; you must keep it for me. My disciples will partake of the other delicacies."

When he had eaten, he said:

"Bury deep in the ground what I have left untouched; the Buddha alone can eat of such meat."

Then he left. The disciples followed.

They had gone only a short distance from Pava when the Master began to feel weary and sick. Ananda grieved, and he cursed Cunda, the blacksmith, for having offered the Master this fatal meal.

"Ananda," said the Master, "do not be angry with Cunda, the blacksmith. Great rewards are reserved to him for the food he gave me. Of all the meals I have ever had, two are most deserving of praise: the one that Sujata, and the other that Cunda, the blacksmith, served to me." He overcame his weariness and presently he reached the banks of the Kakutstha. The river was peaceful and pure. The Master bathed in the limpid waters. After the bath, he drank, then went to a mango grove. There, he said to the monk Cundaka:

"Fold my cloak in four, that I may lie down and rest."

Cundaka cheerfully obeyed. He quickly folded the cloak in four and spread it on the ground. The Master lay down, and Cundaka sat beside him. The Master rested a few hours. Then he set out again, and he finally arrived at Kusinagara. There, on the banks of the Hiranyavati, stood a pleasant, peaceful little wood. The Master said:

"Go, Ananda, and prepare a couch for me between two twin trees. Have the head to the north. I am ill, Ananda."

Ananda prepared the couch, and the Master went and reclined on it.

THE BUDDHA ENTERS NIRVANA

It was not the season for trees to bloom, yet the two trees that sheltered the Master were covered with blossoms. The flowers fell gently upon his couch, and from the sky, sweet melodies slowly drifted down. The Master said to pious Ananda:

"See: it is not the season for flowers, yet these trees have bloomed, and the blossoms are raining down upon me. Listen: the air is joyous with the songs that the happy Gods are singing in the sky in honour of the Buddha. But the Buddha is paid a more enduring honour than this. Monks, nuns, believers, all those who see the truth, all those who live within the law, they are the ones that do the Buddha supreme honour. Therefore you must live according to the law, Ananda, and, even in the most trivial matters, you must follow the sacred path of truth."

Ananda was weeping. He walked away, to hide his tears:

He thought, "For many misdeeds I have not yet been forgiven, and I shall be guilty of many more misdeeds. Oh, I am still far from the saintly goal, and he who took pity on me, the Master, is about to enter nirvana."

The Master called him back and said:

"Do not grieve, Ananda, do not despair. Remember my words: from all that delights us, from all that we love, we must one day be separated. How can that which is born he other than inconstant and perishable? How can that which is born, how can that which is created, endure for ever? Long have you honoured me, Ananda; you have been a devoted friend. Yours was a happy friendship, and you were faithful to it in thought, in word and in deed. You have done great good, Ananda; continue in the right path, and you will be forgiven your former misdeeds."

Night came on. The inhabitants of Kusinagara had heard that the Master was reclining under two twin trees, and they came in great crowds to pay him homage. An aged hermit, Subhadra, appeared, and bowing before the Master, professed his belief in the Buddha, in the law and in the community; and Subhadra was the last of the faithful to have the joy of seeing the Master face to face. The night was beautiful. Ananda was seated beside the Master. The Master said:

"Perhaps, Ananda, you will think, 'We no longer have a Master.' But you must not think that. The law remains, the law that I taught you; let it be your guide, Ananda, when I shall no longer be with you.

He said again:

"Verily, O monks, all that is created must perish. Never cease to struggle."

He was no longer of this world. His face was of luminous gold. His spirit ascended to the realms of ecstasy. He entered nirvana. The earth shook, and thunder rolled across the sky. Near the ramparts, at dawn, they of Kusinagara built a great funeral pile, as though for a king of the world, and there they burned the body of the Blessed One.

7

Buddha's Great Gift to the World

SAMSARA AND NIRVANA

Look about and contemplate life! Everything is transient and nothing endures. There is birth and death, growth and decay; there is combination and separation. The glory of the world is like a flower: it stands in full bloom in the morning and fades in the heat of the day. Wherever you look, there is a rushing and a struggling, and an eager pursuit of pleasure. There is a panic flight from pain and death, and hot are the flames of burning desires.

The world is Vanity Fair, full of changes and transformations. All is Samsara, the turning Wheel of Existence. Is there nothing permanent in the world? Is there in the universal turmoil no resting-place where our troubled heart can find peace? Is there nothing everlasting? Oh, that we could have cessation of anxiety, that our burning desires would be extinguished! When shall the mind become tranquil and composed? The Buddha, our Lord, was grieved at the ills of life. He saw the vanity of worldly happiness and sought salvation in the one thing that will not fade or perish, but will abide for ever and ever. You who long for life, learn that immortality is hidden in transiency. You who wish for happiness without the sting of regret, lead a life of righteousness. You who yearn for riches, receive treasures that are eternal. Truth is wealth, and a life of truth is happiness.

All compounds will be dissolved again, but the varieties which determine all combinations and separations as laws of nature endure for ever and aye. Bodies fall to dust, but the truths of the mind will not be destroyed. Truth knows neither birth nor death; it has no beginning and no end. Welcome the truth. The truth is the immortal part of mind. Establish the truth in your mind, for the truth is the image of the eternal; it portrays the immutable; it reveals the everlasting; the truth gives unto mortals the boon of immortality.

The Buddha has proclaimed the truth; let the truth of the Buddha dwell in your hearts. Extinguish in yourselves every desire that antagonizes the Buddha, and in the perfection of your spiritual growth you will become like unto him. That of your heart which cannot or will not develop into Buddha must perish, for it is mere illusion and unreal; it is the source of your error; it is the cause of your misery.

You attain to immortality by filling your minds with truth. Therefore, become like unto vessels fit to receive the Master's words. Cleanse yourselves of evil and sanctify your lives. There is no other way of reaching truth.

Learn to distinguish between Self and Truth. Self is the cause of selfishness and the source of evil; truth cleaves to no self; it is universal and leads to justice and righteousness. Self, that which seems to those who love their self as their being, is not the eternal, the everlasting, the imperishable. Seek not self, but seek the truth.

If we liberate our souls from our petty selves, wish no ill to others, and become clear as a crystal diamond reflecting the light of truth, what a radiant picture will appear in us mirroring things as they are, without the admixture of burning desires, without the distortion of erroneous illusion, without the agitation of clinging and unrest.

Yet you love self and will not abandon self-love. So be it, but then, verily, you should learn to distinguish between the false self and the true self. The ego with all its egotism is the false self. It is an unreal illusion and a perishable combination. He only who identifies his self with the truth will attain Nirvana; and he who has entered Nirvana has attained Buddhahood; he has acquired the highest good; he has become eternal and immortal. All compound things shall be dissolved again, worlds will break to pieces and our individualities will be scattered; but the words of Buddha will remain for ever.

The extinction of self is salvation; the annihilation of self is the condition of enlightenment; the blotting out of self is Nirvana.

Happy is he who has ceased to live for pleasure and rests in the truth. Verily his composure and tranquility of mind are the highest bliss.

Let us take our refuge in the Buddha, for he has found the everlasting in the transient. Let us take our refuge in that which is the immutable in the changes of existence. Let us take our refuge in the truth that is established through the enlightenment of the Buddha. Let us take our refuge in the community of those who seek the truth and endeavour to live in the truth.

THE SAVIOUR

The things of the world and its inhabitants are subject to change. They are combinations of elements that existed before, and all living creatures are what their past actions made them; for the law of cause and effect is uniform and without exception.

But in the changing things there is a constancy of law, and when the law is seen there is truth. The truth lies hidden in Samsara as the permanent in its changes. Truth desires to appear; truth longs to become conscious; truth strives to know itself.

There is truth in the stone, for the stone is here; and no power in the world, no god, no man, no demon, can destroy its existence. But the stone has no consciousness. There is truth in the plant and its life can expand; the plant grows and blossoms and bears fruit. Its beauty is marvellous, but it has no consciousness. There is truth in the animal; it moves about and perceives its surroundings; it distinguishes and learns to choose. There is consciousness, but it is not yet the consciousness of Truth. It is a consciousness of self only. The consciousness of self dims the eyes of the mind and hides the truth. It is the origin of error, it is the source of illusion, it is the germ of evil. Self begets selfishness.

There is no evil but what flows from self. There is no wrong but what is done by the assertion of self. Self is the beginning of all hatred, of iniquity and slander, of impudence and indecency, of theft and robbery, of oppression and bloodshed. Self is Mara, the tempter, the evildoer, the creator of mischief. Self entices with pleasures. Self promises a fairy's paradise. Self is the veil of Maya, the enchanter. But the pleasures of self are unreal, its paradisian labyrinth is the road to misery, and its fading beauty kindles the flames of desires that never can be satisfied.

Who shall deliver us from the power of self? Who shall save us from misery? Who shall restore us to a life of blessedness?

There is misery in the world of Samsara; there is much misery and pain. But greater than all the misery is the bliss of truth. Truth gives peace to the yearning mind; it conquers error; it quenches the flames of desires; it leads to Nirvana. Blessed is he who has found the peace of Nirvana. He is at rest in the struggles and tribulations of life; he is above all changes; he is above birth and death; he remains unaffected by the evils of life.

Blessed is he who has found enlightenment. He conquers, although he may be wounded; he is glorious and happy, although he may suffer; he is strong, although he may break down under the burden of his work; he is immortal, although he will die. The essence of his being is purity and goodness.

Blessed is he who has attained the sacred state of Buddhahood, for he is fit to work out the salvation of his fellow beings. The truth has taken its abode in him. Perfect wisdom illumines his understanding, and righteousness ensouls the purpose of all his actions. The truth is a living power for good, indestructible and invincible! Work the truth out in your mind, and spread it among mankind, for truth alone is the saviour from evil and misery. The Buddha has found the truth and the truth has been proclaimed by the Buddha! Blessed be the Buddha!

ENLIGHTENMENT

There was in Kapilavatthu a Sakya king, strong of purpose and reverenced by all men, a descendant of the Okkakas, who call themselves Gautama, and his name was Suddhodana or Pure-Rice. His wife Mayadevi was beautiful as the water-lily and pure in mind as the lotus. As the Queen of Heaven, she lived on earth, untainted by desire, and immaculate.

The king, her husband, honoured her in her holiness, and the spirit of truth, glorious and strong in his wisdom like unto a white elephant, descended upon her. When she knew that the hour of motherhood was near, she asked the king to send her home to her parents; and Suddhodana, anxious about his wife and the child she would bear him, willingly granted her request.

At Lumbini there is a beautiful grove, and when Mayadevi passed through it the trees were one mass of fragrant flowers and many birds were warbling in their branches. The Queen, wishing to stroll through the shady walks, left her golden palanquin, and, when she reached the giant sala tree in the midst of the grove, felt that her hour had come. She took hold of a branch. Her attendants hung a curtain about her and retired. When the pain of travail came upon her, four pure-minded angels of the great Brahma held out a golden net to receive the babe, who came forth from her right side like the rising sun bright and perfect.

The Brahma-angels took the child and placing him before the mother said: "Rejoice, O queen, a mighty son has been born unto thee."

At her couch stood an aged woman imploring the heavens to bless the child. All the worlds were flooded with light. The blind received their sight by longing to see the coming glory of the Lord; the deaf and dumb spoke with one another of the good omens indicating the birth of the Buddha to be. The crooked became straight; the lame walked. All prisoners were freed from their chains and the fires of all the hells were extinguished.

No clouds gathered in the skies and the polluted streams became clear, whilst celestial music rang through the air and the angels rejoiced with gladness. With no selfish or partial joy but for the sake of the law they rejoiced, for creation engulfed in the ocean of pain was now to obtain release. The cries of beasts were hushed; all malevolent beings received a loving heart, and peace reigned on earth. Mara, the evil one, alone was grieved and rejoiced not.

The Naga kings, earnestly desiring to show their reverence for most excellent law, as they had paid honour to former Buddhas, now went to greet the Bodhisattva. They scattered before him mandara flowers, rejoicing with heartfelt joy to pay their religious homage.

The royal father, pondering the meaning of these signs, was now full of joy and now sore distressed. The queen mother, beholding her child and the commotion which his birth created, felt in her timorous heart the pangs of doubt.

Now there was at that time in a grove near Lumbini Asita, a rishi, leading the life of a hermit. He was a Brahman of dignified mien, famed not only for wisdom and scholarship, but also for his skill in the interpretation of signs. And the king invited him to see the royal babe.

The seer, beholding the prince, wept and sighed deeply. And when the king saw the tears of Asita he became alarmed and asked: "Why has the sight of my son caused thee grief and pain?"

But Asita's heart rejoiced, and, knowing the king's mind to be perplexed, he addressed him, saying: "The king, like the moon when full, should feel great joy, for he has begotten a wondrously noble son. I do not worship Brahma, but I worship this child; and the gods in the temples will descend from their places of honour to adore him. Banish all anxiety and doubt. The spiritual omens manifested indicate that the child now born will bring deliverance to the whole world.

"Recollecting that I myself am old, on that account I could not hold my tears; for now my end is coming on and I shall not see the glory of this babe. For this son of thine will rule the world. The wheel of empire will come to him. He will either be a king of kings to govern all the lands of the earth, or verily will become a Buddha. He is born for the sake of everything that lives. His pure teaching will be like the shore that receives the shipwrecked. His power of meditation will be like a cool lake; and all creatures parched with the drought of lust may freely drink thereof. On the fire of covetousness he will cause the cloud of his mercy to rise, so that the rain of the law may extinguish it. The heavy gates of despondency will he open, and give deliverance to all creatures ensnared in the self-entwined meshes of folly and ignorance. The king of the law has come forth to rescue from bondage all the poor, the miserable, the helpless." When the royal parents heard Asita's words they rejoiced in their hearts and named their new-born infant Siddhattha, that is he who has accomplished his purpose."

And the queen said to her sister, Pajapati: "A mother who has borne a future Buddha will never give birth to another child. I shall soon leave this world, my husband, the king, and Siddhattha, my child. When I am gone, be thou a mother to him." And Pajapati wept and promised. When the queen had departed from the living, Pajapati took the boy Siddhattha and reared him. And as the light of the moon increases little by little, so the royal child grew from day to day in mind and in body; and truthfulness and love resided in his heart. When a year had passed Suddhodana the king made Pajapati his queen and there was never a better stepmother than she.

THE TIES OF LIFE

When Siddhattha had grown to youth, his father desired to see him married, and he sent to all his kinsfolk, commanding them to bring their princesses that the prince might select one of them as his wife. But the kinsfolk replied and said: "The prince is young and delicate; nor has he learned any of the sciences. He would not be able to maintain our daughter, and should there be war he would be unable to cope with the enemy."

The prince was not boisterous, but pensive in his nature. He loved to stay under the great jambu-tree in the garden of his father, and, observing the ways of the world, gave himself up to meditation. And the prince said to his father: "Invite our kinsfolk that they may see me and put my strength to the test." And his father did as his son bade him.

When the kinsfolk came, and the people of the city Kapilavatthu had assembled to test the prowess and scholarship of the prince, he proved himself manly in all the exercises both of the body and of the mind, and there was no rival among the youths and men of India who could surpass him in any test, bodily or mental. He replied to all the questions of the sages; but when he questioned them, even the wisest among them were silenced.

Then Siddhattha chose himself a wife. He selected his cousin Yasodhara, the gentle daughter of the king of Koli. In their wedlock was born a son whom they named Rahula which means "fetter" or "tie," and King Suddhodana, glad that an heir was born to his son, said: "The prince having begotten a son, will love him as I love the prince. This will be a strong tie to bind Siddhattha's heart to the interests of the world, and the kingdom of the Sakyas will remain under the scepter of my descendants."

With no selfish aim, but regarding his child and the people at large, Siddhattha, the prince, attended to his religious duties, bathing his body in the holy Ganges and cleansing his heart in the waters of the law. Even as men desire to give happiness to their children, so did he long to give peace to the world.

THE THREE WOES

The palace which the king had given to the prince was resplendent with all the luxuries of India; for the king was anxious to see his son happy. All sorrowful sights, all misery, and all knowledge of misery were kept away from Siddhattha, for the king desired that no troubles should come nigh him; he should not know that there was evil in the world.

But as the chained elephant longs for the wilds of the jungles, so the prince was eager to see the world, and he asked his father, the king, for permission to do so. And Suddhodana ordered a jewel-fronted chariot with four stately horses to be held ready, and commanded the roads to be adorned where his son would pass.

The houses of the city were decorated with curtains and banners, and spectators arranged themselves on either side, eagerly gazing at the heir to the throne. Thus Siddhattha rode with Channa, his charioteer, through the streets of the city, and into a country watered by rivulets and covered with pleasant trees. There by the wayside they met an old man with bent frame, wrinkled face and sorrowful brow, and the prince asked the charioteer: "Who is this? His head is white, his eyes are bleared, and his body is withered. He can barely support himself on his staff."

The charioteer, much embarrassed, hardly dared speak the truth. He said: "These are the symptoms of old age. This same man was once a suckling child, and as a youth full of sportive life; but now, as years have passed away, his beauty is gone and the strength of his life is wasted."

Siddhattha was greatly affected by the words of the charioteer, and he sighed because of the pain of old age. "What joy or pleasure can men take," he thought to himself, when they know they must soon wither and pine away!"

And lo! while they were passing on, a sick man appeared on the way-side, gasping for breath, his body disfigured, convulsed and groaning with pain. The prince asked his charioteer: "What kind of man is this?" And the charioteer replied and said: "This man is sick. The four elements of his body are confused and out of order. We are all subject to such conditions: the poor and the rich, the ignorant and the wise, all creatures that have bodies are liable to the same calamity."

And Siddhattha was still more moved. All pleasures appeared stale to him, and he loathed the joys of life.

The charioteer sped the horses on to escape the dreary sight, when suddenly they were stopped in their fiery course. Four persons passed by, carrying a corpse; and the prince, shuddering at the sight of a lifeless body, asked the charioteer: "What is this they carry? There are streamers and flower garlands; but the men that follow are overwhelmed with grief!"

The charioteer replied: "This is a dead man: his body is stark; his life is gone; his thoughts are still; his family and the friends who loved him now carry the corpse to the grave." And the prince was full of awe and terror: "Is this the only dead man, he asked, or does the world contain other instances?"

With a heavy heart the charioteer replied: "All over the world it is the same. He who begins life must end it. There is no escape from death."

With bated breath and stammering accents the prince exclaimed: "O worldly men! How fatal is your delusion! Inevitably your body will crumble to dust, yet carelessly, unheedingly, ye live on." The charioteer observing the deep impression these sad sights had made on the prince, turned his horses and drove back to the city.

When they passed by the palace of the nobility, Kisa Gotami, a young princess and niece of the king, saw Siddhattha in his manliness and beauty, and, observing the thoughtfulness of his countenance, said: "Happy the father that begot thee, happy the mother that nursed thee, happy the wife that calls husband this lord so glorious."

The prince hearing this greeting, said: "Happy are they that have found deliverance. Longing for peace of mind, I shall seek the bliss of Nirvana."

Then asked Kisa Gotami: "How is Nirvana attained?" The prince paused, and to him whose mind was estranged from wrong the answer came: "When the fire of lust is gone out, then Nirvana is gained; when the fires of hatred and delusion are gone out, then Nirvana is gained; when the troubles of mind, arising from blind credulity, and all other evils have ceased, then Nirvana is gained!"

Siddhattha handed her his precious pearl necklace as a reward for the wisdom she had inspired in him, and having returned home looked with disdain upon the treasures of his palace.

His wife welcomed him and entreated him to tell her the cause of his grief. He said: "I see everywhere the impression of change; therefore, my heart is heavy. Men grow old, sicken, and die. That is enough to take away the zest of life."

The king, his father, hearing that the prince had become estranged from pleasure, was greatly overcome with sorrow and like a sword it pierced his heart.

THE BODHISATTVAS RENUNCIATION

It was night. The prince found no rest on his soft pillow; he arose and went out into the garden. "Alas!" he cried "all the world is full of darkness and ignorance; there is no one who knows how to cure the ills of existence." And he groaned with pain. Siddhattha sat down beneath the great jambu-tree and gave himself to thought, pondering on life and death and the evils of decay. Concentrating his mind he became free from confusion. All low desires vanished from his heart and perfect tranquility came over him.

In this state of ecstasy he saw with his mental eye all the misery and sorrow of the world; he saw the pains of pleasure and the inevitable certainty of death that hovers over every being; yet men are not awakened to the truth. And a deep compassion seized his heart.

While the prince was pondering on the problem of evil, he beheld with his mind's eye under the jambu tree a lofty figure endowed with majesty, calm and dignified. "When comes thou, and who may thou be asked the prince.

In reply the vision said: "I am a samana. Troubled at the thought of old age, disease, and death I have left my home to seek the path of salvation. All things hasten to decay; only the truth abides forever. Everything changes, and there is no permanency; yet the words of the Buddhas are immutable. I long for the happiness that does not decay; the treasure that will never perish; the life that knows of no beginning and no end. Therefore, I have destroyed all worldly thought. I have retired into an unfrequented dell to live in solitude; and, begging for food, I devote myself to the one thing needful.

Siddhattha asked: "Can peace be gained in this world of unrest? I am struck with the emptiness of pleasure and have become disgusted with lust. All oppresses me, and existence itself seems intolerable."

The samana replied: "Where heat is, there is also a possibility of cold; creatures subject to pain possess the faculty of pleasure; the origin of evil indicates that good can be developed. For these things are correlatives. Thus where there is much suffering, there will be much bliss, if thou but open thine eyes to behold it. Just as a man who has fallen into a heap of filth ought to seek the great pond of water covered with lotuses, which is near by: even so seek thou for the great deathless lake of Nirvana to wash off the defilement of wrong. If the lake is not sought, it is not the fault of the lake. Even so when there is a blessed road leading the man held fast by wrong to the salvation of Nirvana, if the road is not walked upon, it is not the fault of the road, but of the person. And when a man who is oppressed with sickness, there being a physician who can heal him, does not avail himself of the physician's help, that is not the fault of the physician. Even so when a man oppressed by the malady of wrong-doing does not seek the spiritual guide of enlightenment, that is no fault of the evil-destroying guide."

The prince listened to the noble words of his visitor and said: "Thou bringest good tidings, for now I know that my purpose will be accomplished. My father advises me to enjoy life and to undertake worldly duties, such as will bring honour to me and to our house. He tells me that I am too young still, that my pulse beats too full to lead a religious life."

The venerable figure shook his head and replied: "Thou should know that for seeking a religious life no time can be inopportune."

A thrill of joy passed through Siddhattha's heart. "Now is the time to seek religion," he said; "now is the time to sever all ties that would prevent me from attaining perfect enlightenment; now is the time to wander into homelessness and, leading a mendicant's life, to find the path of deliverance."

The celestial messenger heard the resolution of Siddhattha with approval. "Now, indeed he added, is the time to seek religion. Go, Siddhattha, and accomplish thy purpose. For thou art Bodhisatta, the Buddha-elect; thou art destined to enlighten the world. Thou art the Tathagata, the great master, for thou wilt fulfill all righteousness and be Dharmaraja, the king of truth. Thou art Bhagavat, the Blessed One, for thou art called upon to become the saviour and redeemer of the world. Fulfill thou the perfection of truth.

Though the thunderbolt descend upon thy head, yield thou never to the allurements that beguile men from the path of truth. As the sun at all seasons pursues his own course, nor ever goes on another, even so if thou forsake not the straight path of righteousness, thou shalt become a Buddha. Persevere in thy quest and thou shalt find what thou seekest. Pursue thy aim unswervingly and thou shalt gain the prize. Struggle earnestly and thou shalt conquer. The benediction of all deities, of all saints of all that seek light is upon thee, and heavenly wisdom guides thy steps. Thou shalt be the Buddha, our Master, and our Lord; thou shalt enlighten the world and save mankind from perdition.

Having thus spoken, the vision vanished, and Siddhattha's heart was filled with peace. He said to himself: "I have awakened to the truth and I am resolved to accomplish my purpose. I will sever all the ties that bind me to the world, and I will go out from my home to seek the way of salvation. The Buddhas are beings whose words cannot fail: there is no departure from truth in their speech. For as the fall of a stone thrown into the air, as the death of a mortal, as the sunrise at dawn, as the lion's roar when he leaves his lair, as the delivery of a woman with child, as all these things are sure and certain-even so the word of the Buddhas is sure and cannot fail. Verily I shall become a Buddha."

The prince returned to the bedroom of his wife to take a last farewell glance at those whom he dearly loved above all the treasures of the earth. He longed to take the infant once more into his arms and kiss him with a parting kiss. But the child lay in the arms of his mother, and the prince could not lift him without awakening both. There Siddhattha stood gazing at his beautiful wife and his beloved son, and his heart grieved. The pain of parting overcame him powerfully. Although his mind was determined, so that nothing, be it good or evil, could shake his resolution, the tears flowed freely from his eyes, and it was beyond his power to check their stream. But the prince tore himself away with a manly heart, suppressing his feelings but not extinguishing his memory.

The Bodhisattva mounted his noble steed Kanthaka, and when he left the palace, Mara stood in the gate and stopped him: "Depart not, O my Lord," exclaimed Mara. "In seven days from now the wheel of empire will appear, and will make thee sovereign over the four continents and the two thousand adjacent islands. Therefore, stay, my Lord."

The Bodhisattva replied: "Well do I know that the wheel of empire will appear to me; but it is not sovereignty that I desire. I will become a Buddha and make all the world shout for joy."

Thus Siddhattha, the prince, renounced power and worldly pleasures, gave up his kingdom, severed all ties, and went into homelessness. He rode out into the silent night, accompanied only by his faithful charioteer Channa. Darkness lay upon the earth, but the stars shone brightly in the heavens.

KING BIMBISARA

Siddhattha had cut his waving hair and had exchanged his royal robe for a mean dress of the colour of the ground. Having sent home Channa, the charioteer, together with the noble steed Kanthaka, to King Suddhodana to bear him the message that the prince had left the world, the Bodhisattva walked along on the highroad with a beggar's bowl in his hand.

Yet the majesty of his mind was ill-concealed under the poverty of his appearance. His erect gait betrayed his royal birth and his eyes beamed with a fervid zeal for truth. The beauty of his youth was transfigured by holiness and surrounded his head like a halo. All the people who saw this unusual sight gazed at him in wonder. Those who were in haste arrested their steps and looked back; and there was no one who did not pay him homage.

Having entered the city of Rajagaha, the prince went from house to house silently waiting till the people offered him food. Wherever the Blessed One came, the people gave him what they had; they bowed before him in humility and were filled with gratitude because he condescended to approach their homes. Old and young people were moved and said: "This is a noble muni! His approach is bliss. What a great joy for us!"

And King Bimbisara, noticing the commotion in the city, inquired the cause of it, and when he learned the news sent one of his attendants to observe the stranger. Having heard that the muni must be a Sakya and of noble family, and that he had retired to the bank of a flowing river in the woods to eat the food in his bowl, the king was moved in his heart; he donned his royal robe, placed his golden crown upon his head and went out in the company of aged and wise counsellors to meet his mysterious guest.

The king found the muni of the Sakya race seated under a tree. Contemplating the composure of his face and the gentleness of his deportment, Bimbisara greeted him reverently and said: "O samana, thy hands are fit to grasp the reins of an empire and should not hold a beggar's bowl. I am sorry to see thee wasting thy youth. Believing that thou art of royal descent, I invite thee to join me in the government of my country and share my royal power. Desire for power is becoming to the noble-minded, and wealth should not be despised. To grow rich and lose religion is not true gain. But he who possesses all three, power, wealth, and religion, enjoying them in discretion and with wisdom, him I call a great master."

The great Sakyamuni lifted his eyes and replied: "Thou art known, O king, to be liberal and religious, and thy words are prudent. A kind man who makes good use of wealth is rightly said to possess a great treasure; but the miser who hoards up his riches will have no profit. Charity is rich in returns; charity is the greatest wealth, for though it scatters, it brings no repentance.

"I have severed all ties because I seek deliverance. How is it possible for me to return to the world? He who seeks religious truth, which is the highest treasure of all, must leave behind all that can concern him or draw away his attention, and must be bent upon that one goal alone. He must free his soul from covetousness and lust, and also from the desire for power.

"Indulge in lust but a little, and lust like a child will grow. Wield worldly power and you will be burdened with cares. Better than sovereignty over the earth, better than living in heaven, better than lordship over all the worlds, is the fruit of holiness. The Bodhisattva has recognized the illusory nature of wealth and will not take poison as food. Will a fish that has been baited still covet the hook, or an escaped bird love the net? Would a rabbit rescued from the serpent's mouth go back to be devoured? Would a man who has burnt his hand with a torch take up the torch after he had dropped it to the earth? Would a blind man who has recovered his sight desire to spoil his eyes again?

"The sick man suffering from fever seeks for a cooling medicine. Shall we advise him to drink that which will increase the fever? Shall we quench a fire by heaping fuel upon it?

"I pray thee, pity me not. Rather pity those who are burdened with the cares of royalty and the worry of great riches. They enjoy them in fear and trembling, for they are constantly threatened with a loss of those boons on whose possession their hearts are set, and when they die they cannot take along either their gold or the kingly diadem.

"My heart hankers after no vulgar profit, so I have put away my royal inheritance and prefer to be free from the burdens of life. Therefore, try not to entangle me in new relationships and duties, nor hinder me from completing the work I have begun. I regret to leave thee. But I will go to the sages who can teach me religion and so find the path on which we can escape evil.

"May thy country enjoy peace and prosperity, and may wisdom be shed upon thy rule like the brightness of the noon-day sun. May thy royal power be strong and may righteousness be the scepter in thine hand."

The king, clasping his hands with reverence, bowed down before Sakyamuni and said: "Mayest thou obtain that which thou seekest, and when thou has obtained it, come back, I pray thee, and receive me as thy disciple." The Bodhisattva parted from the king in friendship and goodwill, and purposed in his heart to grant his request.

THE BODHISATTVA'S SEARCH

Alara and Uddaka were renowned as teachers among the Brahmans, and there was no one in those days who surpassed them in learning and philosophical knowledge. The Bodhisattva went to them and sat at their feet. He listened to their doctrines of the atman or self, which is the ego of the mind and the doer of all doings. He learned their views of the transmigration of souls and of the law of karma; how the souls of bad men had to suffer by being reborn in men of low caste, in animals, or in hell, while those who purified themselves by libation, by sacrifices, and by self-mortification would become kings, or Brahmans, or devas, so as to rise higher and higher in the grades of existence. He studied their incantations and offerings and the methods by which they attained deliverance of the ego from material existence in states of ecstasy.

Alara said: "What is that self which perceives the actions of the five roots of mind, touch, smell, taste, sight, and hearing? What is that which is active in the two ways of motion, in the hands and in the feet? The problem of the soul appears in the expressions 'I say,' 'I know and perceive,' 'I come,' and 'I go' or 'I will stay here.' Thy soul is not thy body; it is not thy eye, not thy ear, not thy nose, not thy tongue, nor is it thy mind. The I is the one who feels the touch in thy body. The I is the smeller in the nose, the taster in the tongue, the seer in the eye, the hearer in the ear, and the thinker in the mind. The I moves thy hands and thy feet. The I is thy soul. Doubt in the existence of the soul is irreligious, and without discerning this truth there is no way of salvation. Deep speculation will easily involve the mind; it leads to confusion and unbelief; but a purification of the soul leads to the way of escape. True deliverance is reached by removing from the crowd and leading a hermit's life, depending entirely on alms for food. Putting away all desire and clearly recognizing the non-existence of matter, we reach a state of perfect emptiness. Here we find the condition of immaterial life. As the munja grass when freed from its horny case, as a sword when drawn from its scabbard, or as the wild bird escaped from its prison, so the ego liberating itself from all limitations, finds perfect release. This is true deliverance, but those only who will have deep faith will learn."

The Bodhisattva found no satisfaction in these teachings. He replied: "People are in bondage, because they have not yet removed the idea of the ego. The thing and its quality are different in our thought, but not in reality. Heat is different from fire in our thought, but you cannot remove heat from fire in reality. You say that you can remove the qualities and leave the thing, but if you think your theory to the end, you will find that this is not so.

"Is not man an organism of many aggregates? Are we not composed of various attributes? Man consists of the material form, of sensation, of thought, of dispositions, and, lastly, of understanding. That which men call the ego when they say 'I am' is not an entity behind the attributes; it originates by their co-operation. There is mind; there is sensation and thought, and there is truth; and truth is mind when it walks in the path of righteousness. But there is no separate ego-soul outside or behind the thought of man. He who believes the ego is a distinct being has no correct conception. The very search for the atman is wrong; it is a wrong start and it will lead you in a false direction.

"How much confusion of thought comes from our interest in self, and from our vanity when thinking 'I am so great,' or 'I have done this wonderful deed?' The thought of thine ego stands between thy rational nature and truth; banish it, and then wilt thou see things as they are. He who thinks correctly will rid himself of ignorance and acquire wisdom. The ideas 'I am' and 'I shall be' or 'I shall not be' do not occur to a clear thinker.

"Moreover, if our ego remains, how can we attain true deliverance? If the ego is to be reborn in any of the three worlds, be it in hell, upon earth, or be it even in heaven, we shall meet again and again the same inevitable doom of sorrow. We shall remain chained to the wheel of individuality and shall be implicated in egotism and wrong. All combination is subject to separation, and we cannot escape birth, disease, old age, and death. Is this a final escape?"

Said Uddaka: "Consider the unity of things. Things are not their parts, yet they exist. The members and organs of thy body are not thine ego, but thine ego possesses all these parts. What, for instance, is the Ganges? Is the sand the Ganges? Is the water the Ganges? Is the hither bank the Ganges? Is the hither bank the Ganges? Is the farther bank the Ganges? The Ganges is a mighty river and it possesses all these several qualities. Exactly so is our ego."

But the Bodhisattva replied: "Not so, sir! If we remove the water, the sand, the hither bank and the farther bank where can we find any Ganges? In the same way I observe the activities of man in their harmonious union, but there is no ground for an ego outside its parts."

The Brahman sage, however, insisted on the existence of the ego, saying: "The ego is the doer of our deeds. How can there be karma without a self as its performer? Do we not see around us the effects of karma? What makes men different in character, station, possessions, and fate? It is their karma, and karma includes merit and demerit. The transmigration of the soul is subject to its karma. We inherit from former existences the evil effects of our evil deeds and the good effects of our good deeds. If that were not so, how could we be different?'

The Tathagata meditated deeply on the problems of transmigration and karma, and found the truth that lies in them. "The doctrine of karma, he said, is undeniable, but the theory of the ego has no foundation. Like everything else in nature, the life of man is subject to the law of cause and effect. The present reaps what the past has sown, and the future is the product of the present. But there is no evidence of the existence of an immutable ego-being, of a self which remains the same and migrates from body to body. There is rebirth but no transmigration.

"Is not this individuality of mine a combination, material as well as mental? Is it not made up of qualities that sprang into being by a gradual evolution? The five roots of sense perception in this organism have come from ancestors who performed these functions. The ideas which I think, came to me partly from others who thought them, and partly they rise from combinations of the ideas in my own mind. Those who have used the same sense-organs, and have thought the same ideas before I was composed into this individuality of mine, are my previous existences; they are my ancestors as much as the I of yesterday is the father of the I of today, and the karma of my past deeds affects the fate of my present existence.

"Supposing there were an atman that performs the actions of the senses then if the door of sight were torn down and the eye plucked out, that atman would be able to peep through the larger aperture and see the forms of its surroundings better and more clearly than before. It would be able to hear sounds better if the ears were torn away; smell better if the nose were cut off; taste better if the tongue were pulled out; and feel better if the body were destroyed.

"I observe the preservation and transmission of character; I perceive the truth of karma, but see no atman whom your doctrine makes the doer of your deeds. There is rebirth without the transmigration of a self. For this atman, this self, this ego in the 'I say' and in the 'I will' is an illusion. If this self were a reality, how could there be an escape from selfhood? The terror of hell would be infinite, and no release could be granted. The evils of existence would not be due to our ignorance and wrong-doing, but would constitute the very nature of our being."

Then the Bodhisattva went to the priests officiating in the temples. But the gentle mind of the Sakyamuni was offended at the unnecessary cruelty performed on the altars of the gods. He said: "Ignorance only can make these men prepare festivals and hold vast meetings for sacrifices. Far better to revere the truth than try to appease the gods by shedding blood. What love can a man possess who believes that the destruction of life will atone for evil deeds? Can a new wrong expiate old wrongs? And can the slaughter of an innocent victim blot out the evil deeds of mankind? This is practicing religion by the neglect of moral conduct. Purify your hearts and cease to kill; that is true religion. Rituals have no efficacy; prayers are vain repetitions; and incantations have no saving power. But to abandon covetousness and lust, to become free from evil passions, and to give up all hatred and ill-will, that is the right sacrifice and the true worship." Uruvela.

URUVELA, PLACE OF MORTIFICATION

The Bodhisattva went in search of a better system and came to a settlement of five Bhikkhus in the jungle of Uruvela; and when the Blessed One saw the life of those five men, virtuously keeping in check their senses, subduing their passions, and practicing austere self-discipline, he admired their earnestness and joined their company. With holy zeal and a strong heart, the Sakyamuni gave himself up to meditative thought and a rigorous mortification of the body. Whereas the five bhikkhus were severe, the Sakyamuni was severer still, and so they revered him, their junior, as their master.

So the Bodhisattva continued for six years patiently torturing himself and suppressing the wants of nature. He trained his body and exercised his mind in the modes of the most rigorous ascetic life. At last, he ate each day one hemp grain only, seeking to cross the ocean of birth and death and to arrive at the shore of deliverance.

And when the Bodhisattva was ahungered, lo! Mara, the Evil One, approached him and said: "Thou art emaciated from fasts, and death is near. What good is thy exertion? Deign to live, and thou wilt be able to do good work." But the Sakyamuni made reply: "O thou friend of the indolent, thou wicked one; for what purpose has thou come? Let the flesh waste away, if but the mind becomes more tranquil and attention more steadfast. What is life in this world? Death in battle is better to me than that I should live defeated."

And Mara withdrew, saying: "For seven years I have followed the Blessed One step by step, but I have found no fault in the Tathagata."

The Bodhisattva was shrunken and attenuated, and his body was like a withered branch; but the fame of his holiness spread in the surrounding countries, and people came from great distances to see him and receive his blessing. However, the Holy One was not satisfied. Seeking true wisdom he did not find it, and he came to the conclusion that mortification would not extinguish desire nor afford enlightenment in ecstatic contemplation.

Seated beneath a jambu-tree, he considered the state of his mind and the fruits of his mortification. His body had become weaker, nor had his fasts advanced him in his search for salvation, and therefore when he saw that it was not the right path, he proposed to abandon it. He went to bathe in the Neranjara River, but when he strove to leave the water he could not rise on account of his weakness. Then espying the branch of a tree and taking hold of it, he raised himself and left the stream. But while returning to his abode, he staggered and lay as though dead.

There was a chief herdsman living near the grove whose eldest daughter was called Nanda; and Nanda happened to pass by the spot where the Blessed One had swooned, and bowing down before him she offered him rice-milk and he accepted the gift. When he had partaken of the rice-milk all his limbs were refreshed, his mind became clear again, and he was strong to receive the highest enlightenment.

After this occurrence, the Bodhisattva again took some food. His disciples, having witnessed the scene of Nanda and observing the change in his mode of living, were filled with suspicion. They feared that Siddhattha's religious zeal was flagging and that he whom they had hitherto revered as their Master had become oblivious of his high purpose.

When the Bodhisattva saw the bhikkhus turning away from him, he felt sorry for their lack of confidence, and was aware of the loneliness of his life. Suppressing his grief he wandered on alone, and his disciples said, "Siddhattha leaves us to seek a more pleasant abode."

MARA, THE EVIL ONE

The Holy One directed his steps to that blessed Bodhitree beneath whose shade he was to accomplish his search. As he walked, the earth shook and a brilliant light transfigured the world. When he sat down the heavens resounded with joy and all living beings were filled with good cheer. Mara alone, lord of the five desires, bringer of death and enemy of truth, was grieved and rejoiced not. With his three daughters, Tanha, Raga and Arati, the tempters, and with his host of evil demons, he went to the place where the great samana sat. But Sakyamuni heeded him not. Mara uttered fear-inspiring threats and raised a whirlwind so that the skies were darkened and the ocean roared and trembled.

But the Blessed One under the Bodhi-tree remained calm and feared not. The Enlightened One knew that no harm could befall him.

The three daughters of Mara tempted the Bodhisattva, but he paid no attention to them, and when Mara saw that he could kindle no desire in the heart of the victorious samana, he ordered all the evil spirits at his command to attack him and overawe the great muni. But the Blessed One watched them as one would watch the harmless games of children. All the fierce hatred of the evil spirits was of no avail. The flames of hell became wholesome breezes of perfume, and the angry thunderbolts were changed into lotus-blossoms.

When Mara saw this, he fled away with his army from the Bodhi-tree, whilst from above a rain of heavenly flowers fell, and voices of good spirits were heard: "Behold the great muni! his heart unmoved by hatred.

The wicked Mara's host 'gainst him did not prevail. Pure is he and wise, loving and full of mercy. As the rays of the sun drown the darkness of the world, so he who perseveres in his search will find the truth and the truth will enlighten him."

ENLIGHTENMENT

The Bodhisattva, having put Mara to flight, gave himself up to meditation. All the miseries of the world, the evils produced by evil deeds and the sufferings arising therefrom, passed before his mental eye, and he thought:

"Surely if living creatures saw the results of all their evil deeds, they would turn away from them in disgust.

But selfhood blinds them, and they cling to their obnoxious desires. They crave pleasure for themselves and they cause pain to others; when death destroys their individuality, they find no peace; their thirst for existence abides and their selfhood reappears in new births. Thus they continue to move in the coil and can find no escape from the hell of their own making. And how empty are their pleasures, how vain are their endeavours! Hollow like the plantain-tree and without contents like the bubble. The world is full of evil and sorrow, because it is full of lust. Men go astray because they think that delusion is better than truth. Rather than truth they follow error, which is pleasant to look at in the beginning but in the end causes anxiety, tribulation, and misery."

And the Bodhisattva began to expound the Dharma. The Dharma is the truth. The Dharma is the sacred law. The Dharma is religion. The Dharma alone can deliver us from error, from wrong and from sorrow.

Pondering on the origin of birth and death, the Enlightened One recognized that ignorance was the root of all evil; and these are the links in the development of life, called the twelve nidanas: In the beginning there is existence blind and without knowledge; and in this sea of ignorance there are stirrings formative and organizing. From stirrings, formative and organizing, rises awareness or feelings. Feelings beget organisms that live as individual beings. These organisms develop the six fields, that is, the five senses and the mind. The six fields come in contact with things. Contact begets sensation. Sensation creates the thirst of individualized being. The thirst of being creates a cleaving to things. The cleaving produces the growth and continuation of selfhood. Selfhood continues in renewed birth. The renewed births of selfhood are the causes of sufferings, old age, sickness, and death. They produce lamentation, anxiety, and despair.

The cause of all sorrow lies at the very beginning; it is hidden in the ignorance from which life grows. Remove ignorance and you will destroy the wrong desires that rise from ignorance; destroy these desires and you will wipe out the wrong perception that rises from them. Destroy wrong perception and there is an end of errors in individualized beings. Destroy the errors in individualized beings and the illusions of the six fields will disappear. Destroy illusions and the contact with things will cease to beget misconception. Destroy misconception and you do away with thirst. Destroy thirst and you will be free of all morbid cleaving. Remove the cleaving and you destroy the selfishness of selfhood. If the selfishness of selfhood is destroyed you will be above birth, old age, disease, and death, and you will escape all suffering.

The Enlightened One saw the four noble truths which point out the path that leads to Nirvana or the extinction of self: The first noble truth is the existence of sorrow. The second noble truth is the cause of suffering. The third noble truth is the cessation of sorrow. The fourth noble truth is the eightfold path that leads to the cessation of sorrow.

This is the Dharma. This is the truth. This is religion. And the Enlightened One uttered this stanza:

"Through many births I sought in vain
The Builder of this House of Pain.
Now, Builder, You are plain to see,
And from this House at last I'm free;
I burst the rafters, roof and wall,
And dwell in the Peace beyond them all."

There is self and there is truth. Where self is, truth is not. Where truth is, self is not. Self is the fleeting error of samsara; it is individual separateness and that egotism which begets envy and hatred. Self is the yearning for pleasure and the lust after vanity. Truth is the correct comprehension of things; it is the permanent and everlasting, the real in all existence, the bliss of righteousness.

The existence of self is an illusion, and here is no wrong in this world, no vice, no evil, except what flows from the assertion of self. The attainment of truth is possible only when self is recognized as an illusion. Righteousness can be practiced only when we have freed our mind from passions of egotism.

Perfect peace can dwell only where all vanity has disappeared. Blessed is he who has understood the Dharma.

Blessed is he who does no harm to his fellow-beings. Blessed is he who overcomes wrong and is free from passion. To the highest bliss has he attained who has conquered all selfishness and vanity. He has become the Buddha, the Perfect One.

The First Converts

The Blessed One tarried in solitude seven times seven days, enjoying the bliss of emancipation. At that time Tapussa and Bhallika, two merchants, came travelling on the road near by, and when they saw the great samana, majestic and full of peace, they approached him respectfully and offered him rice cakes and honey. This was the first food that the Enlightened One ate after he attained Buddhahood.

And the Buddha addressed them and pointed out to them the way of salvation. The two merchants, seeing the holiness of the conqueror of Mara, bowed down in reverence and said: "We take our refuge, Lord, in the Blessed One and in the Dharma."

Tapussa and Bhallika were the first that became followers of the Buddha and they were lay disciples.

The Brahma's Request

The Blessed One having attained Buddhahood while resting under the shepherd's Nigrodha tree on the banks of the river Neranjara, pronounced this solemn utterance:

"How sure his pathway in this wood,

Who follows truth's unchanging call!

How blessed, to be kind and good,

And practice self-restraint in all!

How light, from passion to be free,

And sensual joys to let go by!

And yet his greatest bliss will be

When he has quelled the pride of 'I'.

"I have recognized the deepest truth, which is sublime and peace-giving' but difficult to understand; for most men move in a sphere of worldly interests and find their delight in worldly desires. The worldling will not understand the doctrine, for to him there is happiness in selfhood only, and the bliss that lies in a complete surrender to truth is unintelligible to him. He will call resignation what to the enlightened mind is the purest joy. He will see annihilation where the perfected one finds immortality. He will regard as death what the conqueror of self knows to be life everlasting. The truth remains hidden from him who is in the bondage of hate and desire. Nirvana remains incomprehensible and mysterious to the vulgar whose minds are beclouded with worldly interests. Should I preach the doctrine and mankind not comprehend it, it would bring me only fatigue and trouble."

Mara, the Evil One, on hearing the words of the Blessed Buddha, approached and said: "Be greeted, thou Holy One. Thou has attained the highest bliss and it is time for thee to enter into the final Nirvana."

Then Brahma Sahampati descended from the heavens and, having worshipped the Blessed One, said: "Alas! the world must perish, should the Holy One, the Tathagata, decide not to teach the Dharma. Be merciful to those that struggle; have compassion upon the sufferers; pity the creatures who are hopelessly entangled in the snares of sorrow. There are some beings that are almost free from the dust of worldliness. If they hear not the doctrine preached, they will be lost. But if they hear it, they will believe and be saved."

The Blessed One, full of compassion, looked with the eye of a Buddha upon all sentient creatures, and he saw among them beings whose minds were but scarcely covered by the dust of worldliness, who were of good disposition and easy to instruct. He saw some who were conscious of the dangers of lust and wrong doing. And the Blessed One said to Brahma Sahampati: "Wide open be the door of immortality to all who have ears to hear. May they receive the Dharma with faith."

Then the Blessed One turned to Mara, saying: "I shall not pass into the final Nirvana, O Evil One, until there be not only brethren and sisters of an Order, but also lay disciples of both sexes, who shall have become true hearers, wise, well trained, ready and learned, versed in the scriptures, fulfilling all the greater and lesser duties, correct in life, walking according to the precepts-until they, having thus themselves learned the doctrine, shall be able to give information to others concerning it, preach it, make it known, establish it, open it, minutely explain it, and make it clear-until they, when others start vain doctrines, shall be able to vanquish and refute them, and so to spread the wonder-working truth abroad.

I shall not die until the pure religion of truth shall have become successful, prosperous, widespread, and popular in all its full extent-until, in a word, it shall have been well proclaimed among men!"

Then Brahma Sahampati understood that the Blessed One had granted his request and would preach the doctrine.

FOUNDING THE KINGDOM

Upaka Sees the Buddha

Now the Blessed One thought: "To whom shall I preach the doctrine first? My old teachers are dead. They would have received the good news with joy. But my five disciples are still alive. I shall go to them, and to them shall I first proclaim the gospel of deliverance."

At that time the five bhikkhus dwelt in the Deer Park at Benares, and the Blessed One rose and journeyed to their abode, not thinking of their unkindness in having left him at a time when he was most in need of their sympathy and help, but mindful only of the services which they had ministered unto him, and pitying them for the austerities which they practiced in vain.

Upaka, a young Brahman and a Jain, a former acquaintance of Siddhattha, saw the Blessed One while he journeyed to Benares, and, amazed at the majesty and sublime joyfulness of his appearance, said to him: "Thy countenance, my friend, is serene; thine eyes are bright and indicate purity and blessedness."

The holy Buddha replied: "I have obtained deliverance by the extinction of self. My body is chastened, my mind is free from desire, and the deepest truth has taken abode in my heart. I have obtained Nirvana, and this is the reason that my countenance is serene and my eyes are bright. I now desire to found the kingdom of truth upon earth, to give light to those who are enshrouded in darkness and to open the gate of deathlessness."

Upaka replied: "Thou professest then, friend, to be Jina, the conqueror of the world, the absolute one and the holy one.

The Blessed One said: "Jinas are all those who have conquered self and the passions of self; those alone are victorious who control their minds and abstain from evil. Therefore, Upaka, I am the Jina." Upaka shook his head. "Venerable Gautama, he said, "thy way lies yonder," and taking another road he went away.

THE SERMON AT BENARES

On seeing their old teacher approach, the five Bhikkus agreed among themselves not to salute him, nor to address him as a master, but by his name only. "For," so they said, "he has broken his vow and has abandoned holiness. He is no bhikkhu, but Gautama, and Gautama has become a man who lives in abundance and indulges in the pleasures of worldliness." But when the Blessed One approached in a dignified manner, they involuntarily rose from their seats and greeted him in spite of their resolution. Still they called him by his name and addressed him as "friend Gautama."

When they had thus received the Blessed One, he said: "Do not call the Tathagata by his name nor address him as 'friend,' for he is the Buddha, the Holy One. The Buddha looks with a kind heart equally on all living beings, and they therefore call him 'Father.' To disrespect a father is wrong; to despise him, is wicked. The Tathagata, the Buddha continued, does not seek salvation in austerities, but neither does he for that reason indulge in worldly pleasures, nor live in abundance. The Tathagata has found the middle path.

"There are two extremes, O bhikkhus, which the man who has given up the world ought not to follow-the habitual practice, on the one hand, of self-indulgence which is unworthy, vain and fit only for the worldly-minded and the habitual practice, on the other hand, of self-mortification, which is painful, useless and unprofitable.

"Neither abstinence from fish and flesh, nor going naked, nor shaving the head, nor wearing matted hair, nor dressing in a rough garment, nor covering oneself with dirt, nor sacrificing to Agni, will cleanse a man who is not free from delusions. Reading the Vedas, making offerings to priests, or sacrifices to the gods, self-mortification by heat or cold and many such penances performed for the sake of immortality, these do not cleanse the man who is not free from delusions. Anger, drunkenness, obstinacy, bigotry, deception, envy, self-praise, disparaging others, superciliousness and evil intentions constitute uncleanness; not verily the eating of flesh.

"A middle path, O bhikkhus avoiding the two extremes, has been discovered by the Tathagata-a path which opens the eyes, and bestows understanding, which leads to peace of mind, to the higher wisdom, to full enlightenment, to Nirvana! What is that middle path, O bhikkhus, avoiding these two extremes, discovered by the Tathagata-that path which opens the eyes, and bestows understanding, which leads to peace of mind, to the higher wisdom, to full enlightenment, to Nirvana? Let me teach you, O bhikkhus, the middle path, which keeps aloof from both extremes. By suffering, the emaciated devotee produces confusion and sickly thoughts in his mind. Mortification is not conducive even to worldly knowledge; how much less to a triumph over the senses!

"He who fills his lamp with water will not dispel the darkness, and he who tries to light a fire with rotten wood will fail. And how can any one be free from self by leading a wretched life, if he does not succeed in quenching the fires of lust, if he still hankers after either worldly or heavenly pleasures? But he in whom self has become extinct is free from lust; he will desire neither worldly nor heavenly pleasures, and the satisfaction of his natural wants will not defile him. However, let him be moderate, let him eat and drink according to the need of the body.

"Sensuality is enervating; the self-indulgent man is a slave to his passions, and pleasure-seeking is degrading and vulgar. But to satisfy the necessities of life is not evil. To keep the body in good health is a duty, for otherwise we shall not be able to trim the lamp of wisdom, and keep our minds strong and clear. Water surrounds the lotus flower, but does not wet its petals. This is the middle path, O bhikkhus, that keeps aloof from both extremes." And the Blessed One spoke kindly to his disciples, pitying them for their errors, and pointing out the uselessness of their endeavours, and the ice of ill-will that chilled their hearts melted away under the gentle warmth of the Master's persuasion.

Now the Blessed One set the wheel of the most excellent law rolling, and he began to preach to the five bhikkhus, opening to them the gate of immortality, and showing them the bliss of Nirvana.

The Buddha said: "The spokes of the wheel are the rules of pure conduct: justice is the uniformity of their length; wisdom is the tire; modesty and thoughtfulness are the hub in which the immovable axle of truth is fixed. He who recognizes the existence of suffering, its cause, its remedy, and its cessation has fathomed the four noble truths. He will walk in the right path.

"Right views will be the torch to light his way. Right aspirations will be his guide. Right speech will be his dwelling-place on the road. His gait will be straight, for it is right behaviour. His refreshments will be the right way of earning his livelihood. Right efforts will be his steps: right thoughts his breath; and right contemplation will give him the peace that follows in his footprints.

"Now, this, O bhikkhus, is the noble truth concerning suffering: Birth is attended with pain, decay is painful, disease is painful, death is painful. Union with the unpleasant is painful,

painful is separation from the pleasant; and any craving that is unsatisfied, that too is painful. In brief, bodily conditions which spring from attachment are painful. This, then, O bhikkhus, is the noble truth concerning suffering.

"Now this, O bhikkhus, is the noble truth concerning the origin of suffering: Verily, it is that craving which causes the renewal of existence, accompanied by sensual delight, seeking satisfaction now here, now there, the craving for the gratification of the passions, the craving for a future life, and the craving for happiness in this life. This, then, O bhikkhus, is the noble truth concerning the origin of suffering.

"Now this, O bhikkhus, is the noble truth concerning the destruction of suffering: Verily, it is the destruction, in which no passion remains, of this very thirst; it is the laying aside of, the being free from, the dwelling no longer upon this thirst. This, then, O bhikkhus, is the noble truth concerning the destruction of suffering.

"Now, this, O bhikkhus, is the noble truth concerning the way which leads to the destruction of sorrow. Verily, it is this noble eightfold path; that is to say: Right views; right aspirations; right speech; right behaviour; right livelihood; right effort; right thoughts; and right contemplation. This, then, O bhikkhus, is the noble truth concerning the destruction of sorrow.

"By the practice of loving-kindness I have attained liberation of heart, and thus I am assured that I shall never return in renewed births. I have even now attained Nirvana."

When the Blessed One had thus set the royal chariot wheel of truth rolling onward, a rapture thrilled through all the universes. The devas left their heavenly abodes to listen to the sweetness of the truth; the saints that had parted from life crowded around the great teacher to receive the glad tidings; even the animals of the earth felt the bliss that rested upon the words of the Tathagata: and all the creatures of the host of sentient beings, gods, men, and beasts, hearing the message of deliverance, received and understood it in their own language.

And when the doctrine was propounded, the venerable Kondanna, the oldest one among the five bhikkhus, discerned the truth with his mental eye, and he said: "Truly, O Buddha, our Lord, thou has found the truth!" Then the other bhikkhus too, joined him and exclaimed: "Truly, thou art the Buddha, thou has found the truth."

And the devas and saints and all the good spirits of the departed generations that had listened to the sermon of the Tathagata, joyfully received the doctrine and shouted: "Truly, the Blessed One has founded the kingdom of righteousness. The Blessed One has moved the earth; he has set the wheel of Truth rolling, which by no one in the universe, be he god or man, can ever be turned back. The kingdom of Truth will be preached upon earth; it will spread; and righteousness, goodwill, and peace will reign among mankind."

THE SANGHA OR COMMUNITY

Having pointed out to the five bhikkhus the truth, the Buddha said: "A man that stands alone, having decided to obey the truth, may be weak and slip back into his old ways. Therefore, stand ye together, assist one another, and strengthen one another efforts. Be like unto brothers; one in love, one in holiness, and one in your zeal for the truth. Spread the truth and preach the doctrine in all quarters of the world, so that in the end all living creatures will be citizens of the kingdom of righteousness. This is the holy brotherhood; this is the church, the congregation of the saints of the Buddha; this is the Sangha that establishes a communion among all those who have taken their refuge in the Buddha."

Kondanna was the first disciple of the Buddha who had thoroughly grasped the doctrine of the Holy One, and the Tathagata looking into his heart said: "Truly, Kondanna has understood the truth." Therefore the venerable Kondanna received the name "Annata-Kondanna that is, "Kondanna who has understood the doctrine." Then the venerable Kondanna spoke to the Buddha and said: "Lord, let us receive the ordination from the blessed One." And the Buddha said: "Come, O bhikkhus! Well taught is the doctrine. Lead a holy life for the extinction of suffering." Then Kondanna and the other bhikkhus uttered three times these solemn vows: "To the Buddha will I look in faith: He, the Perfect One, is holy and supreme. The Buddha conveys to us instruction, wisdom, and salvation; he is the Blessed One, who knows the law of being; he is the Lord of the world, who yokes men like oxen, the Teacher of gods and men, the Exalted Buddha. Therefore, to the Buddha will I look in faith.

"To the doctrine will I look in faith: well-preached is the doctrine by the Exalted One. The doctrine has been revealed so as to become visible; the doctrine is above time and space. The doctrine is not based upon hearsay, it means 'Come and see'; the doctrine to welfare; the doctrine is recognized by the wise in their own hearts. Therefore to the doctrine will I look in faith.

"To the community will I look in faith; the community of the Buddha's disciples instructs us how to lead a life of righteousness; the community of the Buddha's disciples teaches us how to exercise honesty and justice; the community of the Buddha's disciples shows us how to practice the truth. They form a brotherhood in kindness and charity, and their saints are worthy of reverence. The community of the Buddha's disciples is founded as a holy brotherhood in which men bind themselves together to teach the behests of rectitude and to do good. Therefore, to the community will I look in faith."

The gospel of the Blessed One increased from day to day, and many people came to hear him and to accept the ordination to lead thenceforth a holy life for the sake of the extinction of suffering. And the Blessed One seeing that it was impossible to attend to all who wanted to hear the truth and receive the ordination, sent out from the number of his disciples such as were to preach the Dharma, and said unto them:

> *"The Dharma and the Vinaya proclaimed by the Tathagata shine forth when they are displayed, and not when they are concealed. But let not this doctrine, so full of truth and so excellent, fall into the hands of those unworthy of it, where it would be despised and contemned, treated shamefully, ridiculed and censured.*

I now grant you, O bhikkhus, this permission. Confer henceforth in the different countries the ordination upon those who are eager to receive it, when you find them worthy.

"Go ye now, O bhikkhus, for the benefit of the many, for the welfare of mankind, out of compassion for the world. Preach the doctrine which is glorious in the beginning, glorious in the middle, and glorious in the end, in the spirit as well as in the letter. There are beings whose eyes are scarcely covered with dust, but if the doctrine is not preached to them they cannot attain salvation. Proclaim to them a life of holiness. They will understand the doctrine and accept it." And it became an established custom that the bhikkhus went out preaching while the weather was good, but in the rainy season they came together again and joined their master, to listen to the exhortations of the Tathagata.

YASA, THE YOUTH OF BENARES

At that time there was in Benares a noble youth, Yasa by name, the son of a wealthy merchant. Troubled in his mind about the sorrows of the world, he secretly rose up in the night and stole away to the Blessed One. The Blessed One saw Yasa coming from afar. Yasa approached and exclaimed: "Alas, what distress! What tribulations!"

The Blessed One said to Yasa: "Here is no distress; here are no tribulations. Come to me and I will teach you the truth, and the truth will dispel your sorrows."

When Yasa, the noble youth, heard that there were neither distress, nor tribulations, nor sorrows, his heart was comforted. He went into the place where the Blessed One was, and sat down near him. Then the Blessed One preached about charity and morality. He explained the vanity of the thought "I am"; the dangers of desire, and the necessity of avoiding the evils of life in order to walk on the path of deliverance.

Instead of disgust with the world, Yasa felt the cooling stream of holy wisdom, and, having obtained the pure and spotless eye of truth, he looked at his person, richly adorned with pearls and precious stones, and his heart was shamed. The Tathagata, knowing his inward thoughts, said: "Though a person be ornamented with jewels, the heart may have conquered the senses. The outward form does not constitute religion or affect the mind. Thus the body of a samana may wear an ascetic's garb while his mind is immersed in worldliness. A man that dwells in lonely woods and yet covets worldly vanities, is a worldling, while the man in worldly garments may let his heart soar high to heavenly thoughts. There is no distinction between the layman and the hermit, if but both have banished the thought of self."

Seeing that Yasa was ready to enter upon the path, the Blessed One said to him: "Follow me!" And Yasa joined the brotherhood, and having put on a bhikkhu's robe, received the ordination.

While the Blessed One and Yasa were discussing the doctrine, Yasa's father passed by in search of his son; and in passing he asked the Blessed One: "Pray, Lord, has thou seen Yasa, my son?"

The Buddha said to Yasa's father: "Come in, sir, thou wilt find thy son"; and Yasa's father became full of joy and he entered. He sat down near his son, but his eyes were holden and he knew him not; and the Lord began to preach. And Yasa's father, understanding the doctrine of the Blessed One, said:

> *"Glorious is the truth, O Lord! The Buddha, the Holy One, our Master, sets up what has been overturned; he reveals what has been hidden; he points out the way to the wanderer who has gone astray; he lights a lamp in the darkness so that all who have eyes to see can discern the things that surround them. I take refuge in the Buddha, our Lord: I take refuge in the doctrine revealed by him: I take refuge in the brotherhood which he has founded. May the Blessed One receive me from this day forth while my life lasts as a lay disciple who has taken refuge in him." Yasa's father was the first lay-member who became the first lay disciple of the Buddha by pronouncing the three-fold formula of refuge.*

When the wealthy merchant had taken refuge in the Buddha, his eyes were opened and he saw his son sitting at his side in a bhikkhu's robe. "My son, Yasa, he said, thy mother is absorbed in lamentation and grief. Return home and restore thy mother to life."

Then Yasa looked at the Blessed One, who said: "Should Yasa return to the world and enjoy the pleasures of a worldly life as he did before?" Yasa's father replied: "If Yasa, my son, finds it a gain to stay with thee, let him stay. He has become delivered from the bondage of worldliness."

When the Blessed One had cheered their hearts with words of truth and righteousness, Yasa's father said: "May the Blessed One, O Lord, consent to take his meal with me together with Yasa as his attendant?" The Blessed One, having donned his robes, took his alms-bowl and went with Yasa to the house of the rich merchant. When they had arrived there, the mother and also the former wife of Yasa saluted the Blessed One and sat down near him.

Then the Blessed One preached, and the women having understood his doctrine, exclaimed: "Glorious is the truth, O Lord! We take refuge in the Buddha, our Lord. We take refuge in the doctrine revealed by him. We take refuge in the brotherhood which has been founded by him. May the Blessed One receive us from this day forth while our life lasts as lay disciples who have taken refuge in him." The mother and the wife of Yasa, the noble youth of Benares, were the first women who became lay disciples and took their refuge in the Buddha.

Now there were four friends of Yasa belonging to the wealthy families of Benares. Their names were Vimala, Subahu, Punnaji, and Gavampati.

When Yasa's friends heard that Yasa had cut off his hair and put on bhikkhu robes to give up the world and go forth into homelessness, they thought: "Surely that cannot be a common doctrine, that must be a noble renunciation of the world. And they went to Yasa, and Yasa addressed the Blessed One saying: "May the Blessed One administer exhortation and instruction to these four friends of mine." And the Blessed One preached to them, and Yasa's friends accepted the doctrine and took refuge in the Buddha, the Dharma, and the Sangha.

THE FIRE-WORSHIPPER

At that time there lived in Uruvela the Jatilas, Brahman hermits with matted hair, worshipping the fire and keeping a fire-dragon; and Kassapa was their chief. Kassapa was renowned throughout all India, and his name was honoured as one of the wisest men on earth and an authority on religion. And the Blessed One went to Kassapa of Uruvela the Jatila, and said: "Let me stay a night in the room where you keep your sacred fire."

Kassapa, seeing the Blessed One in his majesty and beauty, thought to himself: "This is a great muni and a noble teacher. Should he stay overnight in the room where the sacred fire is kept, the serpent will bite him and he will die." And he said: "I do not object to your staying overnight in the room where the sacred fire is kept, but the serpent lives there; he will kill you and I should be sorry to see you perish."

But the Buddha insisted and Kassapa admitted him to the room where the sacred fire was kept. And the Blessed One sat down with body erect, surrounding himself with watchfulness. In the night the dragon came, belching forth in rage his fiery poison, and filling the air with burning vapour, but could do him no harm, and the fire consumed itself while the World-honoured One remained composed. And the venomous fiend became very worth so that he died in his anger. When Kassapa saw the light shining forth from the room he said: "Alas, what misery! Truly, the countenance of Gautama the great Sakyamuni is beautiful, but the serpent will destroy him."

In the morning the Blessed One showed the dead body of the fiend to Kassapa, saying: "His fire has been conquered by my fire." And Kassapa thought to himself. "Sakyamuni is a great samana and possesses high powers, but he is not holy like me."

There was in those days a festival, and Kassapa thought: "The people will come hither from all parts of the country and will see the great Sakyamuni. When he speaks to them, they will believe in him and abandon me." And he grew envious. When the day of the festival arrived, the Blessed One retired and did not come to Kassapa. And Kassapa went to the Buddha on the next morning and said: "Why did the great Sakyamuni not come?"

The Tathagata replied: "Did thou not think, O Kassapa, that it would be better if I stayed away from the festival?" And Kassapa was astonished and thought: "Great is Sakyamuni; he can read my most secret thoughts, but he is not holy like me."

The Blessed One addressed Kassapa and said: "Thou sees the truth, but accepts it not because of the envy that dwells in thy heart. Is envy holiness? Envy is the last remnant of self that has remained in thy mind. Thou art not holy, Kassapa; thou has not yet entered the path." And Kassapa gave up his resistance. His envy disappeared, and, bowing down before the Blessed One, he said: "Lord, our Master, let me receive the ordination from the Blessed One."

And the Blessed One said: "Thou, Kassapa, art chief of the Jatilas. Go, then, first and inform them of thine intention, and let them do as thou thinks fit." Then Kassapa went to the Jatilas and said: "I am anxious to lead a religious life under the direction of the great Sakyamuni, who is the Enlightened One, the Buddha. Do as ye think best."

The Jatilas replied: "We have conceived a profound affection for the great Sakyamuni, and if thou wilt join his brotherhood, we will do likewise." The Jatilas of Uruvela now flung their paraphernalia of fire-worship into the river and went to the Blessed One. Nadi Kassapa and Gaya Kassapa, brothers of the great Uruvela Kassapa, powerful men and chieftains among the people, were dwelling below on the stream, and when they saw the instruments used in fire-worship floating in the river, they said: "Something has happened to our brother. And they came with their folk to Uruvela. Hearing what had happened, they, too, went to the Buddha.

The Blessed One, seeing that the Jatilas of Nadi and Gaya, who had practiced severe austerities and worshipped fire, were now come to him, preached a sermon on fire, and said: "Everything, O Jatilas, is burning. The eye is burning, all the senses are burning, thoughts are burning. They are burning with the fire of lust. There is anger, there is ignorance, there is hatred, and as long as the fire finds inflammable things upon which it can feed, so long will it burn, and there will be birth and death, decay, grief, lamentation, suffering, despair, and sorrow. Considering this, a disciple of the Dharma will see the four noble truths and walk in the eightfold path of holiness. He will become wary of his eye, wary of all his senses, wary of his thoughts. He will divest himself of passion and become free. He will be delivered from selfishness and attain the blessed state of Nirvana."

And the Jatilas rejoiced and took refuge in the Buddha, the Dharma, and the Sangha.

THE SERMON AT RAJAGAHA

The Blessed One having dwelt some time in Uruvela went to Rajagaha, accompanied by a number of bhikkhus, many of whom had been Jatilas before. The great Kassapa, chief of the Jatilas and formerly a fire worshipper, went with him.

When the Magadha king, Seniya Bimbisara, heard of the arrival of Gautama Sakyamuni, of whom the people said, "He is the Holy One, the blessed Buddha, guiding men as a driver curbs bullocks, the teacher of high and low," he went out surrounded with his counsellors and generals and came to the grove where the Blessed One was. There they saw the Blessed One in the company of Kassapa, the great religious teacher of the Jatilas, and they were astonished and thought: "Has the great Sakyamuni placed himself under the spiritual direction of Kassapa, or has Kassapa become a disciple of Gautama?"

The Tathagata, reading the thoughts of the people, said to Kassapa: "What knowledge has thou gained, O Kassapa, and what has induced thee to renounce the sacred fire and give up thine austere penances?"

Kassapa said: "The profit I derived from adoring the fire was continuance in the wheel of individuality with all its sorrows and vanities. This service I have cast away, and instead of continuing penances and sacrifices I have gone in quest of the highest Nirvana. Since I have seen the light of truth, I have abandoned worshipping the fire."

The Buddha, perceiving that the whole assembly was ready as a vessel to receive the doctrine, spoke thus to Bimbisara the king: "He who knows the nature of self and understands how the senses act, finds no room for selfishness, and thus he will attain peace unending. The world holds the thought of self, and from this arises false apprehension. Some say that the self endures after death, some say it perishes. Both are wrong and their error is most grievous. For if they say the self is perishable, the fruit they strive for will perish too, and at some time there will be no hereafter. Good and evil would be indifferent. This salvation from selfishness is without merit.

"When some, on the other hand, say the self will not perish, then in the midst of all life and death there is but one identity unborn and undying. If such is their self, then it is perfect and cannot be perfected by deeds. The lasting, imperishable self could never be changed self would be lord and master, and there would be no use in perfecting the perfect; moral aims and salvation would be unnecessary.

"But now we see the marks of joy and sorrow. Where is any constancy? If there is no permanent self that does our deeds, then there is no self; there is no actor behind our actions, no perceiver behind our perception, no lord behind our deeds.

"Now attend and listen: The senses meet the object and from their contact sensation is born. Thence results recollection. Thus, as the sun's power through a burning-glass causes fire to appear, so through the cognizance born of sense and object, the mind originates and with it the ego, the thought of self, whom some Brahman teachers call the lord. The shoot springs from the seed; the seed is not the shoot; both are not one and the same, but successive phases in a continuous growth. Such is the birth of animated life.

"Ye that are slaves of the self and toil in its service from morning until night, ye that live in constant fear of birth, old age, sickness, and death, receive the good tidings that your cruel master exists not. Self is an error, an illusion, a dream. Open your eyes and awaken. See things as they are and ye will be comforted. He who is awake will no longer be afraid of nightmares. He who has recognized the nature of the rope that seemed to be a serpent will cease to tremble.

"He who has found there is no self will let go all the lusts and desires of egotism. The cleaving to things, covetousness, and sensuality inherited from former existences, are the causes of the misery and vanity in the world. Surrender the grasping disposition of selfishness, and you will attain to that calm state of mind which conveys perfect peace, goodness, and wisdom."

And the Buddha breathed forth this solemn utterance:

"Do not deceive, do not despise
Each other, anywhere.
Do not be angry, and do not
Secret resentment bear;
For as a mother risks her life
And watches over her child,
So boundless be your love to all,
So tender, kind and mild.

"Yea cherish goodwill right and left,
For all, both soon and late,
And with no hindrance, with no stint,
From envy free and hate;
While standing, walking, sitting down,
Forever keep in mind:
The rule of life that's always best
Is to be loving-kind.

"Gifts are great, the founding of viharas is meritorious, meditations and religious exercises pacify the heart, comprehension of the truth leads to Nirvana, but greater than all is loving-kindness. As the light of the moon is sixteen times stronger than the light of all the stars, so loving-kindness is sixteen times more efficacious in liberating the heart than all other religious accomplishments taken together. This state of heart is the best in the world. Let a man remain steadfast in it while he is awake, whether he is standing, walking, sitting, or lying down."

When the Enlightened One had finished his sermon, the Magadha king said to the Blessed One: "In former days, Lord, when I was a prince, I cherished five wishes. I wished: O, that I might be inaugurated as a king. This was my first wish, and it has been fulfilled. Further, I wished: Might the Holy Buddha, the Perfect One, appear on earth while I rule and might he come to my kingdom. This was my second wish and it is fulfilled now. Further I wished: Might I pay my respects to him. This was my third wish and it is fulfilled now. The fourth wish was: Might the Blessed One preach the doctrine to me, and this is fulfilled now.

"The greatest wish, however, was the fifth wish: Might I understand the doctrine of the Blessed One. And this wish is fulfilled too.

"Glorious Lord! Most glorious is the truth preached by the Tathagata! Our Lord, the Buddha, sets up what has been overturned; he reveals what has been hidden; he points out the way to the wanderer who has gone astray; he lights a lamp in the darkness so that those who have eyes to see may see. I take my refuge in the Buddha. I take my refuge in the Dharma. I take my refuge in the Sangha."

The Tathagata, by the exercise of his virtue and by wisdom, showed his unlimited spiritual power. He subdued and harmonized all minds. He made them see and accept the truth, and throughout the kingdom the seeds of virtue were sown.

THE KING'S GIFT

Seniya Bimbisara, the king, having taken his refuge in the Buddha, invited the Tathagata to his palace, saying: "Will the Blessed One consent to take his meal with me tomorrow together with the fraternity of bhikkhus?" The next morning the king announced to the Blessed One that it was time for taking food:

"Thou art my most welcome guest, O Lord of the world, come; the meal is prepared."

The Blessed One having donned his robes, took his alms-bowl and, together with a great number of bhikkhus, entered the city of Rajagaha. Sakka, the king of the Devas, assuming the appearance of a young Brahman, walked in front, and said: "He who teaches self-control with those who have learned self-control; the redeemer with those whom he has redeemed; the Blessed One with those to whom he has given peace, is entering Rajagaha Hail to the Buddha, our Lord! Honour to his name and blessings to all who take refuge in him." Sakka intoned this stanza:

"Blessed is the place in which the Buddha walks,

And blessed the ears which hear his talks;

Blessed his disciples, for they are

The tellers of his truth both near and far.

"If all could hear this truth so good

Then all men's minds would eat rich food,

And strong would grow men's brotherhood."

When the Blessed One had finished his meal, and had cleansed his bowl and his hands, the king sat down near him and thought:

"Where may I find a place for the Blessed One to live in, not too far from the town and not too near, suitable for going and coming, easily accessible to all people who want to see him, a place that is by day not too crowded and by night not exposed to noise, wholesome and well fitted for a retired life? There is my pleasure-garden, the bamboo grove Veluvana, fulfilling all these conditions. I shall offer it to the brotherhood whose head is the Buddha."

The king dedicated his garden to the brotherhood, saying: "May the Blessed One accept my gift." Then the Blessed One, having silently shown his consent and having gladdened and edified the Magadha king by religious discourse, rose from his seat and went away.

SARIPUTTA AND MOGGALLANA

At that time Sariputta and Moggallana, two Brahmans and chiefs of the followers of Sanjaya, led a religious life. They had promised each other: "He who first attains Nirvana shall tell the other one."

Sariputta seeing the venerable Assaji begging for alms, modestly keeping his eyes to the ground and dignified in deportment, exclaimed: "Truly this samana has entered the right path; I will ask him in whose name he has retired from the world and what doctrine he professes." Being addressed by Sariputta, Assaji replied: "I am a follower of the Buddha, the Blessed One, but being a novice I can tell you the substance only of the doctrine."

Said Sariputta: "Tell me, venerable monk; it is the substance I want." And Assaji recited the stanza:

"Nothing we seek to touch or see

Can represent Eternity.

They spoil and die: then let us find

Eternal Truth within the mind."

Having heard this stanza, Sariputta obtained the pure and spotless eye of truth and said: "Now I see clearly, whatsoever is subject to origination is also subject to cessation. If this be the doctrine I have reached the state to enter Nirvana which heretofore has remained hidden from me." Sariputta went to Moggallana and told him, and both said: "We will go to the Blessed One, that he, the Blessed One, may be our teacher."

When the Buddha saw Sariputta and Moggallana coming from afar, he said to his disciples, These two monks are highly auspicious." When the two friends had taken refuge in the Buddha, the Dharma and the Sangha, the Holy One said to his other disciples: "Sariputta, like the first-born O son of a world-ruling monarch, is well able to assist the king as his chief follower to set the wheel of the law rolling."

Now the people were annoyed. Seeing that many distinguished young men of the kingdom of Magadha led a religious life under the direction of the Blessed One, they became angry and murmured: "Gautama Sakyamuni induces fathers to leave their wives and causes families to become extinct." When they saw the bhikkhus, they reviled them, saying: "The great Sakyamuni has come to Rajagaha subduing the minds of men. Who will be the next to be led astray by him?"

The bhikkhus told it to the Blessed One, and the Blessed One said: "This murmuring, O bhikkhus, will not last long, it will last seven days. If they revile you, answer them with these words: 'It is by preaching the truth that Tathagatas lead men. Who will murmur at the wise? Who will blame the virtuous? Who will condemn self-control, righteousness, and kindness?" And the Blessed One proclaimed:

"Commit no wrong, do only good,

And let your heart be pure.

This is the doctrine Buddhas teach,

And this doctrine will endure."

ANATHAPINDIKA, THE MAN OF WEALTH

At this time there was Anathapindika, a man of unmeasured wealth, visiting Rajagaha. Being of a charitable disposition, he was called "the supporter of orphans and the friend of the poor." Hearing that the Buddha had come into the world and was stopping in the bamboo grove near the city, he set out on that very night to meet the Blessed One.

And the Blessed One saw at once the sterling quality of Anathapindika's heart and greeted him with words of religious comfort. And they sat down together, and Anathapindika listened to the sweetness of the truth preached by the Blessed One. And the Buddha said: "The restless, busy nature of the world, this, I declare, is at the root of pain. Attain that composure of mind which is resting in the peace of immortality. Self is but a heap of composite qualities, and its world is empty like a fantasy.

"Who is it that shapes our lives? Is it Isvara, a personal creator? If Isvara be the maker, all living things should have silently to submit to their maker's power. They would be like vessels formed by the potter's hand; and if it were so, how would it be possible to practice virtue? If the world had been made by Isvara there should be no such thing as sorrow, or calamity, or evil; for both pure and impure deeds must come from him. If not, there would be another cause beside him, and he would not be self-existent. Thus, thou sees, the thought of Isvara is overthrown.

"Again, it is said that the Absolute has created us. But that which is absolute cannot be a cause. All things around us come from a cause as the plant comes from the seed; but how can the Absolute be the cause of all things alike? If it pervades them, then, certainly, it does not make them.

"Again, it is said that Self is the maker. But if self is the maker, why did it not make things pleasing? The causes of sorrow and joy are real and touchable. How can they have been made by self?

"Again, if we adopt the argument that there is no maker, our fate is such as it is, and there is no causation, what use would there be in shaping our lives and adjusting means to an end? Therefore, we argue that all things that exist are not without cause. However, neither Isvara, nor the absolute, nor the self nor causeless chance, is the maker, but our deeds produce results both good and evil according to the law of causation.

"Let us, then, abandon the heresy of worshipping Isvara and of praying to him; let us no longer lose ourselves in vain speculations or profitless subtleties; let us surrender self and all selfishness, and as all things are fixed by causation, let us practice good so that good may result from our actions."

And Anathapindika said: "I see that thou art the Buddha, the Blessed One the Tathagata, and I wish to open to the my whole mind. Having listened to my words advise me what I shall do. My life is full of work, and having acquired great wealth, I am surrounded with cares. Yet I enjoy my work, and apply myself to it with all diligence. Many people are in my employ and depend upon the success of my enterprises.

"Now, I have heard thy disciples praise the bliss of the hermit and denounce the unrest of the world. 'The Holy One,' they say, 'has given up his kingdom and his inheritance, and has found the path of righteousness, thus setting an example to all the world how to attain Nirvana.' My heart yearns to do what is right and to be a blessing unto my fellows. Let me then ask thee, Must I give up my wealth, my home, and my business enterprises, and, like thyself, go into homelessness in order to attain the bliss of a religious life?"

And the Buddha replied: "The bliss of a religious life is attainable by every one who walks in the noble eightfold path. He that cleaves to wealth had better cast it away than allow his heart to be poisoned by it; but he who does not cleave to wealth, and possessing riches, uses them rightly, will be a blessing unto his fellows. It is not life and wealth and power that enslave men, but the cleaving to life and wealth and power. The bhikkhu who retires from the world in order to lead a life of leisure will have no gain, for a life of indolence is an abomination, and lack of energy is to be despised. The Dharma of the Tathagata does not require a man to go into homelessness or to resign the world, unless he feels called upon to do so; but the Dharma of the Tathagata requires every man to free himself from the illusion of self, to cleanse his heart, to give up his thirst for pleasure, and lead a life of righteousness.

And whatever men do, whether they remain in the world as artisans, merchants, and officers of the king, or retire from the world and devote themselves to a life of religious meditation, let them put their whole heart into their task; let them be diligent and energetic, and, if they are like the lotus, which, although it grows in the water, yet remains untouched by the water, if they struggle in life without cherishing envy or hatred, if they live in the world not a life of self but a life of truth, then surely joy, peace, and bliss will dwell in their minds."

Bibliography

Auboyer, Jeannine: *Buddha: A Pictorial History of His Life and Legacy,* Crossroad, New York, 1983.

Behl, Benoy K.: *The Ajanta Caves: Artistic Wonder of Ancient Buddhist India,* Harry N. Abrams, New York, 1998.

Cummings, Mary: *The Lives of the Buddha in the Art and Literature of Asia,* University of Michigan, Ann Arbor, 1982.

Haldar, J. R.: *Early Buddhist Mythology,* Manohar, New Delhi, 1977.

Horner, I. B.: *The Living Thoughts of Gautama the Buddha,* Cassell, London, 1948.

Ireland, John D.: *The Udana: Inspired Utterances of the Buddha,* Buddhist Publication Society, Kandy, 1990.

John Powers: *The Yogacara School of Buddhism: A Bibliography,* Scarecrow Press, Lanham, 1991.

Miksic, John: *Borobudur: Golden Tales of the Buddha,* Shambala, Boston, 1990.

Pal, Pratapaditya: *Light of Asia: Buddha Sakyamuni in Asian Art,* County Museum of Art, Los Angeles, 1984.

Seneviratna, Anuradha: *King Ashoka and Buddhism,* Buddhist Publication Society, Kandy, 1994.

Snellgrove, David L.: *The Image of the Buddha,* Kodansha International, Tokyo, 1978.

Wray, Elizabeth: *The Ten Lives of the Buddha,* Weatherhill, New York, 1972.

Yushin Yoo: *Books on Buddhism: An Annotated Subject Guide,* Scarecrow Press, Metuchen, 1976).

Zwalf, W.: *Buddhism: Art and Faith,* British Museum Publications, London, 1985.

Index

□□□